Systems Thinking:
Creative Holism for Managers

Systems Thinking: Creative Holism for Managers

Michael C. Jackson

University of Hull, UK

John Wiley & Sons, Ltd

This publication is designed to provide accurate and authoritative information in regard to
the subject matter covered. It is sold on the understanding that the Publisher is not engaged
in rendering professional services. If professional advice or other expert assistance is
required, the services of a competent professional should be sought.

Other Wiley Editorial Offices

John Wiley & Sons Inc., 111 River Street, Hoboken, NJ 07030, USA

Jossey-Bass, 989 Market Street, San Francisco, CA 94103-1741, USA

Wiley-VCH Verlag GmbH, Boschstr. 12, D-69469 Weinheim, Germany

John Wiley & Sons Australia Ltd, 33 Park Road, Milton, Queensland 4064, Australia

John Wiley & Sons (Asia) Pte Ltd, 2 Clementi Loop #02-01, Jin Xing Distripark, Singapore 129809

John Wiley & Sons Canada Ltd, 22 Worcester Road, Etobicoke, Ontario, Canada M9W 1L1

Wiley also publishes its books in a variety of electronic formats. Some content that appears
in print may not be available in electronic books.

British Library Cataloguing in Publication Data

A catalogue record for this book is available from the British Library

ISBN-13 978-0-470-84522-6 (HB)

Project management by Originator, Gt Yarmouth, Norfolk (typeset in $11\frac{1}{2}/13$pt Garamond)

Dust as we are, the immortal spirit grows
Like harmony in music; there is a dark
Inscrutable workmanship that reconciles
Discordant elements, makes them cling together
In one society.

Wordsworth (*The Prelude*, 1850)

Contents

Preface

Managers today are expected to cope with increasing complexity, change and diversity.

Complexity stems from the nature of problems. They rarely present themselves individually, but come related to other problems, in richly interconnected problem situations that are appropriately described by Russ Ackoff as 'messes'. As a result, once you examine them, problems seem to get bigger and to involve more issues and stakeholders.

Change is a product of our era. Organizations, if they are to remain viable, have to respond adroitly to constant shifts in their environments. Customers change their preferences over shorter time spans. Competition can be global and is often fuelled by the onward march of technological innovation. Governments impose new regulations. Transformations in society and in ways of thinking impose fresh responsibilities on managers.

In a world of complexity and change, managers are asked to tackle a much greater diversity of problems. They have to continue to ensure that organizational processes are efficient and that they are served by the latest developments in technology. But this is hardly enough to stay ahead of the game. Staff have to be inspired and the organization's stock of knowledge captured and distributed, so that the organization learns faster than its competitors. This requires the putting in place of flexible structures as well as the demonstration of transformational leadership qualities. Changes in the law and in social expectations require managers to respond positively to eliminate discrimination and to monitor the impact of their organizations' activities.

Faced with increasing complexity, change and diversity, managers have inevitably sought the help of advisers, consultants and academics. So desperate have they become for enlightenment that they have elevated a number of these to the status of management gurus. Too often, however, managers have been peddled panaceas in the form of the latest management fad. We are now awash with quick-fix solutions such as:

- scenario planning;
- benchmarking;
- rightsizing;
- value chain analysis;
- continuous improvement;
- total quality management;
- learning organizations;
- process re-engineering;
- knowledge management;
- balanced scorecard;
- customer relationship management.

Unfortunately, as so many managers have discovered to the cost of themselves and their organizations, these relatively simple solutions rarely work in the face of significant complexity, change and diversity.

Fundamentally, simple solutions fail because they are not holistic or creative enough.

They are not holistic because they concentrate on the parts of the organization rather than on the whole. In doing so they miss the crucial interactions between the parts. They fail to recognize that optimizing the performance of one part may have consequences elsewhere that are damaging for the whole. This fault is known as 'suboptimization'. In its early days, as is now admitted by the originators of the approach, process re-engineering concentrated far too much on the things that can be engineered at the expense of the people in organizations. People reacted and process re-engineering interventions failed in terms of securing overall improvement. Benchmarking encourages looking at the efficiency of the different parts of the organization separately against external comparators. It fails to see that, even if each part is optimized, the performance of the whole organization can be disastrous if the parts do not interact together well.

Management fads also stifle creativity. They pander to the notion that there is one best solution in all circumstances. Sometimes, if this solution tackles only one of the aspects of an organization relevant to its performance, the effect is to reinforce suboptimization. Total quality management, for example, has done a lot to improve process design, but can be criticized for ignoring wider structural issues and the politics of organizations. At other times, even if more parts are considered, there is the danger that they are all viewed from the same perspective. The balanced scorecard claims to embrace different viewpoints on organizational performance while actually requiring users to transfer a machine-like view of organizations to a wider range of their activities. It looks at different things, but in the same way. This inhibits creativity.

Because of the frequent failure of the panaceas they have been offered, managers are looking for alternatives. In increasing numbers they are turning toward systems thinking. Systems thinking managers know that simple solutions are bound to fail when pitched against complex problem situations. They are willing to struggle with more complicated ideas that, at first acquaintance, may be more difficult to understand. They hope to emerge from this engagement with systems thinking better equipped to cope with complexity, change and diversity. This hope is based on the fact that systems thinking is holistic rather than reductionist and, at least in the form of critical systems thinking, does everything possible to encourage creativity.

Holism puts the study of wholes before that of the parts. It does not try to break down organizations into parts in order to understand them and intervene in them. It concentrates its attention instead at the organizational level and on ensuring that the parts are functioning and are related properly together so that they serve the purposes of the whole. Being holistic also means approaching problems ready to employ the systems language. For example, looking at organizations, their parts and their environments as systems, subsystems and suprasystems. All the systems approaches described in this book seek to make use of the philosophy of holism and the systems vocabulary associated with it.

Because of the growing popularity of holistic thinking, there is now a rich storehouse of different systems approaches. While these all employ holism they do not all encourage creativity. Some fall prey to the fault found with so many management fads – they encourage us to look at organizations from only one perspective. Increasingly, being systemic is also coming to mean being able to look at problem situations and knowing how to resolve them from a variety of points of view and using different systems approaches in combination. Critical systems thinking specifically encourages this kind of creativity. Creativity is made possible by this book because it presents a full range of systems approaches and discusses how they can be used together.

Managers, although increasingly interested in systems thinking, have reached different stages in their understanding of it. Some know little except that it might help. Others are employing systems ideas almost instinctively. It is amazing how often systems concepts are heard in the every-day parlance of managers and decision-makers: concepts such as holism, joined-up thinking, partnership, inclusiveness, stakeholding, governance, interconnectivity, globalization and ecology. A few have engaged in more in-depth study of books like Peter Senge's *The Fifth Discipline* (Random House, 1990) or of ideas emanating from the sciences of complexity.

If you are a manager or someone aspiring to be a manager, at whatever stage you are in your study of systems thinking, this book is designed to help. If you are new to the ideas, then it should serve as a solid introduction. If you are familiar with a few of the ideas, but know little about how they are related or can be used to manage organizations, then the book will give you a more rigorous understanding of holism and how to use systems ideas in practice. If you understand some systems approaches but not others, then the book will expand your knowledge and enable you to be creative in your choice and use of systems methodologies and methods. You will also be able to use the book as a guide to further reading about systems thinking.

The genesis of this book goes back to the early 1980s when with Paul Keys, at the University of Hull, I established a research programme to inquire into the theoretical coherence and practical value of systems ideas and different systems approaches. This work continued in the late 1980s and in 1991 I published, with Bob Flood, *Creative Problem Solving: Total Systems Intervention* (Wiley). The success of that volume is the inspiration for this book. *Creative Problem Solving* was very popular and, indeed, is still widely used. However, in some important respects it was flawed and it has in-evitably got somewhat out of date. Having completed a major theoretical tome of my own in 2000 – *Systems Approaches to Management* (Kluwer/Plenum) – I became confident that I had clarified my own thinking about some of the difficult issues surrounding the use of systems ideas. A produc-tive thing to do, I thought, would be to make available the results of the new research in a more popular format. This book, therefore, draws on the strengths of *Creative Problem Solving*, particularly its introductory nature and accessibility, together with the latest research findings. Its name *Systems Thinking: Creative Holism for Managers* stems from the emphasis placed, as we have already discussed, on the creative use of systems approaches.

I am grateful to the following for their permission to reproduce previously published material: Productivity Press, for Figure 5.4; Abacus, for Figure 7.1; Sage, for Figure 7.2; and Plenum Press, for Figure 10.4.

Bob Flood and I could not agree on what a follow-up to *Creative Problem Solving* would be like or on whether we wanted to do one. This volume has to be, therefore, my own interpretation of what a revised and better *Creative*

Problem Solving should be. Nevertheless, there is a debt to the earlier volume, in concept if not in content, and I therefore gratefully acknowledge Bob's contribution to this book.

For helpful comments on individual chapters I would like to thank Paul Keys (Chapter 4), Ted Geerling (Chapter 5), Peter Fryer (Chapter 7), Amanda Gregory (Chapter 8), Russ Ackoff (Chapter 9), Peter Checkland (Chapter 10), Gerald Midgley (Chapter 11), Norma Romm (Chapter 13) and Keith Ellis (Chapter 14). Thanks to Maria Ortegon, Ellis Chung, Gerald Midgley, Keith Ellis and Alvaro Carrisoza for the case studies in Chapters 7, 8, 11, 14 and 15, respectively. Very special thanks to Angela Espinosa who advised on Chapter 6, coauthored Chapter 12 and provided the case studies for those two chapters. I did not always take the advice offered and all the faults that remain are my responsibility.

At John Wiley & Sons, Diane Taylor deserves special credit for having faith in this project and persevering with it – even if it has taken so long to come to fruition that she has already retired. Thanks also to Sarah Booth.

I still write longhand, not very neatly and with whatever biro I can acquire. My PA Doreen Gibbs copes admirably with this as well as offering loads of other support. I am extremely grateful to her for help over the years.

This has been the most difficult book to complete of all those I have written. It has been done at a time when I have been extremely busy as Director of the University of Hull Business School. Everyone I know, either as a colleague, friend or acquaintance, has got used to asking 'how is the book coming on?' Our dog, Kelly, has had even fewer walks than normal. The major sacrifices, however, have been made by my sons Christopher and Richard and my wife Pauline. Thank you so much for having put up with this and I promise it is the last book.

Michael C. Jackson
May, 2003

Introduction

The book is divided into three parts. The first part presents some introductory material on systems ideas and how they came to be applied to management problems. Part II considers and classifies the most significant attempts that have been made to take a holistic approach to improving organizational performance. Many of these holistic approaches employ systems ideas in a manner that enhances creativity. The maximum creative use of holism to assist managers, however, comes from using the different approaches in combination. This is the focus of the final part of the book. Let us now consider how the book is structured based on this overall plan.

In the Preface we noted that systems thinking eschews simple solutions to complex problems. It embraces holism and creativity to handle complexity, change and diversity. These notions are initially a little more difficult to grasp than the fads and panaceas prepared in easily digestible form for managers to consume. We begin therefore, in Chapter 1, by learning the language of systems thinking. Systems concepts have a long history, dating back to early Greek philosophy. They have penetrated and been refined in a variety of different disciplines. We consider the emergence and meaning of the most important systems terms and how they give rise to a language fit for the purpose of dealing with managerial concerns.

It was about the time of the Second World War that the first attempts were made to apply systems ideas to managerial problem-solving. Chapter 2 looks at the birth and development of this applied systems thinking. It is one of the strengths of systems thinking compared with, say, process re-engineering, knowledge management and the balanced scorecard, that it has a reasonably long history of application from which much has been learned. The history of applied systems thinking over the last few decades has seen it continually reframing itself so as to become slicker in dealing with complexity and change in a wider range of problem situations.

The final chapter of Part I relates developments in applied systems thinking to different ways of looking at operations and organizations, and how they should be managed. This is accomplished by considering what assumptions managers make when dealing with problems in organizations. Managers get locked into particular, limited ways of seeing the world and this clearly affects the way they try to change it. The assumptions they make can be revealed if set against the backdrop of the metaphors and paradigms that are used to understand organizations and intervene in them. The various holistic approaches to management themselves build on different metaphors and paradigms. Once this is grasped it becomes possible to understand the strengths and weaknesses of the variety of holistic approaches and to use them in combination to enhance creativity.

Following these introductory chapters on systems concepts, applied systems thinking and creativity enhancement, Part II provides a comprehensive review of the best known and most useful holistic approaches to management. All the approaches considered make use of the systems language presented in Chapter 1 and at least a significant subset of the systems concepts introduced. They are all holistic in character. The use to which they put systems ideas is different however – according to the purposes that they hope to achieve. In particular, the metaphors they employ and the paradigms they embrace make a difference to what is envisaged as the most important aim that systems thinking should pursue. On this basis, holistic approaches can be classified into four types:

- systems approaches for improving goal seeking and viability;
- systems approaches for exploring purposes;
- systems approaches for ensuring fairness;
- systems approaches for promoting diversity.

Part II is divided into four; emphasizing that there are these four 'types' of systems approach (Types A–D) each privileging a different aim.

Chapters 4, 5, 6 and 7 detail those systems approaches that can help goal seeking and viability through increasing the efficiency and efficacy of organizational processes and structures (Type A). Their primary orientation is improving organizational performance in terms of how well the organization does its tasks and responds to changes in its environment. Included in this category are 'hard systems thinking' (Chapter 4), 'system dynamics – the fifth discipline' (Chapter 5), 'organizational cybernetics' (Chapter 6) and 'complexity theory' (Chapter 7).

Type B systems approaches seek to improve organizational performance by exploring purposes and ensuring sufficient agreement is obtained among an organization's stakeholders about purposes. Their primary orientation is to evaluate different aims and objectives, promote mutual understanding, ensure an accommodation is reached and gain commitment to purposes. Discussion around purposes normally involves issues of the effectiveness and elegance of what is being proposed. Chapter 8 considers 'strategic assumption surfacing and testing', Chapter 9 'interactive planning' and Chapter 10 'soft systems methodology'.

Chapter 11 on 'critical systems heuristics' and Chapter 12 on 'team syntegrity' consider Type C systems approaches. The main concern shifts to ensuring fairness in organizations. Organizational performance is seen as improved as discrimination of all kinds is eliminated, full and open participation is encouraged so that people have a say over decisions that involve them, and organizations pay attention to all those affected by their actions. This orientation is reflected in a primary concern with emancipating and empowering disadvantaged groups.

Type D is covered in just one chapter, Chapter 13, on postmodern systems thinking. This sees performance as improved if organizations exhibit a diversity appropriate to the challenges they face in new times. Organizations can become moribund, sterile, boring because they are dominated by particular systems of thought and routinized ways of doing things. Postmodern systems thinking challenges normality and the routine, encouraging difference and fun. It emphasizes the importance of looking for exceptions and of engaging people's emotions when seeking change.

Part II, therefore, presents and considers the most important attempts that have been made to bring holism, and the systems language associated with it, to the attention of managers in ways that they can make use of. Chapters 4–13 set out and critique the main systems approaches to management. As will become apparent the four categories (Types A–D), into which these systems approaches have been divided, can be related back to the different paradigms of thinking about organizations discussed in Chapter 3. Moreover, within each category the differences between the systems approaches selected for consideration can be linked to the variety of metaphors looked at in Chapter 3. This enables us to see clearly the assumptions on which the different systems approaches are based, why they emphasize certain factors as being significant for organizational performance and ignore others, and to understand at a deeper level their strengths and weaknesses.

The role and importance of Part III can now be outlined. Although all the systems approaches considered in Part II embrace holism, and this has many advantages in dealing with complexity, change and diversity, they do so on the basis of particular perspectives on the nature of organizations and how they should be managed to make them work well. It is surely being even more holistic to believe that improving organizational performance, in its very broadest sense, requires an ability to look at organizations from all these perspectives (based on different paradigms and metaphors). And it requires managers to be able to bring to bear, on the complex, diverse and rapidly changing problem situations they confront, holistic approaches based on the variety of possible perspectives. Overall organizational performance must depend on: improving goal seeking and viability; exploring purposes; ensuring fairness; and promoting diversity. Consideration must be given to efficiency, efficacy, effectiveness, elegance, emancipation, empowerment, exception and emotion. Improvement can involve all of these things although, of course, it is necessary for managers to prioritize and to have a different emphasis to their actions at different times.

Part III of the book is called 'creative holism' and is concerned with the use of different systems approaches, reflecting alternative holistic perspectives, in combination. The various systems approaches cannot be used all at once but they can be employed creatively, in an informed and ethical way, to promote together the overall improvement of organizational performance. This is the essence of creative holism.

Part III consists of two chapters. The first looks at 'total systems intervention', as the best known approach to combining different systems approaches. The second describes 'critical systems practice', as the modern expression of creative holism.

A short conclusion closes the argument.

In this introduction I have sought to make clear the structure of the book and the logic underlying that structure. This is summarized in Table I.1.

Table I.1   The structure of the book.

Introduction			
Part I Holism and Systems Practice		Chapter 1	The Systems Language
		Chapter 2	Applied Systems Thinking
		Chapter 3	Creativity and Systems
Part II Systems Approaches	*Type A* *Improving Goal Seeking and Viability*	Chapter 4	Hard Systems Thinking
		Chapter 5	System Dynamics: The Fifth Discipline
		Chapter 6	Organizational Cybernetics
		Chapter 7	Complexity Theory
	Type B *Exploring Purposes*	Chapter 8	Strategic Assumption Surfacing and Testing
		Chapter 9	Interactive Planning
		Chapter 10	Soft Systems Methodology
	Type C *Ensuring Fairness*	Chapter 11	Critical Systems Heuristics
		Chapter 12	Team Syntegrity
	Type D *Promoting Diversity*	Chapter 13	Postmodern Systems Thinking
Part III Creative Holism		Chapter 14	Total Systems Intervention
		Chapter 15	Critical Systems Practice
Conclusion			

Part I

Holism and Systems Practice

The aim of Part I is to provide the reader with the background information needed to understand fully the different systems approaches studied in Part II. Chapter 1 introduces the systems language and some simple systems ideas. It does this by tracing the influence of holism and the emergence of various systems concepts in some important intellectual disciplines, such as philosophy and biology. Chapter 2 considers the development of applied systems thinking since its birth around the time of the Second World War. It tries to put a pattern on events by seeing the different systems approaches that arose as responses, in turn, to the need to improve goal seeking and viability, to explore purposes, to ensure fairness, and to promote diversity. These various requirements themselves originate in the greater complexity, turbulence and variety of problem situations as discussed in the Preface. Chapter 3 steps back a little and sees the development of different systems approaches in terms of a willingness by systems thinkers to explore and enrich various metaphors of organization and alternative sociological paradigms using systems ideas. It is upon an understanding of this process, and of what different metaphors and paradigms have to offer, that the critique of the different systems approaches, exposing their strengths and weaknesses, can be launched in Part II.

The Systems Language $\qquad$ 1

The more we study the major problems of our time, the more we come to realise that they cannot be understood in isolation. They are systemic problems, which means that they are interconnected and interdependent.

Capra (1996)

1.1 INTRODUCTION

Simply defined, a system is a complex whole the functioning of which depends on its parts and the interactions between those parts. Stated like this, it is clear that we can identify systems of very different types:

- physical, such as river systems;
- biological, such as living organisms;
- designed, such as automobiles;
- abstract, such as philosophical systems;
- social, such as families;
- human activity, such as systems to ensure the quality of products.

The traditional, scientific method for studying such systems is known as reductionism. Reductionism sees the parts as paramount and seeks to identify the parts, understand the parts and work up from an understanding of the parts to an understanding of the whole. The problem with this is that the whole often seems to take on a form that is not recognizable from the parts. The whole emerges from the interactions between the parts, which affect each other through complex networks of relationships. Once it has emerged, it is the whole that seems to give meaning to the parts and their interactions. A living organism gives meaning to the heart, liver and lungs; a family to the roles of husband, wife, son, daughter.

It is not surprising therefore that there exists an alternative to reductionism for studying systems. This alternative is known as holism. Holism considers systems to be more than the sum of their parts. It is of course interested in the parts and particularly the networks of relationships between the parts, but primarily in terms of how they give rise to and sustain in existence the new entity that is the whole – whether it be a river system, an automobile, a philosophical system or a quality system. It is the whole that is seen as important and gives purpose to the study.

Holism gained a foothold in many different academic disciplines, benefiting from the failure of reductionism to cope with problems of complexity, diversity and change in complex systems. In what follows we look at the encounter of holism with philosophy, biology, control engineering, organization and management theory, and the physical sciences. We see how the systems language associated with holism was developed and enriched in each case. Particularly fruitful were the encounters with biology and control engineering, which gave birth to systems thinking as a transdiscipline, studying systems in their own right, in the 1940s and 1950s. This produced a language that describes the characteristics that systems have in common, whether they are mechanical, biological or social.

In a conclusion to the chapter I seek to explain why this language is particularly powerful for the purposes of managers.

More detailed accounts of the development of holistic thinking can be found in Checkland (1981) and Jackson (2000).

1.2 PHILOSOPHY

The classical Greek philosophers, Aristotle and Plato, established some important systems ideas. Aristotle reasoned that the parts of the body only make sense in terms of the way they function to support the whole organism and used this biological analogy to consider how individuals need to be related to the State. Plato was interested in how the notion of control, or the art of steersmanship (*kybernetes*), could be applied both to vessels and the State. Ships had to be steered safely toward harbour by a helmsman. A similar role needed to be fulfilled in societies if they were to prosper.

Holism was pushed to the margins of philosophical debate for many centuries, but the golden age of European philosophy, during the 18th and 19th centuries, saw a renewed interest in what it had to offer. Kant and

Hegel were particularly influential in this respect. Kant was an 'idealist' who argued that we could never really know reality or whether it was systemic. However, he believed it was helpful for humans to think in terms of wholes emerging from and sustained by the self-organization of their parts. Hegel introduced process into systems thinking. An understanding of the whole, or the truth, could be approached through a systemic unfolding of thesis, antithesis and synthesis. Each movement through this cycle, with the synthesis becoming the new thesis, gradually enriched our grasp of the whole.

It was these philosophical ideas that impacted on the scientific disciplines, where they were given a more rigorous formulation.

1.3 BIOLOGY

The fruitfulness of the relationship between holism and biology can be accounted for by the complexity of the problems encountered by biologists in trying to understand whole organisms. Whole organisms seemed to resist the attempts of scientific reductionists to reduce them to the sum of their parts. In the 1920s and 1930s, as a response to this, more holistically inclined biologists began to argue that organisms were more than the sum of their parts. They conceived that a hierarchy existed in nature – molecules, organelles, cells, organs, organisms – and, at certain points in the hierarchy, stable levels of organized complexity arose that demonstrated emergent properties, which did not exist at levels below. An organism was one such level.

It was argued that an organism (e.g., an animal) had a clear boundary separating it from its environment and was capable, as its main emergent property, of a degree of autonomy. An organism sustained itself in a steady state by carrying out transactions across this boundary with its environment. It had to be capable of making internal transformations to ensure that it was adapted to its environment. The processes that maintained the steady state were referred to as homeostatic, an example being the self-regulating mechanism controlling body temperature. The behaviour of an organism could not, it seemed, be explained by the properties of its parts in isolation. It arose from the particular interdependence of the parts, which gave rise to a new level of organized complexity. Biology was seen exactly as the science appropriate to this level and could not therefore be reduced to physics or chemistry.

Ludwig von Bertalanffy has become the best known of the biologists who argued that organisms should be studied as complex wholes. In 1950 he published an article in which be made the well-known distinction between closed systems and open systems. A closed system engages in no exchanges with its environment. An open system, such as an organism, has to interact with its environment to maintain itself in existence. Open systems take inputs from their environments, transform them and then return them as some sort of product back to the environment. They depend on the environment for their existence and adapt in reaction to changes in the environment.

Von Bertalanffy's lasting fame and influence has derived from his suggestion that the sorts of behaviour he witnessed in open systems in biology could be seen demonstrated by open systems in other domains. Thus, he initiated and named 'general system theory' (see von Bertalanffy, 1968) – a kind of transdiscipline in which systems were studied in their own right and which allowed insights from one discipline to be transferred to others. General system theory was soon embraced by management thinkers who transferred the open system model to their study of organizations.

The biological system model is represented in Figure 1.1. It shows a system separated from its environment by a distinct boundary. The system has a complex structure, being differentiated into subsystems that themselves have parts (systems arranged in a hierarchy of systems). The close interrelationships of mutual influence between the subsystems must ensure homeostasis – the maintenance of a steady state. One subsystem is acting in a kind of 'management' capacity, trying to ensure integration and co-ordination. The system takes inputs of material, energy and information

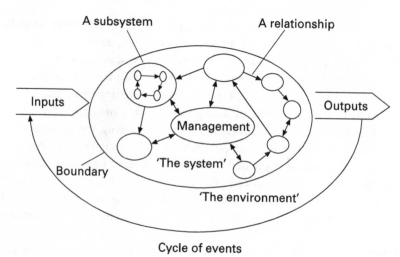

Figure 1.1 The biological system model.

from its environment, uses some to sustain itself and transforms the rest into outputs. These outputs may themselves allow the system to secure, through a cycle of events, more of the useful inputs it needs to survive.

The open systems perspective propounded by von Bertalanffy, and so influential in the 1970s and 1980s, has more recently been challenged by the biologists Maturana and Varela (1980). They emphasize instead the closed system of interactions that occurs in living entities. These interactions ensure the self-production of the system and its autonomy. Such self-producing, or *autopoietic* (from the ancient Greek for self-production), systems respond to environmental disturbances, but not directly or simply; the nature of the response depends on their own internal organizational arrangements. This does not mean that autopoietic systems cannot change their structure, but it does mean that they do this only with a view to keeping their fundamental organizational identity intact. The emphasis on the circular organization of living systems, and their resistance to change, offers a useful corrective to those general system theorists who stress the overriding importance of organization–environment relations.

1.4 CONTROL ENGINEERING

The other figure who stands alongside von Bertalanffy, as a founding father of systems thinking as a transdiscipline, is Norbert Wiener, a mathematician and control engineer. In 1948 Wiener published a book on what he called, borrowing from the Greek, cybernetics – the science of control and communication in the animal and the machine. Cybernetics, Wiener argued, was a new science that had application to many different disciplines because it dealt with general laws that governed control processes whatever the nature of the system under consideration.

The two key concepts introduced by Wiener into the systems lexicon were control and communication. In understanding control, whether in the mechanical, biological or political realm, the idea of negative feedback is crucial. This concept allows a proper, scientific explanation to be given of purposive behaviour – behaviour directed to the attainment of a goal. It was Wiener's insight that all such behaviour requires negative feedback. In this process, information is transmitted about any divergence of behaviour from a present goal and corrective action taken, on the basis of this information, to bring the behaviour back towards the goal. In a central heating system a thermostat monitors the heat of a room against some preset temperature and uses the information that the temperature is too low or high to switch

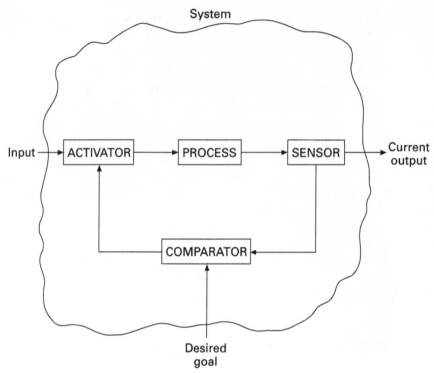

Figure 1.2 A negative feedback system.

the system on or off. Communication is equally significant because if we wish to control the actions of a machine or another human being we must communicate information to that machine or individual.

Figure 1.2 shows a simple, negative feedback system. It operates by sensing the current output of the process that is to be controlled. The output is compared with the desired goal and, if it diverges from this, an activator adjusts the input to bring the process back toward achieving the desired goal. In this way, systems regulate themselves and are controlled, in the face of environmental disturbances, through the effective communication of information. It is of course very important that the sensor and comparator operate continuously and rapidly. This ensures that discrepancies are identified at the earliest possible opportunity and corrective action can immediately be initiated. It is also worth noting that it is not necessary to understand the nature of the process, which might be a complex system, in order to employ the negative feedback device. The controller can regard it as a 'black box' and adjust it simply by manipulating the inputs in order to achieve the desired outputs.

Although it did not impinge much on the consciousness of Wiener, another form of feedback, positive feedback, has become significant for systems thinking. While negative feedback counteracts deviations from a goal, positive feedback amplifies them. For example, one mistimed tackle in a soccer match can lead to a series of deliberate fouls, escalating into uncontrolled aggression from both sides. Identifying situations where the parts of a system are locked into a positive feedback loop, and its behaviour is spinning out of control, is of obvious significance to managers. A good referee can re-establish order with the astute use of a yellow card.

A final systems concept that I need to introduce in this section is 'variety'. Variety is a term first used by Ashby (1956) to refer to the number of possible states a system can exhibit. According to Ashby's law of requisite variety, systems can only be controlled if the would-be controller can command the same degree of variety as the system. Today, systems are complex and change rapidly; they exhibit high variety. Managers need to pay attention to reducing the variety of the system they are seeking to control and/or to increasing their own variety. This process of 'balancing varieties' is known as variety engineering. We shall see how it is done in Chapter 6.

1.5 ORGANIZATION AND MANAGEMENT THEORY

Early attempts to marry holism with organization and management theory took two main forms. In the first some basic systems concepts were incorporated in the prevailing scientific management tradition to yield optimizing approaches, such as systems engineering. In the second there was a wholesale transfer of the biological analogy, especially as refined by von Bertalanffy, to yield systems models of organization emphasizing the importance of subsystems to overall organizational effectiveness and the significance of the organization–environment fit.

Both these early attempts met with difficulties because they failed to recognize that systems containing human beings are, what we now call, purposeful. The systems of components that engineers are used to dealing with are purposive – designed to reach the goal specified by the engineers. Biological systems are adept at survival, but if this is their purpose it is obviously something ascribed to them from the outside and not something they think about themselves. The parts of social systems however – human beings – can generate their own purposes from inside the system, and these might not correspond at all to any purposes prescribed by managers or outsiders. Social and organizational systems, therefore, have multiple purposes: they are purposeful.

It was soon clear that a different kind of terminology would be useful for describing and working with purposeful systems.

A number of roles had to be delimited relevant to purposeful systems and reflecting some alternative sources of purposes. The term 'stakeholder' is used to refer to any group with an interest in what the system is doing. Decision-makers or owners have the power to make things happen in systems; actors carry out basic tasks; customers or clients benefit or suffer from what a system does. Problem-owners worry about the performance of some aspect of a system. Witnesses are affected by systems but unable to influence their behaviour. Problem-solvers or analysts take on board the task of trying to improve systems.

Since purposes emanate from the human mind, attention also has to be given to the different mental models that people bring to their roles. These mental models are made up, in each case, of a mix of the understanding and values that individuals have gathered through their experiences and education. The facts and values that they use in interpreting the world can perhaps themselves be understood in systems terms. They are said to constitute the world view, *Weltanschauung* (a German word meaning 'world image'), or appreciative system employed by an individual or group.

For those who want to manage purposeful systems or intervene to change them the resistance, or otherwise, of *Weltanschauungen* or appreciative systems to change becomes critical. If the only change that can be contemplated takes place in the context of an existing mental model, then you are limited to bringing about first-order learning. If, however, the mental model itself can be changed, and purposes radically altered, then second-order change is possible. The ways in which world views change became a primary focus of 'soft systems thinking' and, within this, Hegel's notion of a 'dialectical debate' between thesis and antithesis was particularly influential.

Finally, in considering purposeful systems, we need to note how significant the concept of boundary becomes. With a machine or organism it is usually very apparent where the boundary of the system lies. For those concerned with purposeful systems, however, this is rarely the case. Where the boundary is seen to be will depend on the world view of the person observing the system. For example, whether the boundary of a business organization should expand to include its natural environment, its local community, unemployed people, etc. are all very much issues open to debate. Values and ethics play a part in such decisions. There is the further matter of who should participate in defining purposes, taking decisions and drawing boundaries. And because resources and interests will be at stake, as well as different philosophies, power and politics will have a significant impact on purposeful systems.

The encounter of holism with management and organization theory has thrown up complications not found when the focus of attention for systems thinking was the natural realm. Part II reveals, however, that this has not been an unequal challenge; holism has stood up to the task well enough.

1.6 THE PHYSICAL SCIENCES

Systems thinking emerged as a transdiscipline, in the 1940s and 1950s, in large part as a reaction to the reductionism of the traditional scientific method and the failure of that reductionism to cope with the complexity inherent in the biological and social domains. It seemed for some time, therefore, that systems thinking was the antithesis of the scientific method. More recently, however, the physical sciences seem to have undergone their own systems revolution and holism, and the concepts associated with it have been welcomed in physics and chemistry as offering new forms of explanation and new avenues of exploration. Quantum theory in physics and the study of dissipative structures in chemistry are examples of a more holistic orientation in the physical sciences.

Because they have undergone their own systems revolution, the physical sciences are now able to make their own contributions to the language of systems thinking more generally. Quantum physics brought to the fore the notion of indeterminacy and gave new meaning to the concept of relationships. From chemistry comes a reinforcement of the process view of systems and the idea of self-organization. Perhaps most important of all, however, has been the birth of a new kind of general system theory in science under the banner of chaos and complexity theory (see Gleick, 1987).

Complexity theory – the more general term and the one we shall use – complements the normal systems concern for order by being equally concerned with disorder. The fact that so many complex systems appear to exhibit disorder, irregularity and unpredictability had seemed to put them beyond the reach of scientific understanding. Complexity theorists did not actually dispute this. Indeed, their early studies reinforced the notion by demonstrating that a small change in the initial conditions of a system can lead to large-scale consequences later on: famously, a butterfly flapping its wings in the Amazon jungle can conceivably lead to storms in the South

China Sea. However, what they also found was that underlying apparent chaos was a surprising degree of pattern. Complex systems seem to be governed in some way by 'strange attractors', which means that although they never repeat exactly the same behaviour, what they do remains within certain limits. The weather in England is notoriously unpredictable in detail, but we never experience extreme cold or extreme heat and, only occasionally, very heavy rainfall and hurricanes. Furthermore, the patterns that govern complex systems seem to be repeated at different levels of the system. The parts of the whole are similar in shape to the whole. Snowflakes and cauliflowers have been used as everyday examples of 'fractal wholes' demonstrating such self-similarity.

Pursuing their research into order and disorder in complex systems, complexity theorists discovered what became known as the 'edge of chaos'. This is a narrow transition zone between order and chaos where systems become capable of taking on new forms of behaviour – of self-organization and particularly innovative activity.

The potential of complexity theory for helping managers is perhaps becoming clear. The organizations they manage seem chaotic and unpredictable. But maybe they too are governed by strange attractors that can, after all, be understood. The environments in which organizations operate are turbulent and ever changing, yet organizations seem slow to adapt. Maybe if they can be driven to the edge of chaos they will be much more creative in the way they behave. A new systems view of organizations has been constructed out of these ideas.

1.7 WHY IS THE SYSTEMS LANGUAGE SO POWERFUL?

In this chapter we have started to become familiar with the systems language. Our undertstanding will be deepened as we start to see how the language can be used to address management problems in Part II. Obviously, it takes effort to learn a new language and we will have to encounter still more new concepts in what follows. In asking you to make this effort I can perhaps rely on the fact that managers are fed up with being offered simple solutions to complex, diverse problems. They recognize that more sophisticated solutions are necessary and that this may demand a more difficult language. I am keen, however, to close the chapter with just four arguments as to why you should bother with the systems language.

First, as we have seen, the emphasis on holism offers a useful corrective to the reductionism that still governs much management thinking. Organizations are complex and the relationships between the parts are crucial. There is a need for joined-up thinking in addressing their problems.

Second is the emphasis modern systems thinking puts on process as well as structure. This stems from systems philosophy, from von Bertalanffy's open systems concept and from complexity theory. It is not always the right approach to design systems according to some predefined blueprint. Allowing a process to take place can lead to innovative behaviour and ways forward that could not have been foreseen before the process was embarked on.

Third is the transdisciplinarity of systems thinking. It draws its ideas and concepts, as we have seen, from a variety of different disciplines and in so doing can draw on their different strengths. Even if analogies derived from physics and biology do not hold strictly when applied to organizations, managers have access to a rich storehouse of insights if they can use other disciplines to provide them with new metaphors for understanding their role.

Finally, the systems language has proven itself more suitable for getting to grips with real-world management problems than that of any other single discipline. It has given rise to a range of powerful systems approaches to management. The next chapter starts to look at the development of this applied systems thinking. In Part II you will get the chance to judge the truth of the claim I am making here for yourself.

REFERENCES

Ashby, W.R. (1956). *An Introduction to Cybernetics*. Methuen, London.

Capra, F. (1996). *The Web of Life: A New Synthesis of Mind and Matter*. Flamingo, London.

Checkland, P.B. (1981). *Systems Thinking, Systems Practice*. John Wiley & Sons, Chichester, UK.

Gleick, J. (1987). *Chaos: The Making of a New Science*. Abacus, London.

Jackson, M.C. (2000). *Systems Approaches to Management*. Kluwer/Plenum, New York.

Maturana, H.R. and Varela, F.J. (1980). *Autopoiesis and Cognition: The Realization of the Living*. D. Reidel, Dordrecht, The Netherlands.

von Bertalanffy, L. (1950). The theory of open systems in physics and biology. In: F.E. Emery (ed.), *Systems Thinking* (pp. 70–85). Penguin, Harmondsworth, UK.

von Bertalanffy, L. (1968). *General System Theory*. Penguin, Harmondsworth, UK.

Wiener, N. (1948). *Cybernetics*. John Wiley & Sons, New York.

Applied Systems Thinking   2

OR [operational research] is regarded by many as being in crisis. If OR is taken to be 'classical OR', this is indisputable ... If, however, the definition of OR is widened to embrace other systems-based methodologies for problem solving, then a diversity of approaches may herald not crisis, but increased competence and effectiveness in a variety of different problem contexts.

Jackson and Keys (1984)

2.1 INTRODUCTION

As systems thinking evolved, and systems concepts developed in the way described in the previous chapter, increasing attention was given to whether it could be used to tackle practical real-world problems. In this chapter we start to consider the work of those involved in a more applied approach to systems thinking, especially those who wanted to apply systems ideas to managerial problem situations. To this end we first consider the nature and limitations of what has come to be called 'hard systems thinking'. We then look at how applied systems thinking developed, during the 1970s, 1980s and 1990s, to overcome some of the weaknesses of hard systems thinking, in the process making itself useful in a much wider range of problem situations. Section 2.4 introduces the main strands of applied systems thinking and picks out the characteristics of the particular approaches we shall be studying in more depth in Part II. A conclusion summarizes the state of applied systems thinking today and leads us to ask questions about how we can make the most creative use of the different modes of holistic intervention that now exist. Part III, on creative holism, will seek to provide the answers.

2.2   HARD SYSTEMS THINKING

When systems practitioners bring together various systems ideas and techniques in an organized way and employ them to try to improve a problem situation, they are said to be using a 'systems methodology' – another technical term to which we shall become accustomed. The attempt to devise such methodologies as a means of tackling real-world problems began around the time of the Second World War. It was during the Second World War, and its immediate aftermath, that the methodologies of Operational Research (OR), Systems Analysis (SA) and Systems Engineering (SE) were born. OR was used extensively to assist the allied war effort (e.g., in increasing the efficiency of radar systems and in optimizing the results of bombing raids on German cities). After the war OR workers migrated into government departments and, especially in Britain, into OR groups established in the large nationalized industries. SA was promoted by the highly influential RAND (acronym for 'Research ANd Development') Corporation and used extensively to help the US military. Somewhat later, in the form of spin-offs, such as cost–benefit analysis, it found willing champions in central and local government departments. SE was an extension of the principles adopted by the engineering profession to large industrial engineering projects (e.g., in the chemical and aerospace industries).

Checkland (1981), recognizing similarities between the approaches of OR, SA and SE, labelled this kind of systems work 'hard systems thinking'. We shall be exploring its nature, strengths and weaknesses more fully in Chapter 4. In essence, however, it offered managers and management scientists a means of seeking to optimize the performance of a system in pursuit of clearly identified goals. Emphasis is placed on the application of a systematic methodology that, having established objectives, is able to identify problems that stand in the way of optimization and rectify them by employing scientific modelling, rational testing, implementation and evaluation processes.

Hard systems thinking was a breakthrough in terms of applying systems thinking to real-world problems. In many cases, as we shall see in Chapter 4, it offers a methodology that remains the most appropriate way of proceeding to tackle such problems. A considerable amount of criticism has, however, been levelled at the limitations of hard systems thinking in the environment inhabited by managers. These criticisms relate to its inability to handle significant complexity, to cope with a plurality of different beliefs and values, and to deal with issues of politics and power.

The extreme complexity and turbulence of problem situations, and of the environments surrounding them, frustrate the aspirations of hard systems thinkers. Hard approaches require an objective account of the system of concern so that a mathematical model can be produced and an optimal solution to the problem recommended. The 'reality' facing today's managers is so complex and subject to change that it is impossible to reduce problem situations to a form that would make them amenable to such modelling. How can we distinguish exactly which elements contribute to the problem situation, identify the relevant interactions between them and quantify their influence?

Another limitation is that hard systems thinking is unable to deal satisfactorily with multiple perceptions of reality. It demands that the goal of the system of concern be known or ascertained before analysis can proceed. OR, for example, requires 'formulation of the problem' on the basis of the objectives to be achieved. In managerial situations the establishment of agreed objectives will often lie at the very heart of the problem to be tackled. Different stakeholders will have diverse opinions about the nature of the system they are involved with and about its proper purposes. Consider, for example, a university – is it primarily a research institution, a teaching factory, a servant of its local community, a supplier of trained labour to employers, a means of passing on the cultural norms of a society, a holiday camp that keeps kids off the street, etc.? Hard methodologies, lacking mechanisms for generating accommodations around objectives, are unable even to get started when confronted with messy situations of this kind.

In need of a clearly defined goal, and an objective account of the situation, it is not surprising that hard systems thinkers should cleave to the point of view of the powerful to progress their analyses. This strategy also increases the chances of having some recommendations implemented. Obviously, however, it leaves hard approaches open to the charge of being unable to deal with politics and power, of serving only influential clients and of limiting their recommendations to those that defend the status quo.

By the 1970s, because of the obvious failings of hard systems thinking, the systems community found itself in something akin to a crisis. In Section 2.3 we shall consider further the nature of this crisis and how applied systems thinking developed in order to overcome it.

2.3 THE DEVELOPMENT OF APPLIED SYSTEMS THINKING

The history of applied systems thinking can be presented in terms of efforts to overcome the weaknesses of hard systems thinking as set out in the previous section. Success in this endeavour has been hard-won, but over the last 30 years or so significant developments have taken place and the systems approach is now valued as making an important contribution to resolving a much wider range of complex problems than hard systems thinking was able to deal with. We can understand these developments best using a framework for classifying systems methodologies, developed by Jackson and Keys in 1984, called the System Of Systems Methodologies (SOSM).

2.3.1 Problem contexts

The starting point in constructing the SOSM is an 'ideal-type' grid of problem situations or problem contexts. This grid has been described and presented in various ways (see Jackson and Keys, 1984; Jackson, 1993, 2000; Flood and Jackson, 1991), but an easily understandable version is shown as Figure 2.1.

We argued earlier in the book that problem contexts become more difficult to manage as they exhibit greater complexity, change and diversity. In very general terms, systems thinkers see increasing complexity, change and diversity as stemming from two sources: the 'systems' managers have to deal with, as they become larger and subject to more turbulence; and the 'participants', those with an interest in the problem situation, as their

		PARTICIPANTS		
		UNITARY	PLURALIST	COERCIVE
SYSTEMS	SIMPLE	Simple–Unitary	Simple–Pluralist	Simple–Coercive
	COMPLEX	Complex–Unitary	Complex–Pluralist	Complex–Coercive

Figure 2.1 Jackson's extended version of Jackson and Keys' 'ideal-type' grid of problem contexts.

values, beliefs and interests start to diverge. This gives rise to the 'systems' and 'participants' dimensions used to establish the grid.

The vertical axis expresses a continuum of system types conceptualized at one extreme as relatively simple, at the other as extremely complex. Simple systems can be characterized as having a few subsystems that are involved in only a small number of highly structured interactions. They tend not to change much over time, being relatively unaffected by the independent actions of their parts or by environmental influences. Extremely complex systems, at the other end of the spectrum, can be characterized as having a large number of subsystems that are involved in many more loosely structured interactions, the outcome of which is not predetermined. Such systems adapt and evolve over time as they are affected by their own purposeful parts and by the turbulent environments in which they exist.

The horizontal axis classifies the relationships that can exist between those concerned with the problem context – the participants – in three types: 'unitary', 'pluralist' and 'coercive'. Participants defined as being in a unitary relationship have similar values, beliefs and interests. They share common purposes and are all involved, in one way or another, in decision-making about how to realize their agreed objectives. Those defined as being in a pluralist relationship differ in that, although their basic interests are compatible, they do not share the same values and beliefs. Space needs to be made available within which debate, disagreement, even conflict, can take place. If this is done, and all feel they have been involved in decision-making, then accommodations and compromises can be found. Participants will come to agree, at least temporarily, on productive ways forward and will act accordingly. Those participants defined as being in coercive relationships have few interests in common and, if free to express them, would hold conflicting values and beliefs. Compromise is not possible and so no agreed objectives direct action. Decisions are taken on the basis of who has most power and various forms of coercion employed to ensure adherence to commands.

Combining the 'systems' and 'participants' dimensions, divided as suggested above, yields six ideal-type forms of problem context: simple–unitary, simple–pluralist, simple–coercive, complex–unitary, complex–pluralist and complex–coercive. This notion of 'ideal type' is crucial in understanding the SOSM and what it is seeking to convey. The grid does not wish to suggest that real-life problem situations can be defined as fitting exactly within any of these boxes. Weber (1969), the originator of the notion, describes ideal types as stating logical extremes that can be used to construct abstract models of general realities. The grid presents some abstract models that reveal various ways in which problem contexts might be typified by managers and management scientists. It is useful to us here if we are able to show, as we seek to do in the next subsection, that the developers of different systems methodologies have themselves been governed by particular ideal-type views of the nature of problem contexts in producing their systems approaches.

2.3.2   Systems methodologies related to problem contexts

The ideal-type grid of problem contexts is useful in helping us to understand how applied systems thinking has developed over the last few decades. It enables us to grasp the variety of responses made by systems practitioners in their attempts to overcome the weaknesses of hard systems thinking in order to tackle more complex problem situations. We are able to discern a pattern in the history of the development of applied systems thinking.

Let us consider initially the assumptions made by hard systems thinking about the nature of problem contexts. It is clear that they assume they are 'simple–unitary'. In other words, hard systems approaches take it for granted that problem contexts are simple–unitary in character and recommend intervening accordingly. It is not surprising given the circumstances in which they were developed that they came to rely on there being a shared and, therefore, readily identifiable goal. If you are trying to win a war or are engaged in postwar reconstruction, it is completely reasonable to make unitary assumptions. Later in the 1960s and 1970s, when hard systems approaches were taken into universities to be further 'refined' by academics, an original bias toward quantification became an obsession with mathematically modelling the system of concern. To believe that this is possible you have to assume that the system you are dealing with is relatively simple. So the underlying assumptions of classical OR (and this is true, if to a lesser extent, of systems analysis and systems engineering) are simple–unitary. Hard systems thinkers remain stuck in that area of the grid of problem contexts where it is assumed that people share values and beliefs and that systems are simple enough to be mathematically modelled. And it is true that these assumptions have served them well in tackling a whole variety of operational issues; in the case of OR for inventory, queuing, scheduling, routing, etc. problems.

Unfortunately, difficulties arose when attempts were made to extend the range of application of hard systems approaches, exactly because of the assumptions embedded within them. As was mentioned earlier, it is often difficult to define precise objectives on which all stakeholders can agree. In these circumstances, methodologies demanding a predefined goal cannot get started because they offer no way of bringing about any consensus or accommodation around a particular goal to be pursued. Similarly, if the system of concern is extremely complex, then any mathematical model produced can only offer a limited and distorted view of reality from a particular perspective – and one which, in a turbulent situation, becomes quickly out of date. In the 1970s, therefore, came a general understanding of the lack of usefulness of hard systems thinking for more complex problem situations, and in problem contexts that were deemed to be more pluralist and coercive in character.

It is to the credit of applied systems thinking that it has not remained stuck in its simple–unitary ghetto. The last 30 or so years have seen an attempt to extend the area of successful application of systems ideas by developing methodologies that assume that problem contexts are more complex, pluralist and/or coercive in nature. This is the progress in applied systems thinking that we now seek to chart.

We begin with the vertical axis of the ideal-type grid of problem contexts, and our concern, therefore, is with those systems practitioners who wanted to move down the axis by assuming that problem contexts were more complex than hard systems thinkers believed. The aim of hard systems thinking was to optimize the system of concern in pursuit of a known goal, and to do this it appeared necessary to model the interactions between all those elements or subsystems that might affect that system of concern. In complex systems, the vast numbers of relevant variables and the myriads of interactions make this an impossible requirement. The solution, suggested by those wishing to progress down the vertical axis, was to identify those key mechanisms or structures that govern the behaviour of the elements or subsystems and, therefore, are fundamental to system behaviour. It is regarded as impossible to mathematically model the relationships between all the variables that 'on the surface' appear to be involved in what the system does. You can, however, determine the most important structural aspects that lie behind system viability and performance. This 'structuralist' approach enables the analyst to determine, at a deeper level, what is going wrong with the present functioning of the system and to learn how to manipulate key design features so that the system can survive and be effective over time by continually regulating itself, and self-organizing, as it adapts to internally and externally generated turbulence.

The systems approaches responsible for making this shift down the vertical axis show a common concern for understanding the nature of complex adaptive systems and with ensuring they are designed to have a capacity for goal seeking and remaining viable in turbulent environments. In this book we concentrate on 'system dynamics', 'organizational cybernetics' and 'complexity theory' as systems approaches that assume, in this manner, that problem contexts are extremely complex and need tackling in a 'structuralist' fashion. In each case, as we shall see, they identify different key structural aspects that need to be understood and manipulated in dealing with complexity. In the case of system dynamics it is the relationships between positive and negative feedback loops that can give rise to 'archetypes' of system behaviour. In the case of organizational cybernetics it is cybernetic laws that can be derived from the concepts of black box, feedback and variety. With complexity theory it is 'strange attractors' and the variables that have to be adjusted to ensure that an 'edge of chaos' state is achieved.

Applied systems thinkers have also made considerable progress along the horizontal axis of the ideal-type grid of problem contexts. If we move part way along that axis we find that a number of methodologies have been developed that assume that problem contexts are pluralist and provide recommendations for analysis and intervention on that basis. This tradition of work has become known as 'soft systems thinking' to distinguish it from the hard systems thinking that was left behind.

Soft systems thinkers abandoned the notion that it was possible to assume easily identifiable, agreed-on goals that could be used to provide an objective account of the system and its purposes. This was seen to be both impossible and undesirable given multiple values, beliefs and interests. Instead, attention had to be given to ensuring sufficient accommodation between different and sometimes conflicting world views in order that temporary coalitions could be fashioned in support of particular changes. The solution was to make subjectivity central, working with a variety of world views during the methodological process. In Checkland's 'soft systems methodology' (1981), a highly developed approach of this kind, systems models expressing different viewpoints, and making explicit their various implications, are constructed so that alternative perspectives can be explored systemically, compared and contrasted. The aim is to generate a systemic learning process in which the participants in the problem situation came to appreciate more fully alternative world views, and the possibilities for change they offer, and as a result an accommodation, however temporary, becomes possible between those who started with and may still hold divergent values and beliefs.

Systems practitioners seeking to progress along the horizontal dimension emphasize the crucial importance of values, beliefs and philosophies. Their primary interest is in exploring the culture and politics of organizations to see what change is feasible and in gaining commitment from participants to agreed courses of action. Such soft systems thinkers are not trying to devise system models that can be used over and over again to reveal how real-world systems can be improved. This is felt not to be relevant or useful because of the widely different viewpoints about purposes that will be present in pluralist problem contexts. Instead, what is usefully replicated, as Checkland argues, is the methodology employed. The same approach to bringing about consensus or accommodation is tried again and again and is gradually improved. As well as studying Checkland's 'soft systems methodology' we will be considering 'strategic assumption surfacing and testing' and Ackoff's 'interactive planning'. All these soft systems approaches have by now been well researched. As a result we know much better than previously about some methodological processes that can assist in bringing about accommodations between different value positions and generate commitment among participants to implement agreed changes.

If we shift further along the horizontal axis of the grid of problem contexts, the issue arises of how to intervene in problem situations that are regarded as coercive. Soft systems thinking fails to respond appropriately because of its pluralist bias that consensus, or at least accommodation, between different stakeholders can be achieved. Systems practitioners have, therefore, sought to formulate 'emancipatory' systems approaches based on the assumption that problem situations can be coercive. Ulrich's 'critical systems heuristics' allows questions to be asked about who benefits from particular system designs and seeks to empower those affected by management decisions but not involved in them. Beer's 'team syntegrity' seeks to specify an arena and procedures that enable all stakeholders to debate openly and democratically the issues with which they are confronted. Both these approaches are considered.

Finally, there are systems practitioners who worry about the claims of any systems methodology to be able to guarantee generalized improvement. They advocate postmodern systems practice in the face of the massive and impenetrable complexity and coercion that they see as inherent in all problem contexts. Suppressed viewpoints must be surfaced and diversity encouraged as in the emancipatory systems approach. All that is possible however is contested, local improvement justified on the basis that it feels right given local circumstances. Chapter 13 is devoted to this version of applied systems thinking.

In short, the argument of this section is that applied systems thinking has developed over the past few decades taking into account the characteristics of a much wider range of the ideal-type problem contexts represented in

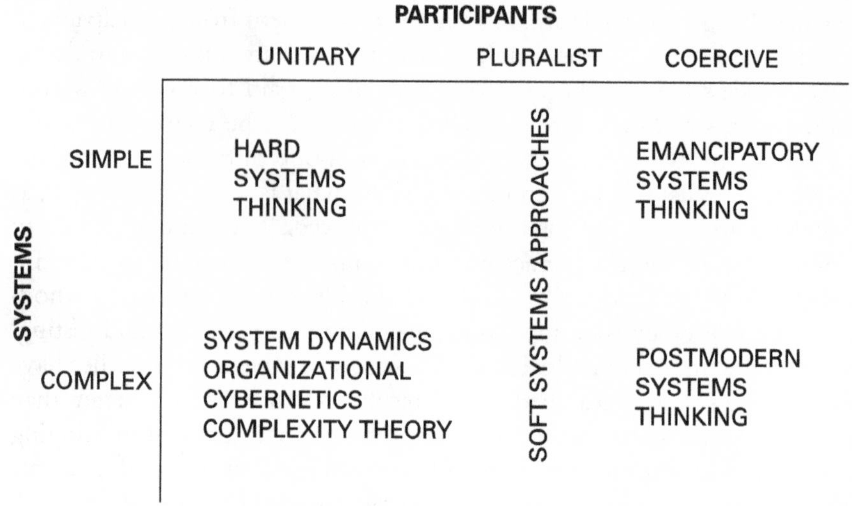

PARTICIPANTS

	UNITARY	PLURALIST	COERCIVE
SIMPLE	HARD SYSTEMS THINKING		EMANCIPATORY SYSTEMS THINKING
COMPLEX	SYSTEM DYNAMICS ORGANIZATIONAL CYBERNETICS COMPLEXITY THEORY		POSTMODERN SYSTEMS THINKING

(Left axis: SYSTEMS. Center column label, vertical: SOFT SYSTEMS APPROACHES)

Figure 2.2 Systems approaches related to problem contexts in the System of Systems Methodologies (SOSM).

the grid. It has progressed along the vertical dimension to take greater account of complexity. It has progressed along the horizontal dimension acknowledging that problem contexts can be defined as pluralist and coercive. These conclusions are summarized in Figure 2.2. The intersecting lines that constructed the particular problem contexts in the grid of Figure 2.1 have been removed in this representation of the SOSM. This should be taken to mean that it is only indicative of the assumptions made by different systems approaches about the nature of problem contexts. There is no intention to pigeon-hole methodologies and a more sophisticated treatment of their underlying assumptions will be presented in Part II.

2.4 THE MAIN STRANDS OF APPLIED SYSTEMS THINKING

It is worth taking time at this point to build on the work of the previous section and to explain briefly the rationale behind the grouping of systems approaches in Part II. In Part II, 10 systems approaches are divided into 4 types according to whether their primary orientation is improving goal seeking and viability, exploring purposes, ensuring fairness or promoting diversity. These are not mutually exclusive possibilities, but they offer a reasonable guideline as to where the main emphasis of an approach lies and, therefore, to what managerial end it most easily lends itself.

Type A systems approaches are dedicated to improving goal seeking and viability. This is a fairly broad category that ranges from optimizing approaches, single-mindedly concerned with reaching predefined goals, to approaches where much more attention is given to capacity building in those areas of organizational behaviour and design perceived as necessary if viability is to be ensured, and so goal seeking made possible. In all cases, however, the measures of success are 'efficiency' (are the minimum resources used in goal seeking?) and/or 'efficacy' (do the means employed enable us to realize our goals?).

The kinds of systems approach we are discussing here are those that have tended to take the nature of the purposes to be served by the system of concern for granted. They have assumed that participants are in a unitary relationship so that goals are already clear or can be easily determined. Their efforts have concentrated on the vertical axis of the grid of problem contexts where they have sought to optimize the system of concern to achieve its goals or reconfigure it to enable it to deal with internally and externally generated complexity and turbulence.

The original form of applied systems thinking, the hard systems approach, endeavours as we saw to find the best means of getting from the present state of the system to some optimum state. Mathematical modelling is often seen as crucial to the success of this. The other three approaches considered under Type A are more 'structuralist' in nature in terms of the analysis of Section 2.3. They seek to understand and manipulate the mechanisms, operating at a 'deeper' level, that give rise to system behaviour.

System dynamics sees the key to system behaviour as lying in the inter-relationships between the positive and negative feedback loops within which important system elements are bound. If these can be understood, then the manager can be guided as to how he or she should intervene in order that system behaviour is controlled close to what is regarded as desirable. Organizational cybernetics uses a cybernetic model, the Viable System Model (VSM), to try to manage issues of complexity and turbulence that are beyond the capacity of hard systems approaches to handle. The VSM seeks to help managers to design complex organizations according to cybernetic prescriptions so that they remain viable in rapidly changing environments. Managers can learn how to use the VSM to diagnose problems in organizations and put them right so that viability is secured and goal seeking becomes possible. Complexity theory is often associated with unpredictability and with the study of disorder. However, an equally important finding of complexity theory is that, underlying chaos, it is possible over time to recognize patterns occurring in the way systems develop.

Managers with access to these patterns can identify points of leverage that they can exploit to ensure that desirable system behaviour is forthcoming.

Type B systems approaches are dedicated to exploring and clarifying the purposes stakeholders want to pursue through the operations or organization in which they have an interest. The three approaches covered are alternative examples of 'soft systems thinking' and so advocate facilitating a learning process in which the importance of subjectivity is fully respected. Stakeholders can benefit from being made aware of the systemic implications of the values and beliefs they hold and by being confronted with different visions of the future and the changes necessary to achieve it. Debate can then be organized around the different viewpoints about purposes that exist and accommodations teased out that stakeholders can commit to in planning systemic improvement. The measures of success for soft methodologies are 'effectiveness' (are we actually achieving what we want to achieve?) and elegance (do the stakeholders find what is proposed tasteful?).

The kinds of systems approach we are discussing here are those that have concentrated their efforts on the horizontal axis of the grid of problem contexts. They have seen the main failing of hard systems thinking as being its inability to deal with pluralism. They see much the most important task of systems thinking as being able to handle the disagreements and conflicts that occur between stakeholders because of the different values, beliefs and philosophies they hold. If these can be managed, then solutions to problems become more or less straightforward.

Strategic assumption surfacing and testing concentrates attention on the different assumptions, multiple perspectives and diverse world views that are likely to exist in any problem situation. It takes advantage of these to articulate a dialectical learning process of thesis, antithesis and synthesis. Conflict is thus harnessed to assist with problem resolution. Interactive planning seeks to win stakeholder approval for and commitment to an 'idealized design' for the system they are involved with. This is meant to ensure that the maximum creativity is brought to the process of dissolving the current mess the stakeholders are confronted by and replacing it with a future they all desire. Appropriate means for achieving the idealized design are then sought. Soft systems methodology enables managers to work with and change the value systems, cultures and philosophies that exist in organizations. It aims to institutionalize continuous learning by seeking and challenging accommodations between the world views of the different stakeholders concerned with a problem situation.

Type C systems approaches are dedicated to ensuring fairness in systems design and in the consequences that follow from it. The two approaches considered are examples of 'emancipatory systems thinking' that have ventured along the horizontal axis of the grid of problem contexts, into areas where the value of soft systems approaches is threatened by lack of fairness or by coercion. To that extent their aims are similar. They want to support those disadvantaged by present systemic arrangements so that they can make their full contribution to systems design and receive the benefits to which they are entitled from the operation of the system of concern. This may not be happening at the moment for all sorts of reasons. There may be a lack of recognition of the rights of some stakeholder group. And it may be that this is the result of some form of conscious or unconscious discrimination based on class, sex, race, sexual orientation, disability, etc. Emancipatory approaches focus attention on matters of this kind that can easily be missed by other sorts of systems thinking. They are, of course, of huge significance in society and of increasing importance for all organizations.

The measures of success for emancipatory approaches are 'empowerment' (are all individuals and groups able to contribute to decision-making and action?) and 'emancipation' (are disadvantaged groups being assisted to get what they are entitled to?). Critical systems heuristics and team syntegrity address these emancipatory concerns from differing perspectives. The former seeks to ensure the full participation of those who are affected by systems designs who might not otherwise be involved. The latter provides for the creation of a democratic milieu in which outcomes result from consensus and the better argument rather than power, status and/or hierarchy.

Type D are postmodern systems approaches that seek to promote diversity in problem resolution. Such approaches are, in a sense, antisystemic in that systems of domination (e.g., dominating discourses) have to be challenged and broken down in order to let suppressed voices have their say. They are less well established than other types of systems methodology (because they are more recent) and one chapter is enough to hint at the value of some of the postmodern methods now being developed. Postmodern systems thinkers are phased by what they see as the immense complexity and coercion that are intertwined in all problem situations. They are therefore sceptical of appeal to any universal guarantees for the success of action. They would however want to justify and evaluate their interventions on the basis of 'exception' (what otherwise marginalized viewpoints have we managed to bring to the fore?) and 'emotion' (does the action that is now being proposed feel appropriate and good in the local circumstances in which we are acting?).

This section has sought to link our account of the development of applied systems thinking to the arrangement of systems approaches that will be found in Part II. Further justification for seeing four major strands in contemporary systems thinking will be given in the next chapter when the four strands are linked to four overarching social science paradigms. The systems approaches detailed as part of the four strands are not, of course, an exhaustive set. In particular, I regret the omission due to space constraints of Miller's 'living systems theory', which contributes significantly to dealing with systems complexity, and Warfield's 'interactive management', a well-regarded soft systems approach. More information about other systems approaches (including these two), together with full references, can be found in Jackson (2000).

2.5 CONCLUSION

In this chapter we have covered a lot of ground, looking at the development of applied systems thinking. The systems approaches available today have resulted from attempts to correct the original problems found when trying to use hard systems thinking in practice. They have also arisen from theoretical developments in the transdiscipline of systems thinking as new problem contexts have been envisioned and their implications for practice have been explored. As we have seen it is reasonable to conclude that there are now four main strands of applied systems thinking embracing a whole variety of individual systems approaches.

Awareness of the different strands of applied systems thinking and of the variety of systems methodologies leads us to ask whether it might not assist creative problem solving to use them in combination in the same intervention. The SOSM has after all helped to demonstrate the relationships between the different approaches and made it possible to understand that they do not necessarily clash with one another. They all do rather different things. It is this insight – that we need to make creative use of the different forms of holistic inquiry – which inspired the 'creative holism' that is the focus of Part III. Before we can appreciate that, however, we need to understand exactly how creativity can be enhanced by using systems approaches in combination. That is the subject of the next chapter.

REFERENCES

Checkland, P.B. (1981). *Systems Thinking, Systems Practice*. John Wiley & Sons, Chichester, UK.

Flood, R.L. and Jackson, M.C. (1991). *Creative Problem Solving: Total Systems Intervention*. John Wiley & Sons, Chichester, UK.

Jackson, M.C. (1993). The system of systems methodologies: A guide to researchers. *Journal of the Operational Research Society*, **44**, 208–209.

Jackson, M.C. (2000). *Systems Approaches to Management*. Kluwer/Plenum, New York.

Jackson, M.C. and Keys, P. (1984). Towards a system of systems methodologies. *Journal of the Operational Research Society*, **35**, 473–486.

Weber, M. (1969). *The Methodology of the Social Sciences*. Free Press, New York.

Creativity and Systems   3

People who learn to read situations from different (theoretical) points of view have an advantage over those committed to a fixed position. For they are better able to recognise the limitations of a given perspective. They can see how situations and problems can be framed and reframed in different ways, allowing new kinds of solutions to emerge.

Morgan (1986)

3.1 INTRODUCTION

This book is concerned with encouraging creativity in viewing management problems and in resolving those problems creatively using systems thinking. Viewing problems creatively allows us to see them as parts of 'messes' – as interdependent and as arising for a whole variety of reasons – and therefore to approach their resolution in a more integrated manner, in terms of the 'system' in which they are embedded. Systems thinking offers us a number of different approaches, often distilled into methodologies, for resolving problems. Systems approaches are holistic and use 'joined-up' thinking, and therefore tackle problems in a more profound way. Using them in combination opens up another dimension of creativity.

The chapter begins by considering the importance of metaphors in enabling us to be more creative. The history of management thought is a story of the use of different metaphors to understand organizations. At first, organizations were thought of as being 'machines' and attention was focused on fitting well-designed jobs into appropriate structures in order to ensure efficient goal seeking (scientific management, bureaucracy theory, administrative management). Later they were studied as 'organisms': complex systems in close interrelationship with their environments and with subsystems meeting their survival needs. With the birth of cybernetics it became possible to see organizations as 'brains' or information processing systems and, as a result, interest developed in decision-making, learning and decentralized control. More recently, organizations have been portrayed as cultures and attention has been given to values and beliefs, and to the engineering of corporate philosophies that can be shared by all employees. Also achieving greater prominence is the notion of organizations as 'political systems'. Learning to view problem situations through the lens provided by each of these metaphors, as in Section 3.2, can help us to be much more creative in recognizing problems and the reasons for their existence.

Another way to be creative is to view organizations, and the social world of which they are part, through the lenses offered by different sociological paradigms. The four most commonly recognized paradigms in social theory are the 'functionalist', 'interpretive', 'emancipatory' and 'post-modern'. The nature of these different paradigms, and the implications of viewing problem situations from inside each paradigm, are explored in Section 3.3.

It is useful in enhancing creativity to be able to view problem situations through different metaphors and paradigms. It is useful, as we argued earlier, to be holistic in addressing problem situations. How much better might it be if we can be both creative and holistic at the same time? Fortunately, we can and this is the lesson of the 'creative holism' presented in Part III.

3.2   CREATIVITY AND METAPHOR

When we take conscious action in the world (e.g., intervening to improve an organization), we do so on the basis of how we see and understand the world. Different viewpoints, therefore, give rise to very different actions and each of these is rational according to the viewpoint that encourages and justifies it. If we want to act creatively, it follows we have to think creatively.

Learning to think differently, to inhabit different viewpoints, is not easy. The educational system, which is often said to be about absorbing structured chunks of information that can then be reproduced in examinations, can constrain creativity. For whatever reason, very few managers find it easy to think in different ways about the operations and organizations they are responsible for and, as a result, they manage in predictable and restricted ways.

A simple experiment will confirm this judgement. Ask any group of managers, perhaps on a management development course, to draw a picture representing their organization and showing their position in the organization. Over 90% will draw a conventional organizational chart setting out the hierarchy of authority that binds together different groupings. I have found, sadly, that this is the case even among managers who have allegedly been exposed to systems thinking. I would not feel happy, at the end of a course in creative holism, if managers did not feel comfortable drawing their organizations in at least four different ways, hopefully many more. It is essential to increasing the creative capacity of managers that they feel equally at home using a variety of different perspectives on problem situations and how they might be tackled.

One of the best ways of challenging our taken for granted assumptions is by exposing them to some alternatives. This process can be much aided if we learn to work with metaphors. For example, if we want to find out what mental model we carry with us as managers, we might ask whether we primarily see organizations as 'machines', 'organisms', 'brains', 'cultures', 'political systems', 'instruments of domination', etc. Using metaphors in this way helps us to bring clarity to what otherwise would be a hidden and unquestioned mental model. Metaphors are very good at this because they ask us to understand something in terms of a name or description that is not literally applicable to it. Usually, the thing described will be less well known, more intangible and the description will be more familiar; for example, when we describe an organization as a machine. Nevertheless, they will have some things in common and the metaphor will draw these out and highlight them. Thus, we become truly conscious of the biases inherent in our own favoured viewpoint. Original thinking can then be encouraged by making use explicitly of other metaphors to reveal alternative perspectives.

Metaphors are extremely good at allowing us to explore our own world views and to assist with creative thinking. Morgan (1986, 1997) has done some very interesting work on different 'images' of organization that have proved insightful to managers. He selects some familiar metaphors (e.g., 'organizations as machines'), some newer ones (e.g., 'organizations as flux and transformation') and some that are challenging (e.g., 'organizations as psychic prisons') with which to explore issues of management. For each metaphor, Morgan describes the salient characteristics that allow us to gain a greater insight into organizations and their problems, and indicates also its limitations – for all metaphors are limited and offer ways of not seeing as well as ways of seeing. This study is helpful in allowing us to elaborate and be explicit about the frameworks that dominate our particular management perspective and in allowing us access to alternatives.

Morgan selects eight important images of organization in his study, and we add a ninth, 'organizations as carnivals', from Alvesson and Deetz (1996). The nine metaphors are:

- organizations as machines;
- organizations as organisms;
- organizations as brains;
- organizations as flux and transformation;
- organizations as cultures;
- organizations as political systems;
- organizations as psychic prisons;
- organizations as instruments of domination;
- organizations as carnivals.

The main characteristics of these nine metaphors are now outlined.

The machine view dominated management theory during the first half of the 20th century and, as we suggested, has been remarkably difficult to shift from managers' minds. It represents organizations as rational instruments designed to achieve the purposes of their owners or controllers. The task to be achieved is broken down into parts, and rules are established that govern the behaviour of these parts. A hierarchy of authority exercises co-ordination and control. Efficiency in achieving the predetermined purposes is the most highly valued attribute of the organization as a machine. This metaphor is seen as neglecting the individuals who make up the organization and as producing organizational designs that are too rigid in volatile environments.

The organism metaphor looks at organizations as wholes made up of interrelated parts. These parts function in such a way as to ensure the survival of the organization as an organism. Survival, therefore, replaces goal seeking as the *raison d'être* of the enterprise. Furthermore organizations, according to this view, are open systems that must secure favourable interchanges with their environments, adapting to environmental disturbances as required. Managers influenced by this metaphor play close attention to the demands of the environment and ensure that subsystems are meeting the organization's needs. Critics argue that the organismic viewpoint forgets that individuals or groups in organizations may not share the organization's overall purposes. They are not like the parts of the body in this respect. As a result the metaphor hides conflict and internally generated change.

The brain metaphor, deriving directly from cybernetics, emphasizes active learning rather than the rather passive adaptability that characterizes the organismic view. This leads to attention being focused on decision-making, information processing and control. The organization having decided on its purposes must be designed as a complex system to respond to environmental disturbances relevant to those purposes. In turbulent environments this necessitates decentralized control because not all the information necessary to cope with change can be processed at the top of the organization. The organization must manage single-loop learning, correcting deviations from prescribed goals; it also needs to be capable of double-loop learning, changing the nature of its purposes if these become unattainable as the environment shifts. The brain metaphor is criticized for the lack of consideration it gives to individuals and their motivations, to power and conflict, and to how purposes are actually derived.

The flux and transformation metaphor is concerned with revealing what Morgan calls the 'logics of change' that give rise to the behaviour we see on the surface of organizations. We referred to this in Chapter 2 as a more structuralist orientation, seeking the mechanisms, or hidden processes, that shape those aspects of organizational activity to which managers normally devote their attention. The flux and transformation metaphor, therefore, asks managers to be less superficial in the way they read what is happening in their organizations. Instead, they should map the counterintuitive behaviour that is produced by interacting positive and negative feedback loops. Or they should seek to understand the consistent patterns that underlie the behaviour of even the most complex and apparently unpredictable of systems. Critics of this metaphor, as applied to organizations, doubt whether there are any deep, structural 'laws' that social organizations obey and worry about the unregulated power that might be given to experts if they manage to convince others that such laws do indeed exist.

According to the culture metaphor, successful managers should devote their attention to the people associated with their organizations and to the values, beliefs and philosophies held dear by those people. People act according to how they see the world, and it is through the interactions between people that organizations take their form and derive their success or failure. Corporate culture refers to the familiar and persistent ways of seeing and acting in a particular organization. Managers need to be stewards of corporate culture ensuring there is sufficient shared ground so that people pull together and damaging long-term conflict is avoided, but also maintaining enough freedom of thought to encourage original thinking and innovation. Critics of the culture metaphor claim that it distracts attention from other important aspects of organizational success, such as achieving goals, designing appropriate structures, managing resources, etc. It can also lead to the ideological manipulation of employees.

The political metaphor looks at how organizations are governed, at the pursuit and use of power and at the micropolitics of organizational life. Individuals in organizations can be competitive as well as co-operative, pursuing different interests that may conflict. Often, as in the System Of Systems Methodologies (SOSM) (see Chapter 2), the possible political relationships that can obtain between participants in an organization are represented as being either unitary, pluralist or coercive – signalling greater conflict and reliance on power, as a means of settling disputes, as we move along that spectrum. However refreshing this perspective might be, critics suspect that it can overemphasize and, by doing so, contribute to the politicization of organizational life. And it does so to the neglect of other factors crucial to the health of organizations.

The psychic prison and instruments of domination metaphors concentrate on the negative aspects of organizational life. The psychic prison perspective emphasizes the impact it can have on the free development of our thinking. Certain organizational forms are seen by psychoanalytic theory as born of and contributing to repression. While the ideologies that sustain capitalist organizations are regarded by Marxist thinkers as preventing individuals from realizing their full potential. Employees become 'alienated', as the jargon has it. The instruments of domination perspective shifts from the individual to the group level and fixes attention on the way certain groups are exploited by others through organizations. The classical picture is of managers using hierarchy and control of the labour process to extract surplus value from the workers in order to benefit shareholders. This is extended, however, in the metaphor to embrace all other groups who might be exploited by organizations or at least excluded from decisions that impact on them – other employee groups, women, the disabled, those of a different sexual orientation, minority races, those in the community affected by the organization, the environment, etc. Critics see organization theorists and management scientists who overuse these two metaphors as being themselves ideologically driven. They have swallowed a radical political agenda that they hope to thrust on others. They are characterized as being intellectual elitists who, for some reason, resent employees who are happy pursuing a nice house and car rather than self-actualizing themselves. They are seen as guardians of 'political correctness'.

The metaphor of the carnival can help point to at least two aspects of organizational life that get suppressed by the other metaphors. At carnival time normal order is suspended and creativity, diversity and ambivalence are encouraged. This helps us to see the fragility of the social order that is sustained in organizations and to recognize as well the presence of other voices and other aspects that are usually suppressed or marginalized. Carnivals are also meant to be light and bright, and to be places where people have fun. There is much in organizations too that can be explained if we pay attention to playfulness, sex, irony, etc. Critics, of course, would see the overemphasis placed by the carnival metaphor on the 'irrational' aspects of organizational life as trivializing. Organizations are important social institutions and the well-being of all of us depends on them functioning well.

These metaphors have been elaborated to help managers be explicit about the biases that inform their own thinking and to enable them to consider some alternative assumptions about organizations and their management. Undoubtedly, readers will feel much more comfortable with some metaphors and the vision presented of the world they inhabit than others. It is important, however, to persevere until you become reasonably comfortable looking at the management task from the perspective offered by each of the nine metaphors.

3.3   CREATIVITY AND PARADIGMS

Another way to look at the problem situations managers face is to view them from the perspectives offered by different sociological paradigms. The word paradigm is now commonly used to refer to something like world view or way of seeing things. Originally, however, it had a technical meaning, provided by Kuhn (1970), and referred to the tradition of research regarded as authoritative by a particular scientific community. It was the set of ideas, assumptions and beliefs that shaped and guided their scientific activity. I will keep this technical meaning here because it enables a firm distinction to be kept between metaphor and paradigm.

Metaphors, as we saw, are clearly partial representations of what is observed. They highlight some things and hide others. It follows that, while they emphasize different things, they can hardly be regarded as in fundamental conflict with one another. Adherents of different paradigms, to the contrary, usually believe that they are offering the best account available of the nature of the 'reality' that is being observed. For this reason 'paradigm wars' are frequent and paradigms are often said to be 'incommensurable', meaning that the accounts offered by different paradigms cannot be reconciled. Managers listening to advisers basing their thinking about organizations in different paradigms will therefore receive contradictory advice and will themselves have to mediate.

It is possible to explain now why creativity is best encouraged if we embrace different paradigms as well as different metaphors. Although metaphors provide various viewpoints on problem situations they do not demand that radically different alternative perspectives are always entertained. Paradigms do – because they rest on assumptions that are incompatible with those of other paradigms. Without adding paradigm creativity to metaphor creativity, it would be too easy to choose a set of metaphors that fitted well together and corresponded with existing cherished beliefs. Exploring different paradigms, however, always ensures that a challenging encounter with rigorously formulated, alternative theoretical positions takes place.

We are of course concerned with sociological paradigms because managers, in trying to improve the operations, services or organizations they manage, have to contend with social systems. A review of the work of Burrell and Morgan (1979) on sociological paradigms and organizational analysis, complemented by that of Alvesson and Deetz (1996) to take account of postmodernism, suggests that there are four common paradigms in use in social theory today. These are:

- the functionalist paradigm;
- the interpretive paradigm;
- the emancipatory paradigm;
- the postmodern paradigm.

I will now briefly describe each of these, at the same time relating them to the metaphors discussed in Section 3.2.

The functionalist paradigm takes its name from the fact that it wants to ensure that everything in the system is functioning well so as to promote efficiency, adaptation and survival. It is optimistic that an understanding can be gained of how systems work by using scientific methods and techniques to probe the nature of the parts of the system, the interrelationships between them and the relationship between the system and its environment. The expertise it provides should put managers more in control of their operations and organizations, and enable them to eliminate inefficiency and disorder. Associated with this paradigm can usually be found the machine, organism, brain, and flux and transformation metaphors.

The interpretive paradigm takes its name from the fact that it believes social systems, such as organizations, result from the purposes people have and that these, in turn, stem from the interpretations they make of the situations in which they find themselves. Organizations happen, and people act and interact in organizations, as a result of their interpretations. This paradigm wants to understand the different meanings people bring to collaborative activity and to discover where these meanings overlap, and so give birth to shared, purposeful activity. Managers can be guided to seek an appropriate level of shared corporate culture in their organizations. They can take decisions, on the basis of participative involvement, that gain the commitment of key stakeholders. Usually associated with this paradigm are the culture and political system metaphors.

The emancipatory paradigm takes its name from the fact that it is concerned to 'emancipate' oppressed individuals and groups in organizations and society. It is suspicious of authority and tries to reveal forms of power and domination that it sees as being illegitimately employed. It criticizes the status quo and wants to encourage a radical reformation of, or revolution in, the current social order. It pays attention to all forms of discrimination, whether resting on class, status, sex, race, disability, sexual orientation, age, etc. Usually associated with this paradigm are the psychic prison and instruments of domination metaphors.

The postmodern paradigm takes its name from the fact that it opposes the 'modernist' rationality that it sees as present in all the other three paradigms. It challenges and ridicules what it regards as their 'totalizing' attempts to provide comprehensive explanations of how organizations function. From the postmodern perspective organizations are far too complex to understand using any of the other paradigms. It takes a less serious view of organizations and emphasizes having fun. It also insists that we can learn much by bringing conflict to the surface, claiming a space for disregarded opinions and thus encouraging variety and diversity. The carnival metaphor fits well with this paradigm.

To understand how these different paradigms can encourage creativity, try to picture any organization known to you from the point of view of each paradigm in turn. How would you manage that organization according to the very different perspectives offered by each paradigm?

3.4 CONCLUSION

This chapter has concentrated on the importance of creativity for problem-solving. We have seen how problem situations can be viewed creatively through the different lenses provided by alternative metaphors and paradigms (see also Flood and Jackson, 1991). Now we need to discover how we can be holistic at the same time. Fortunately, as the previous chapter demonstrates, this is possible because systems thinking has developed a variety of problem resolving approaches to match the variety of the problem contexts we can envisage.

In the previous chapter we charted the history of applied systems thinking in terms of progress along the two dimensions of the SOSM. A different and equally enlightening way of conceptualizing this history is to see it as being about the exploration and opening up of different metaphors and paradigms by applied systems thinking.

Hard systems thinking clearly depends on the machine metaphor. System dynamics and complexity theory can then be seen as abandoning that for the flux and transformation metaphor, while organizational cybernetics builds additionally on insights from the organism and brain metaphors. The soft systems approaches (strategic assumption surfacing and testing, interactive planning, soft systems methodology) reject the machine meta-phor in order to build their foundations on the culture and political systems metaphors. Critical systems heuristics and team syntegrity are based on the psychic prison and instruments of domination metaphors, while postmodern systems thinking privileges the carnival metaphor.

Paradigm analysis can be used to paint a similar picture of the develop-ment of applied systems thinking – this time in terms of the range of types of social theory it has been prepared to embrace. System dynamics, organiza-tional cybernetics and complexity theory did not jettison the functionalism of hard systems thinking although they did take it in a more structuralist direction. Soft systems thinking, however, made a paradigm break with hard systems thinking and created systems methodologies for problem-solving based on the interpretive paradigm. Critical systems heuristics and team syntegrity make sense in terms of the emancipatory paradigm. Post-modern systems approaches were created to accurately reflect the new orientation and the new learning about intervention that could be derived from the postmodern paradigm.

In short, not only can we be creative about problem situations by employ-ing metaphors and paradigms, we can also respond to them, trying to solve, resolve or dissolve them, using forms of holistic intervention con-structed on the basis of different metaphors and paradigms. This relationship is more fully considered in Part II, and, looking ahead to Part III, modern systems thinking sees value in all the different metaphors of organization and sociological paradigms, and seeks to make appropriate use of the variety of systems approaches reflecting different metaphors and paradigms.

Creative holism conceives the different systems approaches as being used in combination, ensuring for the manager the benefits of both creativity and holism.

REFERENCES

Alvesson, M. and Deetz, S. (1996). Critical theory and postmodernist approaches to organizational studies. In: S.R. Clegg, C. Hardy and W.R. Nord (eds), *Handbook of Organization Studies* (pp. 191–217). Sage, London.

Burrell, G. and Morgan, G. (1979). *Sociological Paradigms and Organizational Analysis*. Heinemann, London.

Flood, R.L. and Jackson, M.C. (1991). *Creative Problem Solving: Total Systems Intervention*. John Wiley & Sons, Chichester, UK.

Kuhn, T. (1970). *The Structure of Scientific Revolutions* (2nd edn). University of Chicago Press, Chicago.

Morgan, G. (1986). *Images of Organisation*. Sage, London.

Morgan, G. (1997). *Images of Organisation* (2nd edn). Sage, London.

Part II

Systems Approaches

The aim of Part II is to outline and critique 10 applied systems approaches, demonstrating how they are holistic and why they are significant from the point of view of managers. Each approach is reviewed (Chapters 4–13) in the same way.

First, a description of the approach is provided in terms of historical background, philosophy/theory underlying the approach (according to its originators), the methodology used to translate the philosophy/theory into practical application and the methods – different models, tools and techniques – usually associated with the approach. The distinction between methodology and methods is crucial here. Methodology is a higher order term that refers to the logical principles that must govern the use of methods in order that the philosophy/theory embraced by the approach is properly respected and appropriately put into practice. Methodology is not detachable from the philosophy/theory of the particular systems approach or, therefore, from the approach itself. Methods, however, concerned as they are with achieving more specific procedural outcomes, are detachable and can be used in the service of other systems approaches with varying degrees of success or failure. Each description concludes with a review of 'recent developments' in the systems approach under consideration.

Second, an example is offered of the approach in action, concentrating particularly on how the methodology and associated methods contribute to the outcomes. Third, a critique of the approach is provided, setting out its particular strengths and weaknesses. This is conducted by looking at the systems concepts emphasized by the approach and at how the particular metaphors and the paradigm it embraces facilitate its ability to achieve certain things for managers while constraining it in other respects. Finally, drawing on all the previous sections, attention is devoted to what exactly each systems approach offers to managers in terms of improving their ability to handle complexity, change and diversity.

The 10 systems approaches are divided in Part II into 'Types', reflecting four basic orientations – goal seeking and viability, exploring purposes, ensuring fairness and promoting diversity. A brief introduction to each of Types A–D establishes and details the nature of these general orientations.

Type A

Improving Goal Seeking and Viability

Here we detail four systems approaches that aim to assist managers improve goal seeking and viability. These approaches are hard systems thinking, system dynamics, organizational cybernetics and complexity theory. They were developed because of the failure of reductionism to cope with problem situations exhibiting increased complexity and turbulence. They emphasize the efficient use of resources in the achievement of goals and the efficacious design of organizations so that adaptability is ensured in the face of complexity and environmental change. In sociological terms they are functionalist in character and orientated toward achieving prediction and control so that better regulation of the enterprise can be obtained. The four approaches differ from one another in the manner in which they seek to progress in dealing with complexity down the vertical axis of the System Of Systems Methodologies (SOSM). This is indicated by the particular metaphors they emphasize within the usual functionalist set of machine, organism, brain, and flux and transformation.

Hard Systems Thinking 4

Many elements of such [sociotechnical] systems exhibit forms of regular behaviour, and scientific scrutiny has yielded much knowledge about these regularities. Thus, many of the problems that arise in socio-technical systems can be addressed by focusing such knowledge in appropriate ways by means of the logical, quantitative, and structural tools of modern science and technology.

Quade and Miser (1985)

4.1 INTRODUCTION

Hard systems thinking, as we saw in Chapter 2, is a generic name given by Checkland (1981) to various systems approaches for solving real-world problems developed during and immediately after the Second World War. The approaches most commonly associated with this label are operational research (operations research in the USA), systems analysis and systems engineering. These, however, gave rise to a myriad of other variants of hard systems thinking, such as decision science, cost–benefit analysis, planning–programming–budgeting systems and policy analysis. All these approaches took on a common form, which Checkland identified and classified as 'hard systems thinking' and which we will be examining below.

The pioneers of hard systems thinking were immensely proud of the fact that they applied the scientific method to problems of real significance to decision-makers. They were not the first to do this. Frederick Taylor had abandoned the laboratory as the place to practise science much earlier in the century, when he invented scientific management. They were, however, the first to recognize that in modifying the scientific method, to make it applicable to real-world problems, one of its main tenets – reductionism – had to be thoroughly questioned. Might not holism offer a better handle on the complex sociotechnical problems that managers face?

4.2 DESCRIPTION OF HARD SYSTEMS THINKING

4.2.1 Historical development

The term 'operational research' was invented about 1937 in the context of a project in which UK scientists sought to assist military leaders to maximize the benefits to be gained from using radar to detect enemy aircraft. What justified the new name was that this was scientific research carried out into operational processes rather than into natural phenomena. From the RAF, operational research soon spread to the army and navy and to other countries, such as Canada, the USA, France and Australia. In the USA its first usage was in the Naval Ordnance group dealing with mine warfare. After the war it found civilian application in government departments and, particularly, in the newly nationalized industries of the UK such as coal, gas, steel and transport. The 1950s saw professional societies being formed to promote Operational Research (OR) and the beginnings of the academic study of the subject.

Systems analysis is said by its protagonists to have emerged out of operations research and to be broader in scope. The name was first applied to research being done for the US Air Force on future weapon systems in the late 1940s. In the 1950s and 1960s the approach was promoted by the influential RAND (an acronym for 'Research ANd Development') Corporation, a non-profit body in the advice-giving business, and its use became widespread in the defence and aerospace industries. In 1965 President Johnson gave systems analysis (under the label 'planning–programming–budgeting systems') a further boost by ordering its adoption in all departments of the US federal government. In 1972 the International Institute for Applied Systems Analysis (IIASA) was established in Austria, on the initiative of the academies of science (or equivalent) of 12 nations, with the remit to apply systems analysis to world problems (e.g., energy, food supply and the environment). Since that time IIASA has become the official guardian of the development of systems analysis as a discipline and profession.

Systems engineering grew out of engineering in the 1940s and 1950s as that discipline sought to extend its scope to the design of more complex systems involving many interacting components. It was pioneered in the USA at Bell Telephone Laboratories to meet the networking challenges faced in the communications industry. It spread rapidly to the defence, space and energy industries and, in the 1960s and 1970s, various guidelines and standards were established for the use of systems engineering to develop military systems and in civilian aerospace and energy programmes. In manufacturing industry, systems engineering had to encompass even more of the 'whole' as it was forced to concern itself with interacting sets of processes (e.g., in petrochemical plants) and how these could be optimized in the prevailing market conditions. Today, the International Council on Systems Engineering (INCOSE) sees the approach as relevant to problems as wide and diverse as transportation, housing, infrastructure renewal and environmental systems (www.incose.org).

4.2.2 Philosophy and theory

Much of the philosophy and theory underpinning hard systems thinking is taken for granted and not declared openly. This is not surprising because so much of it is borrowed directly from the natural sciences. Discussion does however sometimes focus on the adjustments that have to be made to the scientific method to make it applicable to the real-world problems that interest hard systems thinkers. We can tease out these adjustments by looking at the common features of well-known definitions of OR, Systems Analysis (SA) and Systems Engineering (SE).

The British Operational Society for many years defined OR as:

> *the application of the methods of science to complex problems arising in the direction and management of large systems of men, machines, materials and money in industry, business, government and defence. The distinctive approach is to develop a scientific model of the system, incorporating measurements of factors such as chance and risk, with which to predict and compare the outcomes of alternative decisions, strategies or controls. The purpose is to help management determine its policy and actions scientifically.*

Quade and Miser (1985), in the first *Handbook of Systems Analysis*, state that:

> *the central purpose of systems analysis is to help public and private decision and policy-makers to solve the problems and resolve the policy issues that they face. It does this by improving the basis for their judgement by generating information and marshalling evidence bearing on their problems and, in particular, on possible actions that may be suggested to alleviate them. Thus commonly, a systems analysis focuses on a problem arising from the operations of a sociotechnical system, considers various responses to this problem and supplies*

evidence about the costs, benefits, and other consequences of these responses.

INCOSE propounds a definition of systems engineering with several components:

(1) it is an interdisciplinary approach and means to establish a sound system concept, (2) it defines and validates clear and concise system requirements, (3) it creates an effective system design or solution, and (4) it ensures that the developed system meets client and user objectives in the operational environment.

Although the commitment to science is explicit in all these definitions, it is also clear that the purpose of using science differs from that normally associated with the scientific enterprise. Its primary purpose in hard systems thinking is to serve the interests of clients, managers, decision-makers, policy-makers, etc., not to bring about the advancement of knowledge for its own sake.

Another point follows. In hard systems thinking scientists are required to address real-world problems and the solutions they produce must work in the operational domain, not in the laboratory. Furthermore, it is usually too costly or simply unethical to carry out experiments using large sociotechnical systems. They are cut off, therefore, from the usual experimental methods employed to test hypotheses under controlled laboratory conditions. An alternative to the laboratory has to be found.

All varieties of hard systems thinking propose that models, primarily mathematical models, can perform in management science the role that the laboratory plays in the natural sciences. Models, in hard systems thinking, are designed to capture the essential features of the real world. Sometimes these will be regularities in behaviour, which detailed observation and measurement reveal in particular types of sociotechnical system. At other times the systems practitioner will have to rely on insight and whatever incomplete information that happens to be available. Whatever is the case, it is seen as essential that some type of model is built.

Models are so crucial in hard systems thinking because they aim to capture as accurately as possible the workings of the system underlying the problems being investigated. Forced to deal with complex problem situations in the real world, the hard systems thinker replaces the traditional notion of a scientific object with that of 'system' as the focus of study. Once the model has been constructed it can be used to explore how the real-world system behaves without actually taking any action that might alter and damage the real-world system itself. In particular, different possible ways of improving system behaviour from the point of view of the clients can be tested.

Finally, it is clearly recognized in the definitions offered that no one field of science is likely to be able to deal with any real-world problem. Such problems simply do not fit into the domains of the established scientific disciplines. The hard systems thinker, being problem- rather than discipline-centred, will therefore have to draw on a range of disciplinary areas or be interdisciplinary in his or her approach.

4.2.3 Methodology

Cutting through the arguments of the advocates of different strands of hard systems thinking that their favoured approach is more comprehensive than the others, Checkland (1981) used an examination of methodology to demonstrate that all variants of hard systems thinking are in fact similar in character. Methodology in applied systems thinking, the reader will recall, refers to the guidance given to practitioners about how to translate the philosophy and theory of an approach into practical application. Looking at the methodologies proposed by hard systems thinkers, Checkland concluded that they all take the same form. They largely assume that they can define an objective for the system they are seeking to improve and see their task as the systematic pursuit of the most efficient means of achieving that objective. We can now review this conclusion in relation to the specific methodologies of OR, SA and SE.

The first full expression of the classical OR methodology appeared in Churchman, Ackoff and Arnoff's textbook on OR published in 1957. The authors establish that OR is the application of the most advanced scientific techniques by interdisciplinary teams to the overall problems of complex organizations and that a systems approach is essential. They then set out a six-stage methodology:

- formulating the problem;
- constructing a mathematical model to represent the system under study;
- deriving a solution from the model;
- testing the model and the solution derived from it;
- establishing controls over the solution;
- putting the solution to work (implementation).

There is, therefore, the expected emphasis on problem formulation (specifying the decision-makers and their objectives, and the system involved), on a modelling phase and an implementation phase.

Many different styles of systems analysis developed out of the early RAND Corporation military applications. It is, however, reasonable to take the three IIASA handbooks, edited by Miser (1995), and Miser and Quade (1985, 1988), as representing the current state of the art as far as systems analysis methodology is concerned. The handbooks make clear that systems analysis always starts with the recognition by someone involved with a sociotechnical system that a problem exists. This problem will require proper formulation. Once that is achieved the methodology prescribes a research phase during which a scientific approach is brought to bear on the problem. The research should be multidisciplinary. It requires identifying alternative ways of tackling the problem and building models that can be used to test the alternatives. The alternative means are then evaluated and ranked according to the decision-makers' preferences, bearing in mind costs, benefits and other consequences. Finally, assistance is given with implementation and with evaluation of outcomes. The Figure 4.1 representation of systems analysis methodology appears in all three of the handbooks.

For A.D. Hall (see Keys, 1991), reflecting on his experiences with the Bell Telephone Laboratories, systems exist in hierarchies and should be engineered with this in mind to best achieve their objectives. The systems engineer is charged with co-ordinating a multidisciplinary team that must discover the objectives and then ensure the optimum integration and consistency of system and subsystems in pursuit of those objectives. Jenkins (1972), a British systems engineer, provides a detailed elaboration of the steps required:

1. Systems analysis –
   1.1 formulation of the problem;
   1.2 organization of the project;
   1.3 definition of the system;
   1.4 definition of the wider system;
   1.5 objectives of the wider system;
   1.6 objectives of the system;
   1.7 definition of an overall economic criterion;
   1.8 information and data collection.
2. Systems design –
   2.1 forecasting;

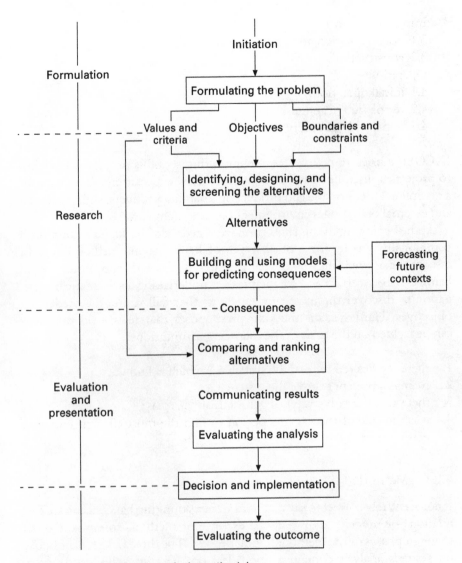

Figure 4.1 The systems analysis methodology.
From Miser and Quade (1988), reproduced by permission of John Wiley & Sons.

2.2 model building and simulation;
2.3 optimization;
2.4 control;
2.5 reliability.

3. Implementation –
    3.1 documentation and sanction approval;
    3.2 construction.
4. Operation –
    4.1 initial operation;
    4.2 retrospective appraisal;
    4.3 improved operation.

INCOSE's brief guide to systems engineering sees this process as bringing to projects a disciplined vision of stakeholders' expectations together with a disciplined focus on the end product, its enabling products, and its internal and external operational environment (i.e., a system view).

At the beginning of this subsection we stated that Checkland recognized a commonality in the form of all types of hard systems methodology. In essence, he argued, they take what is required (the ends and objectives) as being easy to ascertain and see their task as undertaking a systematic investigation to discover the most efficient 'how' that will realize the predefined objectives. Hard systems thinking presupposes that real-world problems can be tackled on the basis of the following assumptions:

1. there is a desired state of the system S_1, which is known;
2. there is a present state of the system S_0;
3. there are alternative ways of getting from S_0 to S_1;
4. it is the role of the systems person to find the most efficient means of getting from S_0 to S_1.

4.2.4 Methods

It is not entirely correct to say that hard systems thinking has concentrated on methods of model building at the expense of methods to support other stages or phases of the methodological process. The three IIASA handbooks on systems analysis contain a good deal on the craft skills necessary to support problem formulation, communication with decision-makers and implementation. The rapid development of 'soft OR' in the 1980s and 1990s in the UK is evidence of a tradition of work that has paid attention to the process of operational research. Successful practitioners of all strands of hard systems thinking have of necessity had to develop well-tuned social and political skills. Nevertheless, it is true that the mainstream academic literature in journals and textbooks certainly does show an overwhelming bias in the direction of perfecting methods of modelling. It is not surprising, therefore, that this is the area in which hard systems thinking has most to offer.

Models are explicit, simplifying interpretations of aspects of reality relevant to the purpose at hand. They seek to capture the most important variables and interactions giving rise to system behaviour. They are used to experiment on as surrogates for the real-world system. The literature of hard systems thinking identifies various types of models: iconic, analogic, analytic, simulations, gaming, judgemental and conceptual. Let us consider these in turn.

Iconic models are simply scale (usually reduced scale) representations of what is being modelled, such as an aircraft model used in wind tunnel testing or an architect's three dimensional model of a new building. Analogue models are very different in appearance to the reality, but, nevertheless, seek to mimic the behaviour of what they represent. An example would be an electrical network used to represent water flowing through pipes.

Analytic models are mathematical models that are used to represent the logical relationships that are believed to govern the behaviour of the system being investigated. They are widely used in operational research. Wilson (1990) helpfully provides a matrix (reproduced as Figure 4.2) that divides analytic models into four classes depending on whether they represent behaviour over time (dynamic) or at one point in time (steady state) and whether the behaviour is described by fixed rules (deterministic) or statistical distribution (non-deterministic).

Algebraic equations can be used to formulate, for example, problems about the most appropriate way to allocate productive resources in order to maximize profit when many alternatives exist and resources are limited. The linear programming technique has been developed to provide an

	Steady state	Dynamic
Deterministic	Algebraic equations	Differential equations
Non-deterministic	Statistical and probability relationships	Discrete-event simulation

Figure 4.2 Types of analytic model.

optimal solution in this type of situation. Statistical and probability relationships can be employed to determine the degree of dependence of one variable on another in the absence of complete knowledge about the interrelationships in a system. Wilson shows how the linear regression technique can provide a model, for example, showing how total electricity sales are related to the level of industrial production. Differential equations provide a modelling language for the dynamic deterministic category. Wilson demonstrates how the problem of designing a suspension system for a vehicle can be tackled on the basis of differential equations solved by computer. Dynamic non-deterministic systems require simulation, which we are treating here as another type of modelling.

Simulation of quite complex systems, in which the relationships between variables are not well understood and change over time, has been made possible with the advance in computing power. It refers to the process of mapping item by item and step by step the essential features of the system we are interested in. The model produced is subject to a series of experiments and the outcomes documented. The likely behaviour of the system can then be predicted using statistical analysis. For example, the essential features of a traffic flow system can be represented in a computer simulation as long as the key factors impacting on traffic flow can be identified. Computer-generated random numbers determine amount of traffic, numbers turning left, etc., so that the system's behaviour can be monitored under different conditions. A sophisticated type of simulation modelling, system dynamics, is described in Chapter 5.

Gaming is a kind of modelling in which human actors play out the roles of significant decision-makers in a system. They are supposed to behave as would their real-world counterparts in order that matters of choice, judgement, values and politics can be investigated.

Judgemental models usually rest on group opinion of the likelihood of particular events taking place. Techniques such as 'Delphi' (developed at the RAND Corporation) and 'scenario writing' are used in systems analysis to develop the best group models from the individual mental models of members of multidisciplinary teams. Delphi employs an anonymous, iterative process to guide experts and other knowledgeable individuals toward a reasonable consensus about an issue. Scenario writing explores the likelihood of particular future states of affairs coming about.

Conceptual models, as the name suggests, are qualitative models used to make explicit the particular mental models held by parties interested in a decision. They are more frequently employed in soft systems thinking than in hard systems thinking.

4.2.5 Recent developments

The most important recent developments in hard systems thinking relate to continued attempts to extend the scope of the approach beyond the somewhat technical problem situations, in which it has proved very successful, to situations of greater complexity and in which people and politics play the central role. INCOSE has declared its intention to expand systems engineering into non-traditional domains, such as transportation, housing, infrastructure renewal and environmental systems – although, it must be said, little work has been done yet on how the approach might have to change to make it so applicable. The IIASA handbooks declare that systems analysis needs to be extended to more 'people-dominated' problems. In this field considerable effort has gone into documenting the 'craft skills' needed to cope with people and politics. But this still remains a long way from developing appropriate concepts and an appropriate language that would allow these matters to be discussed theoretically so that continuous learning can be generated. The greatest progress has been made in OR, with the establishment of 'soft OR' in the UK as a complementary practice to 'hard OR'. Soft OR differs markedly from the classical version we have been studying in this chapter and does put people at the centre of problem resolving and decision-making. The collection of papers in Rosenhead and Mingers (2001) is a good introduction.

In general, the question needs asking whether hard systems thinking really can be adapted in the way certain visionaries believe. Would it not lose the capacity to be good at what it does well now? Would it not be better for us to look to other systems approaches, developed for other purposes, to complement hard systems thinking where it is weak?

4.3 HARD SYSTEMS THINKING IN ACTION

Given the range of hard systems approaches covered in this chapter, it is difficult to provide one representative example of hard systems thinking in action. We shall tackle this problem by showing different aspects of use for each of OR, SE and SA.

Once the original pioneering spirit had faded, operational researchers, or at least those of a more academic persuasion, began to concentrate their efforts on developing mathematical models to apply to what they recognized as frequently occurring types of problems. Each problem type was assumed to have a particular form and structure, which determined its nature and how it could be tackled, regardless of the context in which it was found – military, manufacturing industry, service sector, etc. Fortuin et al. (1996) present 15 case studies of OR at work in application areas as diverse as transport and logistics, product and process design, maintenance and financial services, health care and environmental decision-making. Keys (1991), and Cavaleri and Obloj (1993), provide good introductory material on the most common OR problems; a typical list being:

- queuing problems;
- inventory problems;
- allocation problems;
- replacement problems;
- co-ordination problems;
- routing problems;
- competitive problems;
- search problems.

Queuing models seek an optimum trade-off between the costs of providing service capacity and keeping customers happy. Inventory models aim to establish the optimum reorder point for stocks of resources so that production flow can be maintained while the costs of holding excess inventory are minimized.

Allocation models seek to apportion scarce resources in the most efficient manner, maximizing output or minimizing costs, while achieving overall objectives. Keys comments on an example involving a farming enterprise that both reared cattle for beef and produced crops that could themselves be sold or, alternatively, used to feed the cattle. A linear programming-type model was constructed containing 640 constraints and 1,801 variables. A solution that maximized profit was discovered in 34 seconds of computer time.

Replacement models help to minimize costs by identifying the point at which acquisition of new assets is justifiable. Co-ordination techniques, such as PERT (Programme Evaluation and Review Technique) and critical path analysis, calculate how tasks must be sequenced in a project to ensure completion in minimum time and at minimum cost. The goal of routing models is to determine the most efficient route between different locations in a network. Competitive problems are conceptualized in terms of games, the aim being to maximize outcomes for one or more participants. Search models try to maximize the efficiency of a search (say, for a location for a new factory) by minimizing both costs and the risks of error.

A recent INCOSE document (see www.incose.org) sets out systems engineering profiles for 18 different application domains: agriculture, commercial aircraft, commercial avionics, criminal justice system and legal processes, emergency services, energy systems, environmental restoration, facilities systems engineering, geographic information systems, health care, highway transportation systems, information systems, manufacturing, medical devices, motor vehicles, natural resources management, space systems, and telecommunications. There are also profiles for seven cross-application domains: e-commerce, high-performance computing, human factors engineering, Internet-based applications, Internet banking, logistics, and modelling and simulation. Not surprisingly, a number of these profiles are rudimentary, with the most extensive being in areas of traditional systems engineering practice, such as the design and development of commercial aircraft.

The commercial aircraft industry operates in a very competitive environment and depends on complex manufacturing processes arising from highly integrated subsystems, advanced technologies, use of advanced materials, detailed specifications and very rigorous testing. The systems engineering specifications for this domain insist on the principle that commercial aircraft are considered as wholes, and not as collections of parts. Both customer and regulatory requirements are first identified. Aircraft architecture is then seen as a hierarchy in which the functions and constraints operating at the top level, the aircraft system itself, flow down into requirements for the subsystems. A typical decomposition of the aircraft system into parts would identify the mechanical, propulsion, environmental, airframe, avionics, interiors, electrical and auxiliary subsystems. These subsystems are then further decomposed into subordinate components with their own requirements deriving from those of the subsystems. Thorough monitoring and control is essential at all stages of design and construction to ensure that requirements at the different levels are verified and validated by testing.

The IIASA handbooks provide some comprehensive descriptions of SA applications, which are then referred to and analysed throughout the three volumes. The main illustrations are of improving blood availability and utilization (also described in Jackson, 2000), improving fire protection, protecting an estuary from flooding, achieving adequate amounts of energy for the long-range future, providing housing for low-income families and controlling a forest pest in Canada. Of these examples, the fire protection case is regarded as one that closely follows the prescribed systems analysis methodology.

The fire protection study began in 1973 in Wilmington, DE and was conducted by a local project team with technical assistance from the New York-based RAND Institute. The eight existing firehouses in Wilmington were getting old and the mayor wanted to find out if they offered adequate protection, whether they were located in the right places and whether any new firehouses needed building. The main objectives of fire protection were pretty obviously to protect lives and safeguard property while, at the same time, keeping costs low. Unfortunately, there was no reliable way of evaluating how different deployment strategies related directly to these objectives. Three 'proxy' measures were therefore developed: approximate travel time to individual locations, average travel time in a region and company workload. The consequences of changes in locations and numbers of firehouses were then considered against these.

The next stage required the analysts to build models that could be used to test various deployment alternatives. The primary tools employed to encapsulate the data were a parametric allocation model, based on a mathematical formula for allocating companies to different regions, and a more descriptive, simulation model, known as the firehouse site evaluation model. The transparency of this latter model was crucial as it enabled city officials to be involved in suggesting alternatives.

The recommendations to close one of the fire companies and reposition most of the remainder provoked a long battle with the firefighters union before they were eventually implemented. When the results were finally evaluated it was found that the fire protection service was just as effective as before, but with costs significantly reduced.

4.4 CRITIQUE OF HARD SYSTEMS THINKING

Hard systems thinking has sought to bring scientific rigour to the solution of management problems. It wants to produce objective results, free from the taint of personality and vested interests, through a process in which assumptions, data and calculations are made clear, and which is validated in order to inform the work of other scientists facing similar problems.

At the same time, hard systems thinkers are clear that they do not seek knowledge for its own sake. They do research aimed at serving the interests of clients, decision-makers and problem owners. This shift to valuing knowledge directly relevant to application rather than simply to the advancement of a scientific discipline was revolutionary and enabled management scientists to steal a march on other disciplinary areas that, to this day, are still struggling to put in place the conceptual apparatus that would enable them to make their findings more relevant (e.g., see Tranfield and Starkey, 1998, on the struggle to establish more application-oriented management research).

In tackling actual management problems hard systems thinkers pioneered the use of multidisciplinary teams of researchers and became advocates of an interdisciplinary approach. Particularly valuable to them, in this respect, was the existence of various systems ideas and concepts. Reductionism was useless because of the complexity and unbounded character of real-world problems and because of the interactive nature of their parts. What was required was a more holistic, integrating approach that sought to be comprehensive by drawing the boundaries of the system of concern more widely. The systems language, employing concepts such as system, subsystem, hierarchy, boundary and control, was perfect for this purpose.

Another problem that hard systems thinkers were able to overcome was how to test the hypotheses they developed. They could not carry out experiments directly on the systems they were hoping to improve – it was too dangerous because of expense, ethics or both. Unlike natural scientists, the problems they faced were too interconnected to be broken up and taken into the laboratory for analysis. The solution was to construct a model or models that accurately captured the behaviour of the real-world system and to run tests on those. Considerable progress had to be made by hard systems thinkers on the techniques of mathematical and computer-based modelling if this approach was to succeed.

We considered the main weaknesses of hard systems thinking in Chapter 2, when we were looking at why other strands of systems thinking had emerged and established themselves over the last few decades. To recap, these related to the failure of hard systems thinking in the face of extreme complexity, multiple perceptions of reality and the need for radical change.

The extreme complexity of the problem situations that managers confront, and the fact that they are subject to very different interpretations, frustrate hard systems thinkers in their search for an objective account of the system of concern that can be used to construct a mathematical model. Modelling is about simplification, but it is often not clear how complex problem situations can be simplified without bias creeping in. There is also the danger of leaving out of account factors that cannot be quantified.

Hard systems approaches demand that the goal of the system of concern be clearly established before analysis can proceed. This makes it difficult even to get started in many problem situations, where multiple stakeholders bring different perceptions to bear on the nature of the system and its objectives. Hard systems thinking tends to leave the human aspect of systems aside. People are treated as components to be engineered, not as actors whose commitment must be won if solutions are to be implemented and plans realized.

Hard systems thinking is also accused of conservatism. It privileges the values and interests of its clients and customers, and lends its apparent expertise to their realization. It thus gives the facade of objectivity to changes that help to secure the status quo.

In general terms, despite its many strengths and achievements, hard systems thinking is today thought of as having a limited domain of application. It is fine when world views converge and the problem becomes one of finding the most efficient means of arriving at agreed-on objectives. Such well-structured problems, usually arising at the tactical level in organizations, are meat and drink to an approach that employs a systematic methodology to seek out alternative means and evaluate them against well-defined measures of performance.

All this is easily understood when we recognize how totally hard systems thinking embraces the functionalist paradigm. Its interest is in ensuring the efficient engineering of systems to achieve known goals. Their behaviour has to be predicted and they have to be regulated in pursuit of their controllers' objectives. The concerns of the interpretive paradigm in bringing about mutual understanding among those with different values and beliefs, of the emancipatory paradigm in alleviating disadvantage and the postmodern paradigm in unpredictability and diversity, do not get a look-in.

Within functionalism, hard systems thinking is further constrained by its adherence to the machine metaphor. The language of goals, rationality, efficient means and control dominates. Other metaphors that might bring to the fore the environment or cultural and political matters are not exploited.

4.5 THE VALUE OF HARD SYSTEMS THINKING TO MANAGERS

Although managers need to employ expert practitioners to get the most value out of hard systems thinking, there are at least five lessons to be learned from it that can easily be absorbed and would benefit them in their everyday work:

• Scientific expertise can help managers at least in dealing with a significant set of the operational problems that they confront.

- The insistence of the systems approach on holism, rather than reduction-ism, in tackling real-world problems can assist managers to obtain comprehensive and integrated solutions. Suboptimization can be avoided.
- The use of a systematic methodology to tackle problems is usually prefer-able to an *ad hoc* approach based on the manager's common sense.
- It is extremely helpful, in seeking to improve problem situations, if man-agers can clearly set objectives, seek alternative means of achieving those objectives and evaluate those alternative means on the basis of precise measures of performance. This is especially the case in the public and voluntary sectors where the market does not operate to ensure efficiency.
- Faced with the complexity of problem situations, managers inevitably use models. Whether these models are mathematical or not, it can assist learning if managers are explicit about the models they are using and the assumptions on which they are based.

4.6 CONCLUSION

The hard systems approach established many of the tenets of applied systems thinking that have since served it well in dealing with problem situations in the context of complexity and change. It had limitations, however, that became obvious to both theoreticians and practitioners in the 1970s and 1980s. New thinking was needed before the systems approach could get going on the road to creative holism.

REFERENCES

Cavaleri, S. and Obloj, K. (1993). *Management Systems: A Global Perspective.* Wadsworth, Belmont, CA.

Checkland, P.B. (1981). *Systems Thinking, Systems Practice.* John Wiley & Sons, Chichester, UK.

Churchman, C.W., Ackoff, R.L. and Arnoff, E.L. (1957). *Introduction to Operations Research.* John Wiley & Sons, New York.

Fortuin, L., van Beek, P. and van Wassenhove, L. (eds) (1996). *OR at Work.* Taylor & Francis, London.

Jackson, M.C. (2000). *Systems Approaches to Management.* Kluwer/Plenum, New York.

Jenkins, G.M. (1972). The systems approach. In: J. Beishon and G. Peters (eds), *Systems Behavior* (pp. 78–104). Open University Press, London.

Keys, P. (1991). *Operational Research and Systems: The Systemic Nature of Operational Research*. Plenum, New York.

Miser, H.J. (ed.) (1995). *Handbook of Systems Analysis: Cases*. John Wiley & Sons, New York.

Miser, H.J. and Quade, E.S. (1985). *Handbook of Systems Analysis: Overview of Uses, Procedures, Applications and Practice*. North Holland, New York.

Miser, H.J. and Quade, E.S. (1988). *Handbook of Systems Analysis: Craft Issues and Procedural Choices*. John Wiley & Sons, New York.

Quade, E.S. and Miser, H.J. (1985). The context, nature, and use of systems analysis. In: H.J. Miser and E.S. Quade (eds), *Handbook of Systems Analysis: Overview of Uses, Procedures, Applications and Practice* (pp. 1–41). North Holland, New York.

Rosenhead, J. and Mingers, J. (eds) (2001). *Rational Analysis for a Problematic World Revisited*. John Wiley & Sons, Chichester, UK.

Tranfield, D. and Starkey, K. (1998). The nature, social organization and promotion of management research: Towards policy. *British Journal of Management*, **9**, 341–353.

Wilson, B. (1990). *Systems: Concepts, Methodologies and Applications*. John Wiley & Sons, Chichester, UK.

System Dynamics: The Fifth Discipline 5

Systems thinking is a discipline for seeing the 'structures' that underlie complex situations, and for discerning high from low leverage change ... Ultimately, it simplifies life by helping us to see the deeper patterns lying beneath the events and the details.

Senge (1990)

5.1 INTRODUCTION

Jay W. Forrester's ambition in developing system dynamics was to extend the range of applied systems thinking to more strategic problems. He believed Operational Research (OR) was losing touch with the real concerns of managers as it concentrated more and more on specific tactical issues, amenable to mathematical modelling because they involve just a few variables in linear relationships with one another. System dynamics, by contrast, would employ the science of feedback, harnessed to the power of the modern digital computer, to unlock the secrets of complex, multiple-loop non-linear systems. Social systems are seen as being of this kind and as causing no particular problems of their own for system dynamics because the impacts of the decisions of human actors can be modelled according to the same rules.

Forrester and his team, at the Massachusetts Institute of Technology (MIT), did all the solid groundwork necessary to establish system dynamics as a rigorous and respected applied systems approach. It was Peter Senge, however, with his book *The Fifth Discipline* (1990), who popularized it. This volume, promoting system dynamics (the 'fifth discipline' of the title) as the key to creating 'learning organizations', hit the best-seller lists worldwide.

5.2 DESCRIPTION OF SYSTEM DYNAMICS

5.2.1 Historical development

In 1956 Forrester, with a background in the computer sciences and control engineering, became a professor in the Sloan School of Management at MIT. He directed the System Dynamics Program there until 1989. The approach he pioneered was originally called 'industrial dynamics' and was announced to the world in a 1958 article for the *Harvard Business Review* titled 'Industrial dynamics: A major breakthrough for decision makers'. Later, as Forrester extended his scope, he renamed the approach 'system dynamics'. The titles of his books over the years signal his increasing aspirations for system dynamics: *Industrial Dynamics* appeared in 1961, followed by *Principles of Systems* and *Urban Dynamics* in 1968 and 1969, respectively, and *World Dynamics* in 1971.

The attempt to encompass and understand the workings of the world as a system, in *World Dynamics* and its sequel *The Limits to Growth* (D. Meadows et al.,1972), was, as might be expected, particularly controversial. Taking five basic parameters as representative of the world system (population, natural resources, industrial production, agricultural production and pollution) and studying their behaviour and interactions, Forrester and his collaborators produced a model which indicated that growth at current levels was unsustainable. In order to avoid catastrophe brought about by pollution or complete exhaustion of natural resources, it was necessary to establish a kind of 'global equilibrium'. Inevitably, the authors were seen as doomsday-mongers.

Forrester, in fact, always saw encouragement of 'learning' as an important element in system dynamics. If managers could learn about how complex systems worked, they could act on them to bring about improvement. Nevertheless, the central feature of his approach was the development of rigorous, computer-based simulation models that could be tested for validity against the behaviour of the real-world systems they were supposed to represent. More recently, in some sections of the system dynamics community, there has been a burgeoning interest in using the approach to promote learning *per se*.

5.2.2 Philosophy and theory

According to the theory of system dynamics, the multitude of variables existing in complex systems become causally related in feedback loops that themselves interact. The systemic interrelationships between feedback loops constitute the structure of the system, and it is this structure that is the prime determinant of system behaviour. For example, a firm that successfully launches a new product on the market may generate sufficient extra cash to enable it to invest in a mass advertising campaign, generating more sales, giving greater revenue, encouraging further advertising, etc. These variables are linked in a positive reinforcing feedback loop. If at the same time the product grabs favourable media attention it may become extremely fashionable, generating more sales and even greater media exposure. A second positive feedback loop is then established supporting the first, and growth in demand can become huge. At this point pressure on the production process may get too great and quality suffer. The product might then acquire a poor reputation and sales decline. A linked negative feedback loop has come into being, which counteracts the original growth loops. The three feedback loops, and the way they interact, give rise to the structure of the system, which in this case can lead to the failure of the product to sustain itself in the market. The aim of system dynamics is to provide managers with an understanding of the structure of complex systems so that they can intervene to ensure behaviour that fits with their goals.

To get an appropriate understanding of structure it is necessary to establish four things:

- the boundary of the system;
- the network of feedback loops;
- the 'rate' or 'flow', and 'level' or 'stock' variables;
- the 'leverage' points.

The boundary must be drawn so as to include all important interacting components and to exclude all those that do not impact on behaviour. It is hereon assumed that all significant dynamic behaviour arises from the interactions of components inside the system boundary. Feedback loops within that boundary are then identified, their nature (positive or negative) deduced and their interrelationships charted. The substructure of the loops is detailed in terms of 'rate' or 'flow', and 'level' or 'stock' variables. A level is a quantity of some element that has accumulated in the system and can change over time. Rates are relationships between elements, often resulting from management decisions, that lead to changes in levels. In a simple inventory system, for example, manufacturing rate and delivery rate will together determine whether the stock level increases or decreases. The complexity involved usually makes it necessary at this point to represent the system in a computer model using one of the programming languages custom-built for system dynamics. This simulation will reveal which are the dominant feedback loops and predict the effect of any time delays that might occur in the system. Managers can experiment to gauge the impact of possible interventions. They will be looking for 'leverage' points – those areas of the system at which they can direct action in order to achieve maximum payback in terms of their objectives. This may demand, for example, breaking existing links or adding new feedback loops.

The growth in power of the digital computer was a major inspiration to Forrester at the time he was developing system dynamics. As suggested above, he believed that the complexity of the structure of many systems was too difficult for the human mind to grasp. As far as humans are concerned, the dynamic behaviour of such systems appears as counterintuitive. The computer, by contrast, is capable of tracing the interactions of innumerable variables and thus of taking complexity in its stride.

Senge (1990; Senge et al., 1994) has identified a number of the counterintuitive aspects of complex systems and elevated them into 11 'laws of the fifth discipline'. So, for example: 'The cure can be worse than the disease'. This means that easy solutions, which seem to offer instant relief, can become addictive and make the system weaker in the long term – as might drinking as a response to stress. Or: 'Cause and effect are not closely related in time and space'. We have to be careful, therefore, in assigning outcomes to particular actions. Or: 'There is no blame'. People tend to be criticized for behaviour of which we disapprove, but the real problem is more likely to be the system of relationships in which they are embedded. If we are to avoid becoming slaves to misunderstandings, we need to see the deeper structural patterns that give rise to problems. System dynamics, Senge insists, can provide the necessary insight and enable us to learn more appropriate responses.

5.2.3 Methodology

The methodology specified by Forrester (1961, 1971) for applying system dynamics in practice is directly derived from the philosophy and theory of the approach. As a first step, the problem worrying the decision-makers is clarified and the variables that impact on the problem are identified. Second, a feedback loop model is constructed that reveals the relationships between the variables. This must then be turned into a mathematical model that, on the basis of rates and levels, captures the basic interactions in the system and, using custom-built software, can be transformed into a computer simulation. In a fourth step the model is validated by comparing its behaviour with real-world activity and, once a decent correspondence has been achieved, experiments are conducted on the model to see how alternative decisions can improve performance. Finally, recommendations are made on how the decision-makers might change the situation to make it better.

Forrester (1971) argues that this methodology combines the power of the human mind with the strengths of today's computers. The human mind is best in the early stages, when the problem is being structured and creativity is necessary to identify the relevant variables and possible feedback loops. The computer takes over to reveal the unexpected consequences that arise from complexity and the dynamic behaviour of the system. The human mind comes into its own again to secure implementation.

To ensure that both these aspects of system dynamics get equal attention, Wolstenholme (1990) likes to think in terms of a qualitative and a quantitative phase to the methodology. Although moving to the quantitative phase, the computer simulation, is highly desirable, the qualitative phase can be valuable in its own right for explicating the decision-makers' understanding of the nature of the system of concern. Wolstenholme is adamant that the decision-makers are central to the qualitative phase, and he insists that they should remain involved during any quantitative steps. Only in this way can implementation of the recommendations be assured.

A more recent five-phase statement of system dynamics methodology, by Maani and Cavana (2000), is careful to include the learning potential inherent in the approach, as emphasized by Senge. The five phases are:

- problem structuring;
- causal loop modelling;
- dynamic modelling;
- scenario planning and modelling;
- implementation and organizational learning.

The first three are relatively routine although early attention is given to trying to identify common patterns of behaviour ('system archetypes' in Senge's terminology) and key leverage points. In the final two, however, new techniques are incorporated specifically designed to encourage learning. Phase 4 develops the idea of using scenarios – testing strategies under varying external conditions – to engage managers. The final phase is more concerned to extend learning among all the relevant stakeholders than to reach specific decisions. 'Microworlds' (or 'management flight simulators') are constructed based on the simulation models. These are interactive and provide managers with a user-friendly interface that allows them to experiment with the models. A 'learning laboratory' is designed to provide for the structured learning of groups of managers engaging with a microworld, and this is then employed to facilitate and diffuse learning throughout the organization.

5.2.4   Methods

The four methods most frequently used to support the various stages of the system dynamics methodology are the 'signed digraph' or 'causal loop diagram', system archetypes, computer simulation software packages and microworlds.

The identification of significant feedback loops and their causal structure is central in system dynamics to understanding system behaviour. A signed digraph can help because it is a causal loop diagram annotated to show the direction of feedback. The example given in Subsection 5.2.2 is shown in Figure 5.1 in signed digraph form. A new product is launched successfully and picks up sales rapidly due to the increased revenue available for mass advertising and some favourable media attention that makes it extremely fashionable. The two positive feedback loops (marked by a plus sign) that yield this result are produced because an increase in any of the variables shown in the loop leads to a corresponding increase in the variable on which it impacts. In signed digraphs, relationships that produce a change in the same direction (either increase or decrease) are marked by a positive sign. As we can see in Figure 5.1, in the positive feedback loops all the signs are positive. The problem arises for this product because as production levels increase, to meet sales demand, quality declines, so does the reputation of the product for quality and sales suffer. The relationship between production and quality is shown with a negative sign to reflect the fact that as production increases quality falls. Note that the links between quality and reputation, and sales remain 'positive' because a decrease in quality leads to a corresponding decrease in reputation for quality and then sales. The one negative sign, between production and quality, produces a negative feedback loop (marked by a minus sign) that counteracts the other two growth loops.

If nothing is done, then the 'dominance' relationships between the loops will determine the fate of the product. For example, if the product becomes exceptionally fashionable, then sales may continue to grow because the quality of the product is regarded as being less significant. Managers are likely to want to ensure a favourable outcome, however, by intervening at

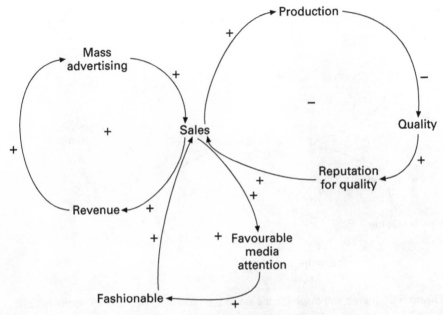

Figure 5.1 A signed digraph: a new product launch.

high leverage points – which may be through contacts with the media to strengthen that loop or by re-engineering the production process to improve quality and so turn that loop positive as well. They will also need to be on the lookout for other possible negative feedback loops – competition brought into the market attracted by their success or a change in how fashionable the product is seen as being.

Senge (1990; Senge et al., 1994) has studied reinforcing (positive) feedback processes and balancing (negative) feedback processes, together with the phenomenon of 'delays', which occur when the impact of a feedback process takes a long time to come through. He concludes that it is possible to identify certain system archetypes that show regular patterns of behaviour, due to particular structural characteristics, that continually give rise to management problems. Once mastered by managers, according to Senge, they open the door to systems thinking. One such is the 'limits to growth' archetype, when reinforcing growth loops inadvertently set off a balancing, negative loop that slows down success or even sends it into reverse. The successful product launch discussed above, which led to the need for higher production levels, giving rise to quality problems, provides an example.

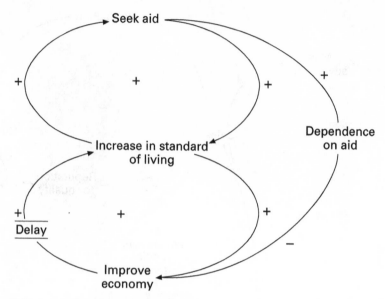

Figure 5.2 Increasing dependence on aid: an example of the 'shifting the burden' archetype.

Other well-known archetypes are 'shifting the burden', 'balancing process with delay', 'accidental adversaries', 'eroding goals', 'escalation', 'success to the successful', 'tragedy of the commons', 'fixes that fail' and 'growth and underinvestment'. The 'shifting the burden' archetype can be illustrated if we consider a developing country wishing to increase the standard of living for its people. It may need to make some fundamental adjustments to its economy in order to achieve this. In the interim it seeks aid to ensure a reasonable standard of living. The danger is that the country becomes 'addicted' to the aid before it sees any benefits coming through from the changes to its economy. Once addicted it loses its capacity for self-reliance, the economy is weakened rather than strengthened and the country becomes completely dependent upon aid. All of these archetypes are easily represented using causal loop diagrams. Our example is shown in Figure 5.2. If managers can learn to recognize system archetypes, they can save themselves a lot of wasted and misdirected effort and target their interventions to points of maximum leverage.

Once the feedback structure of a system is understood and captured in a model, it is possible to further elaborate by building a computer simulation

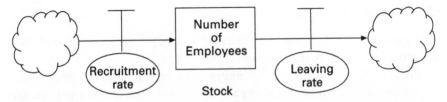

Figure 5.3 Stock-and-flow diagram.

designed to represent its dynamic behaviour. Indeed, 'serious' system dynamicists see this step as essential – regarding causal loop diagrams and
system archetypes as mere 'training wheels' for systemic thinking (see
Sterman, 2000). Building the simulation involves plotting the systemic
impacts of the various feedback loops on the 'levels' and 'rates' that exist
within the system. Stock-and-flow diagrams (where the stocks are the levels
and the flows are the rates) are used for this purpose. In Figure 5.3 we see
some of the typical symbols used in stock-and-flow diagrams. The stock
level of interest in this case is the number of employees in a company. This
is shown as a rectangular 'vessel'. The recruitment rate is a flow, shown as a
kind of valve, which adds to the number of employees. There is another
flow of staff leaving, which subtracts from the stock of employees. Employees are recruited from a 'source', shown as a cloud, and return to a 'sink',
similarly represented, when they leave. Suffice it to say that much user-
friendly software is now available that allows conversion of causal loop and
stock-and-flow diagrams into sophisticated computer simulations. Popular
examples are DYNAMO, STELLA, ithink, DYSMAP, VENSIM and
POWERSIM.

The software also facilitates the creation of microworlds or management
flight simulators (see Morecroft and Sterman, 1994). These present managers
with an easily understood control panel that hides the complexity of the
simulation and provides something much more like a gaming environment.
Managers can try out different decisions on a representation of the situation
they are facing at work and see what consequences ensue. Care is taken in
designing proper settings to maximize the benefits of the learning process.
These settings are called 'learning laboratories'. The aim is to get groups of
managers to question their existing mental models. In particular, they
should come to recognize the interdependence of the issues they deal with
and to replace superficial explanations of problems with a more systemic
understanding.

5.2.5   Recent developments

Recent developments in system dynamics have focused further on its ability to promote learning in organizations.

Senge (1990) regards system dynamics, presented as 'the fifth discipline', as the most important tool that organizations must master on the route to becoming 'learning organizations'. Only system dynamics can reveal the systemic structures that govern their behaviour. Nevertheless, it is essential to support study of the fifth discipline with research on the other four disciplines seen as significant in the creation of learning organizations. These are 'personal mastery', 'managing mental models', 'building shared vision' and 'team learning'. Personal mastery involves individuals in continually clarifying and deepening understanding of their own purposes. The discipline of managing mental models requires organizations continually to question the taken-for-granted assumptions that underpin the world views governing their current behaviour. Shared vision requires unearthing visions of the future that inspire consensus and commitment. Team learning, if properly encouraged and enhanced, allows an organization to get the benefits of synergy from the knowledge held by individuals. Although system dynamics is more fundamental than any of these and in effect underpins them, they are nevertheless worthy of study in their own right.

Vennix's (1996) influential work on 'group model building' centres on integrating individual mental models, each of which initially offers only a limited perspective on the causal processes at work. The approach depends heavily on the skills of the facilitator who helps the group to elaborate the initial models into a system dynamics model that reflects a shared social reality and a consensus around the nature of the problem. The whole group is involved throughout, and this enhances team learning and creates commitment to the resulting decisions.

Sterman (2000) holds out a bright future for system dynamics interacting, through computer technology, with fields such as complexity science and artificial intelligence, and in qualitative areas of research concerned with mental models, learning and strategic decision making.

5.3   SYSTEM DYNAMICS IN ACTION

One of the interventions most frequently used to illustrate the power of the system dynamics approach is that conducted by the MIT System Dynamics Group with Hanover Insurance (see Senge and Sterman in Morecroft and

Sterman, 1994; Maani and Cavana, 2000; Cavaleri and Obloj, 1993). The case reveals that apparently rational action taken by management to reduce the costs of settling claims and to maintain customer satisfaction actually led to an erosion of quality of service and increased settlement costs. The system dynamics study demonstrated, through an analysis of the interacting feed-back loops, exactly why this happened, suggested less obvious but more efficacious ways of tackling the problems faced and led to the development of a microworld and learning laboratory to spread the learning obtained throughout the company.

Hanover Insurance had undergone an amazing transformation in the 1970s and early 1980s pulling itself from the bottom of the industry to become a leader in the property and liability field. During this period it grew 50% faster than the industry as a whole. Nevertheless, it could not escape the many problems and resulting runaway costs that impacted on the industry during the 1980s. Automobile insurance premiums doubled causing a public backlash, the number of product liability cases increased massively and the average size of claims settled in court increased fivefold. It was easy to blame dishonest policy holders, biased juries, greedy lawyers and the increased litigiousness of society. Senior managers in Hanover, however, determined to look at how their own management practices were contributing to the problem situation. A good starting point was the claims management operation responsible now, because of increasing numbers and complexity of claims, for more than 67% of total company expenses.

The project began with a team from Hanover, consisting of the senior vice-president for claims and two of his direct subordinates, meeting regu-larly with some MIT researchers. A vision statement expressed the desire to be pre-eminent among claims organizations and to provide 'fair, fast, and friendly' service. From this it was possible to derive an image of the ideal claims adjuster and the performance measures he or she would be required to meet. The problem was finding a coherent path from the reality to the ideal. There were lots of candidate strategies, but these seemed disjointed. A more systemic solution was required.

STELLA was used with the Hanover team to build computer-based simulation models. These were subject to basic reality checks and employed to test the results of current strategies and to seek improvements in manage-ment practices. Expert judgement was used, alongside whatever quantitative data were available, to estimate the many 'soft variables' involved and their effects. The final model was both sophisticated in its treatment of problem dynamics and fully owned by the Hanover team. Figure 5.4, reproduced

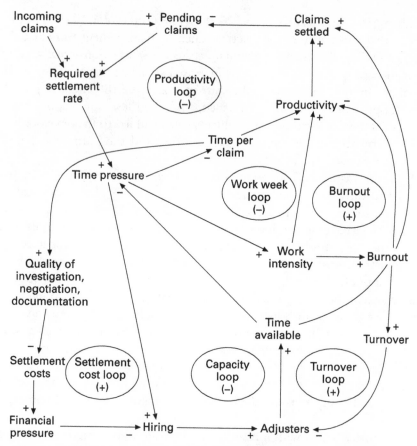

Figure 5.4 System dynamics of claims processing in the insurance industry. Feedback loops controlling claims settlement, with processes causing self-reinforcing erosion of quality and increasing settlement costs. Arrows indicate the direction of causality. Signs ('+' or '−') at arrowheads indicate the polarity of relationships: a '+' denotes that an increase in the independent variable causes the dependent variable to increase, *ceteris paribus* (and a decrease causes a decrease). Similarly, '−' indicates that an increase in the independent variable causes the dependent variable to decrease. Positive loop polarity (denoted by (+) in the loop identifier) indicates a self-reinforcing (positive feedback) process. Negative (−) loop polarity indicates a self-regulating (negative feedback) process.

From Senge and Sterman (1994), reproduced by permission of Productivity Press.

from Senge and Sterman, is a causal diagram that expresses the problem dynamics.

The existing, implicit strategy of Hanover, in the face of pressure from increased claims, was captured in the productivity loop and the work week loop of Figure 5.4. The operating norm for claims adjusters was simply to work faster and work harder. Working faster helped reduce pending claims because less time was spent per claim and therefore more claims could be settled. Working harder helped reduce pending claims because of the effect on productivity of working longer hours and taking shorter and fewer breaks. In the short term these 'fixes' might appear to work. In the longer term, however, other relationships bring about unintended consequences (initially hidden because of the existence of 'delays') that make matters worse rather than better. They are examples of the 'fixes that fail' archetype.

The unintended consequences of working faster are shown in the settlement cost loop of Figure 5.4. Spending less time per claim reduces the quality of settlements, and this leads to increased settlement costs. Less time to investigate and negotiate claims means that inflated settlements are agreed. Other customers become dissatisfied with the amount of time devoted to them by the adjuster and are more ready to resort to law. Where litigation results, inadequate documentation means longer preparation time and less successful outcomes.

The unintended consequences of working harder are shown in the burnout loop and turnover loop of Figure 5.4. Working harder leads to fatigue, ill health and staff burnout, which impacts adversely on productivity. Burnout also increases staff turnover, which means fewer assessors and even greater time pressure on those that remain.

Through the settlement cost, burnout and turnover loops, therefore, the initial fixes provoke longer term unintended consequences that reduce quality, increase time pressures and increase costs. Because this feedback is delayed and its causes are not easy to trace, management will tend to react by relying further on the original fixes. In an insurance industry facing runaway costs the temptation to require claims adjusters to work even faster and harder was virtually irresistible. The idea of addressing the problem by hiring new claims adjusters seemed ridiculous. In archetype terms, therefore, the burden was shifted from capacity expansion to quality erosion.

Hanover, at the time of the study, had the highest number of assessors per claim in the industry. Nevertheless, because the Hanover team had been involved in building the model themselves and, through the model, had come to appreciate the interconnections that produced the counterintuitive behaviour of the claims adjustment system, they were prepared to embrace the only fundamental solution to the problem. This, as is shown by the capacity loop in Figure 5.4, was increasing adjuster capacity. However well it compared with the rest of the industry, only by hiring new adjusters and training them properly could Hanover genuinely address issues of service quality and increased costs.

The next challenge for the project was to extend the learning gained to the entire company. As implied earlier, there was a tendency to blame outside factors, and not internal management practices, for the travails of the insurance industry. Furthermore, in Hanover responsibility for decision-making is widely distributed. If there was to be a real change in the way the company behaved it was essential that all those managers with influence experienced for themselves the counterintuitive behaviour of the claims processing system. To achieve this a claims learning laboratory, incorporating a computer simulation game (or management flight simulator), was developed. Managers were familiarized with causal loop diagrams and helped to think through the variables and relationships associated with the claims system. The design of the game ensured that they were forced to make explicit their mental models and to challenge them when the results of the strategies they championed defied their expectations. As a result 'double-loop' learning was facilitated.

As is demonstrated by the many excellent examples in Sterman's (2000) *Business Dynamics*, system dynamics is applicable to a wide range of industrial and public policy issues.

5.4   CRITIQUE OF SYSTEM DYNAMICS

The strengths of system dynamics rest on the power of its claim that structure is the main determinant of system behaviour and that structure can be described in terms of the relationships between positive and negative feedback loops. If this claim is granted, then system dynamics becomes a unifying interdisciplinary framework, capable of seeing beyond the surface detail presented by individual disciplines to the deeper patterns that are really responsible for generating behaviour. System dynamics can help managers penetrate complexity and get their hands on the real levers of change and improvement in social systems.

Again, once the claim is ceded, then some interesting explanations for organizational ills become available, based on the behaviour of interrelated feedback systems. It seems that problems arise: when we treat symptoms rather than fundamental causes; when we become addicted to easy solutions; when we forget that it takes time for interventions to show significant outcomes; when we try to change systems drastically rather than look for small changes that can produce big results; when we blame others or outside circumstances rather than seeing that our own actions also contribute to the relationships that determine system behaviour; and so forth. An understanding of feedback systems, and the common dysfunctional system archetypes to which they give rise, enable managers to cope with complexity and take more efficient and efficacious decisions in pursuit of their goals.

This is even more the case because system dynamic models help to pinpoint key decision points. The actions of decision-makers are included in the models, and it is therefore easy to establish the consequences of present policies and to explore alternative strategies. This leads to the emphasis on learning that is particularly prominent in Senge's writings. Managers, unaware of the systemic relationships to which their actions contribute, are prone to act in ways that exacerbate existing problems. If they are involved in building causal loop models, however, they become aware of the underlying structures at work. They are more willing to question the mental models that contribute to the consolidation of damaging archetypes.

Combine these powerful theoretical insights with the advances made in methodology, quantitative modelling, computer simulation and software packages, and there is much to support the argument that system dynamics has achieved Forrester's ambition for systems thinking of making it more applicable to strategic problems.

Critics, however (Keys, 1991; Flood and Jackson, 1991; Jackson, 2000), urge considerable caution. To those working in specific disciplines and trained in the scientific method, system dynamics can seem imprecise and lacking in rigour. Sometimes, system dynamicists seem to jump to building their models without doing their homework. They simply ignore existing theories in the field they are exploring. At other times, if insufficient data are known about an area of concern, they remain prepared to plough on, building their models without bothering to collect all the relevant data that others would regard as essential. Judgement rather than proper scientific research is used to fill in the gaps. Forrester's claim, in the early 1970s, that we know enough to make useful models of social systems reeks of arrogance.

Senge's work can appear 'unscientific', even to others working within system dynamics. Forrester was reacting against the tendency in OR to reduce management science to a limited number of mathematical models. Senge seems to be repeating the mistake in believing that key management problems can be explored using a limited set of system archetypes. Forrester insisted that rigorous computer simulation, designed to tease out the counterintuitive behaviour of social systems, was central to system dynamics. Senge appears to replace this, as the core of the approach, with managers learning about feedback relationships.

If system dynamics models are imprecise, then they cannot give very accurate predictions of future system states and, therefore, will be of limited usefulness to decision-makers. This criticism is reinforced if we take seriously insights derived from chaos and complexity theory (see Chapter 7). Complexity theory insists on the 'butterfly' effect – the idea that small changes in a system's initial conditions can alter its long-term behaviour very significantly. If system dynamics has no accurate grasp on initial conditions or of the exact impact different relevant variables have on one another, then the claim to make accurate predictions must appear as preposterous. This can be illustrated if we take Cavaleri and Obloj's (1993) example of a causal loop diagram outlining the systemic relationships supposed to determine the future political direction of Russia. Using this diagram readers are invited to suggest which of six scenarios has the greatest likelihood of occurring: 'confusion reigns', 'a return to communism', 'the "Russian" state', 'Chile revisited', 'European-style democratic socialism' or 'New York on the Volga'. I have no idea, using the diagram, how anyone could attempt to answer this question.

Another line of criticism against system dynamics sees its theory, methodology and methods as simply unsuitable to the subject matter of its concern. To these critics, human beings, through their intentions, motivations and actions, shape social systems. If we want to learn about social systems we need to understand the subjective interpretations of the world that individual social actors employ. Social structure emerges through a process of negotiation and renegotiation of meaning. System dynamics misses the point when it tries to study social systems 'objectively', from the outside. And in trying to grasp the complexity of social reality using models built on feedback processes, system dynamics presents itself with an impossible task.

To critics of this persuasion, system dynamics, the *raison d'être* of which is to tackle greater complexity, is itself the perpetrator of gross simplification. It is easy to show, using simple feedback diagrams, that providing aid to a developing country is not a long-term solution to its economic problems (to take our earlier example), that increasing police recruitment may not be the best way of reducing crime, that building more roads may not ease road congestion, that reducing cost might not be the best solution to declining profits. But, in my experience, these things are hardly enlightening to actual decision-makers, who are well aware of them as well as of the myriad of other pragmatic, cultural, ethical and political factors that prevent them acting in the rational way prescribed by system dynamics. None of these problems are as simple as system dynamics makes them out to be. Few management problems are as simple as Senge's archetypes suggest.

The emphasis in system dynamics on understanding objectively the underlying structure of social systems, and the relative neglect of subjectivity, has other consequences as well. Little attention is given to the variety of purposes that different social actors might see social systems as serving. There is a tendency, in a unitary fashion, to assume that purposes have already been agreed or, in a coercive manner, to take for granted the objectives of powerful decision-makers. And system dynamicists can sometimes contribute to disenfranchising other stakeholders if they present themselves as elite technicians capable of providing objective accounts of the nature of social systems.

We can see the debate we have just been examining as one between those adhering to the functionalist and the interpretive paradigms. System dynamics, despite the recent emphasis on mental models and learning, is essentially functionalist in nature. It sees system structure as the determining force behind system behaviour and tries to map that structure in terms of the relationships between feedback loops. The aim is to better predict the behaviour of social systems so that managers can control them. Improving goal seeking, or at least ensuring that stability is maintained so that goals can be achieved, is to the fore. The guiding rationales behind other systems approaches – exploring purposes, ensuring fairness and promoting diversity – receive much less support. The work of Senge (1990) and Vennix (1996), it is true, edges closer to the interpretive paradigm and a greater concern with ensuring mutual understanding through group problem-solving. If system dynamics leans too far in this direction, however, it risks jettisoning the claim to our attention it derives from the functionalist presumption that it can unearth laws that govern the behaviour of systems. If humans are free to construct social systems as they wish, what determining influence does system structure have? And what confidence can we have in the power of causal loop analysis to predict system behaviour? This tension between determinism and free will is unresolved in, for example, the work of Senge, and eats at its credibility. System dynamics, to be worthy of our attention, must maintain its functionalist aspirations. Otherwise, it becomes simply an undertheorized soft systems approach.

The functionalism that underpins system dynamics differs somewhat from the functionalism of hard systems thinking in embracing a structuralist rather than positivist epistemology. In other words, its claim to knowledge is that it gives access to the underlying structures that determine system behaviour rather than to the surface details that, once logically examined, explain what is happening. A belief in the existence of these deeper patterns governing surface events, and its ability to unearth them, gives to system dynamics an ability to cut through apparent complexity. This is why the approach can claim to be broader in scope and more powerful than hard systems thinking.

A broader range of system concepts is employed in system dynamics than in hard systems thinking. Notions such as stocks and flows, positive and negative feedback, causal loops, structure, behaviour and learning are added to the ideas of system, subsystem, hierarchy and boundary. There is a much more dynamic orientation, which is due to the 'flux and transformation' metaphor dominating over the machine metaphor in system dynamics – even if somewhat tempered by a mechanical equilibrium slant. The culture metaphor is beginning to assume greater importance, but remains in a supportive role. Metaphors that would point to the significance of environmental relations or the play of power and politics are not employed.

5.5 THE VALUE OF SYSTEM DYNAMICS TO MANAGERS

As with hard systems thinking, managers need the help of experts in order to get the most out of system dynamics. Nevertheless, it is worth following the pattern begun in the previous chapter by trying to pick out five lessons that managers can easily learn from system dynamics that can certainly benefit their practice:

- It is often helpful to look beyond the apparent mess presented by surface appearances to see if there are any underlying patterns of feedback loops that are determining system behaviour. Occasionally, computer simulation can help to tease out the effects that the relationships between variables and loops are producing.
- An understanding of how feedback loops interact to cause system behaviour can inform the way managers work. For example, they become much more aware of the dangers of unintended consequences, of treating symptoms rather than causes, of the importance of 'delays', etc.
- Rather than jumping to what appear to be obvious solutions to problems, managers need to appreciate that complex systems often behave in subtle and unexpected ways. It is worth spending time

looking for smaller interventions that, nevertheless, may be the levers to bring about substantial changes.

- System dynamics supports the conclusion that 'no man is an island'. It is no good, therefore, blaming the environment or other people for our problems. Our decisions are part of the set of relationships giving rise to the difficulties that we face.

- System dynamic models, management flight simulators, etc. can assist managers to appreciate the systemic relationships in which they are involved and to which their decisions contribute. They teach managers that they often need to radically change their thinking before improvement can become possible. The double-loop learning involved in changing mental models is crucial to successful management practice.

5.6 CONCLUSION

The system dynamics approach can provide insight for managers in many circumstances. In basic terms it is an advance down the vertical, systems dimension of the SOSM (see Chapter 2). It offers better prospects for dealing with system complexity than hard systems thinking. Many would want to claim more for it and, like Senge, seize the label 'systems thinking' for the system dynamics strand within the systems approach. This is to push too far. System dynamics has a particular, limited competence that it would do well to consolidate and cultivate. Those system dynamics authors who tread beyond functionalism risk losing touch with their core competence and come into competition with systems thinkers who have been exploring other paradigms for some time and, as a result, have developed methodologies and methods more attuned to those paradigms. Rather than believing that system dynamics can do everything, a critical systems thinker is likely to want to combine the strengths of system dynamics with what other systems approaches have learned to do better.

REFERENCES

Cavaleri, S. and Obloj, K. (1993). *Management Systems: A Global Perspective*. Wadsworth, Belmont, CA.

Flood, R.L. and Jackson, M.C. (1991). *Creative Problem Solving: Total Systems Intervention*. John Wiley & Sons, Chichester, UK.

Forrester, J.W. (1958), Industrial dynamics: A major breakthrough for decision makers. *Harvard Business Review*, **36**, 37–48.

Forrester, J.W. (1961). *Industrial Dynamics*. Productivity Press, Portland, OR.

Forrester, J.W. (1968). *Principles of Systems*. Productivity Press, Portland, OR.

Forrester, J.W. (1969). *Urban Dynamics*. Productivity Press, Portland, OR.

Forrester, J.W. (1971). *World Dynamics*. Productivity Press, Portland, OR.

Jackson, M.C. (2000). *Systems Approaches to Management*. Kluwer/Plenum, New York.

Keys, P. (1991). *Operational Research and Systems: The Systemic Nature of Operational Research*. Plenum, New York.

Maani, K.E. and Cavana, R.Y. (2000). *Systems Thinking and Modelling*. Pearson Education, New Zealand.

Meadows, D.H., Meadows, D.L., Randers, J. and Behrens, III, W.W. (1972). *The Limits to Growth*. Universe Books, New York.

Morecroft, J.D.W. and Sterman, J.D. (eds) (1994). *Modelling for Learning Organizations*. Productivity Press, Portland, OR.

Senge, P. (1990). *The Fifth Discipline: The Art and Practice of the Learning Organization*. Random House, London.

Senge, P. and Sterman, J.D. (1994). Systems thinking and organizational learning: Acting locally and thinking globally in the organization of the future. In: J.D.W. Morecroft and J.D. Sterman (eds), *Modelling for Learning Organizations* (pp. 195–216). Productivity Press, Portland, OR.

Senge, P., Kleiner, A., Roberts, C., Ross, R. and Smith, B. (1994). *The Fifth Discipline Fieldbook*. Century, London.

Sterman, J.D. (2000). *Business Dynamics – Systems Thinking and Modelling in a Complex World*. McGraw-Hill, New York.

Vennix, J.A.C. (1996). *Group Model Building: Facilitating Team Learning Using System Dynamics*. John Wiley & Sons, Chichester, UK.

Wolstenholme, E.F. (1990). *Systems Enquiry: A System Dynamics Approach*. John Wiley & Sons, Chichester, UK.

Organizational Cybernetics 6

Our institutions are failing because they are disobeying laws of effective organisation which their administrators do not know about, to which indeed their cultural mind is closed, because they contend that there exists and can exist no science competent to discover those laws.

Beer (1974)

6.1 INTRODUCTION

Cybernetics, as we saw in Chapter 1, was originally defined as the science of control and communication in the animal and the machine. Inevitably, however, ideas from this powerful interdisciplinary science soon began to be transferred to the managerial domain. Initially, they were used simply as a bolt-on to existing hard systems approaches. Employing the negative feedback mechanism, for example, was recognized as essential to ensuring conformance to externally defined goals. In this 'management cybernetics' guise, the usefulness of cybernetics was constrained by the machine metaphor. The work of Stafford Beer on 'organisational cybernetics' changed all that.

Beer was determined to break with traditional management thinking. He looked at company organization charts and regarded them as totally unsatisfactory as a model for complex enterprises. They suggested that the person at the top of the organization needed a brain weighing half a ton – since all information flowed up to him and all decisions appeared to be his responsibility. As Beer commented, peoples' heads do not get bigger toward the top of an organization, except perhaps in a metaphorical sense. Drawing upon a wider range of cybernetic concepts, and important insights from neurophysiology, he redefined cybernetics as the 'science of effective organisation' and set out to construct a more accurate and useful model. The result was his influential 'viable system model', which, as its name suggests, is a model of the key features that any viable system must exhibit.

6.2 DESCRIPTION OF ORGANIZATIONAL CYBERNETICS

6.2.1 Historical development

According to Beer, the cybernetic concepts of black box, negative feedback and variety, which we met in Chapter 1, are ideal for helping us to understand and improve complex systems, like organizations, that are characterized by extreme complexity, self-regulation and probabilism. The black box technique reminds us that we should not try to break systems down into their parts to understand them, but rather control them through monitoring their outputs and manipulating their inputs appropriately. The negative feedback mechanism can then be employed to ensure that they are regulated to achieve preferred goals. Variety engineering offers a means of ensuring control of probabilistic systems, the behaviour of which cannot be predicted in advance.

Beer reasoned that if he wanted to understand further the principles of viability underpinning the behaviour of complex organizations, it would be useful to take a known-to-be-viable system as a model. The human body, controlled by the nervous system, is perhaps the richest and most flexible viable system of all. In his book *Brain of the Firm* (1972), therefore, Beer takes this example and builds from it a neurocybernetic model consisting of five essential subsystems, which can be identified in the brain and body in line with major functional requirements. This is the basis of the 'Viable System Model' (VSM), which he then seeks to show is equally relevant to social organizations.

In a later book, *The Heart of Enterprise* (1979), the same model, consisting of five subsystems and appropriate feedback loops and information flows, is derived from the original cybernetic laws. This demonstrates that the VSM is generally applicable to all systems, and to organizations large and small. Indeed, in a one-person enterprise all five functions will still need to be performed by that one individual if viability is to be ensured.

The year 1985 saw the publication of *Diagnosing the System for Organizations* in which Beer introduces the VSM, and offers advice for applying it, in the form of a handbook or manager's guide. A second edition of *Brain of the Firm* (1981) details the most ambitious use of the model in support of the Allende Government in Chile. Many other applications are described in

Beer's books, as they are in Espejo and Harnden (1989), and Espejo and Schwaninger (1993).

6.2.2 Philosophy and theory

Beer's organizational cybernetics, like system dynamics, is 'structuralist' in nature. In the case of system dynamics (see Chapter 5) it was the relationships between feedback processes operating at the deep structural level that gave rise to system behaviour at the surface level. With organizational cybernetics it is cybernetic laws and principles at work below the surface that generate the phenomena we observe and the relationships between them. Beer advocates a rigorous scientific procedure to unearth these cybernetic laws. Modelling is crucial and, as we saw Beer doing in *Brain of the Firm*, it is possible to use precise models developed in one scientific discipline to inform developments in another field. In this way, the management scientist can get beyond mere metaphor and analogy to produce models that can be shown, by logic and mathematics, to be homomorphic in nature because they express genuinely interdisciplinary laws. The VSM is Beer's attempt to demonstrate, in as simple a way as possible, how cybernetic laws underpin the operation of all complex systems. We shall study this in Subsection 6.2.3.

One of the most important findings of organizational cybernetics is that complex systems have a 'recursive' nature. This refers to the fact that systems exist in hierarchies, and that the organizational form of higher level systems can be found repeated in the parts. The second characteristic is, of course, a consequence of the first since, according to cybernetics, all viable systems exhibit the same organizational characteristics. The VSM respects the recursive nature of systems, and its applicability to different system levels allows elegant representations of organizations to be constructed and acts as a great variety reducer for managers and management scientists. The same viable system principles can be used to model a subsystem (a division) in an organization, that organization and its suprasystem (the system of which the organization is a part). Using the VSM, lower level systems, which inevitably appear as 'black boxes' when the organization as a whole is being observed, can become the focus of interest in their own right with only a slight adjustment of attention.

In later discussions of the VSM, Beer also makes use of the theory of autopoiesis developed by Maturana and Varela (e.g., 1980). Autopoietic systems are self-producing systems, and viable systems necessarily therefore need to be autopoietic. However, as Beer notes, it is essential that this property be embodied only in the system as a whole and in its key operational elements. In a company, that means the company itself and the business units. If support services become autopoietic, seeking to produce themselves for their own benefit, then bureaucracy ensues.

Another insight from the theory of autopoiesis is that the VSM captures and describes the essential 'organization' of systems rather than particular structures. Organization, in this sense, is what defines a system and enables it to maintain autonomy and identity. Structure concerns itself with the variety of arrangements between components that might enable the 'organization' to be realized. This emphasis on essential organization rather than particular structures goes a long way toward accounting for the generality of the model.

6.2.3   Methodology

The VSM embodies in a highly usable way the various cybernetic laws and principles that Beer regards as essential to improving the performance of organizations. It is not surprising, therefore, to find it at the very centre of the approach I am calling organizational cybernetics. Nevertheless, it is worth remembering that the VSM itself is a model rather than a methodology and can be used for purposes other than those prescribed by Beer.

When the VSM is employed as part of organizational cybernetics its role is to reveal whether enterprises obey cybernetic laws or flout them. If used in a 'design' mode its gaze is focused on plans for new organizations, and it aims to ensure they are constructed according to good cybernetic principles. The model can also be used in a 'diagnostic' mode. Here it acts as an exemplar of good organization against which the structures and processes of an actually existing system can be checked. In this mode, the organizational physician can 'X-ray' the actual system and judge what is going wrong on the basis of his or her knowledge of what a healthy organization should look like.

Our starting point for understanding the VSM must be the concept of 'variety' and Ashby's (1956) law of requisite variety: 'only variety can destroy variety'. Figure 6.1 shows the situation facing the managers of a complex set of operations in these terms. It can be assumed that the environment is of much greater variety (it can exhibit more system states) than the operations, which are in turn of much greater variety than the management. However, as Ashby's law tells us, for management to be able to control the operations and if the operations are to be sustainable in the environment, varieties must be balanced. This requires variety engineering

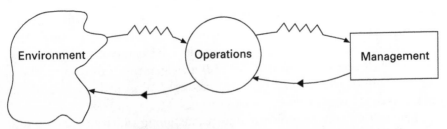

Figure 6.1 Variety engineering.

– the attenuation of the variety of high-variety systems and the amplification of the variety of low-variety systems.

The VSM is in part a sophisticated working through of the implications of Ashby's law of requisite variety for enterprises. In the process a crucial conundrum facing organizations has to be resolved – that of centralization versus decentralization. As can be gleaned from study of Figure 6.1, management will be keen to control the operations in order to realize agreed-on goals. At the same time, if the operations are to be responsive to changes in the environment, they will require the maximum capacity to act in an autonomous manner. If management restricts the variety of the operations too much, then the organization will not be adaptive to changes in the environment. If management effects too little control over operations, then the organization will drift and be incapable of achieving goals. The VSM claims to demonstrate to managers a solution whereby the maximum autonomy is granted to operations consistent with the maintenance of systemic cohesion and thus goal-seeking capability.

Use of the VSM can now be outlined. The first step is to agree on the identity of the organization in terms of the purposes it is to pursue. The policy-making function of the system ('System 5', as we shall see) must express and represent these purposes, but, obviously, should not be the sole repository of identity. Ideally, it should reflect purposes that emerge from and are accepted by the operational elements. Equally clearly, purposes need to be derived taking into account the state of the organization's environment and the opportunities and threats that exist. Proper management of this first step in the methodology attenuates environmental variety by helping to determine what aspects of the environment are actually relevant to the system.

The second stage involves 'unfolding' the complexity of the organization by deciding what operational or business units will enable it best to achieve its purposes. According to the logic of the model these units will be made as autonomous as possible within the constraints of overall systemic cohesion. The strategy of unfolding complexity, therefore, increases the variety of the organization with respect to its environment. It also reduces the overwhelming variety that the overall management of the organization would otherwise have to face because this can be 'absorbed', and decisions can be taken at lower levels in the enterprise.

There will always be a choice of 'dimensions' along which an organization can unfold its complexity. A university, for example, might decide that its primary activities should be teaching and learning, research and reach-out; or arts, social sciences, sciences, medicine and business; or undergraduate, postgraduate, postexperience and part-time teaching. It is in making this decision that the VSM requires of its users perhaps the greatest creativity. The key is to find the best expression of identity and purpose given what the nature of the organization and its environment will allow. So, a university that had chosen to be teaching-centred or been forced by history and circumstances in this direction would be unwise to adopt the first of those options provided above.

Once a decision has been made about primary divisions, it is usual to focus the VSM analysis on three levels of recursion. At level 1 resides the system with which we are currently most concerned, called the 'system in focus'. In the university example, this might be the university itself. At level 0 is the wider system of which the university is part, which might be universities in the north of England, or universities in the UK. At recursion level 2 lie the primary activities that have now been determined – perhaps arts, social sciences, sciences, medicine and business. This can be seen in Figure 6.2 where University X is our system in focus. As Figure 6.2 suggests, if the management of the university wished to delve into what for it is normally the 'black box' of the business school, it could go down to what would be recursion level 3 and use the VSM to ask questions about the various activities in the business school.

The aim then, paying particular attention to the 'system in focus', is to use the VSM to model at three levels of recursion. The VSM itself is shown in Figure 6.3, and we must now elaborate on its essential organization. It is made up of five elements (Systems 1 to 5), which we can label implementation, co-ordination, operational control (including services management), development and policy. The functions handled by these five elements must, cybernetics dictates, be adequately performed in all systems that wish to remain viable. I will now describe the five systems in turn and the information flows that connect the bits of the model.

System 1 consists of the various parts of the organization concerned with

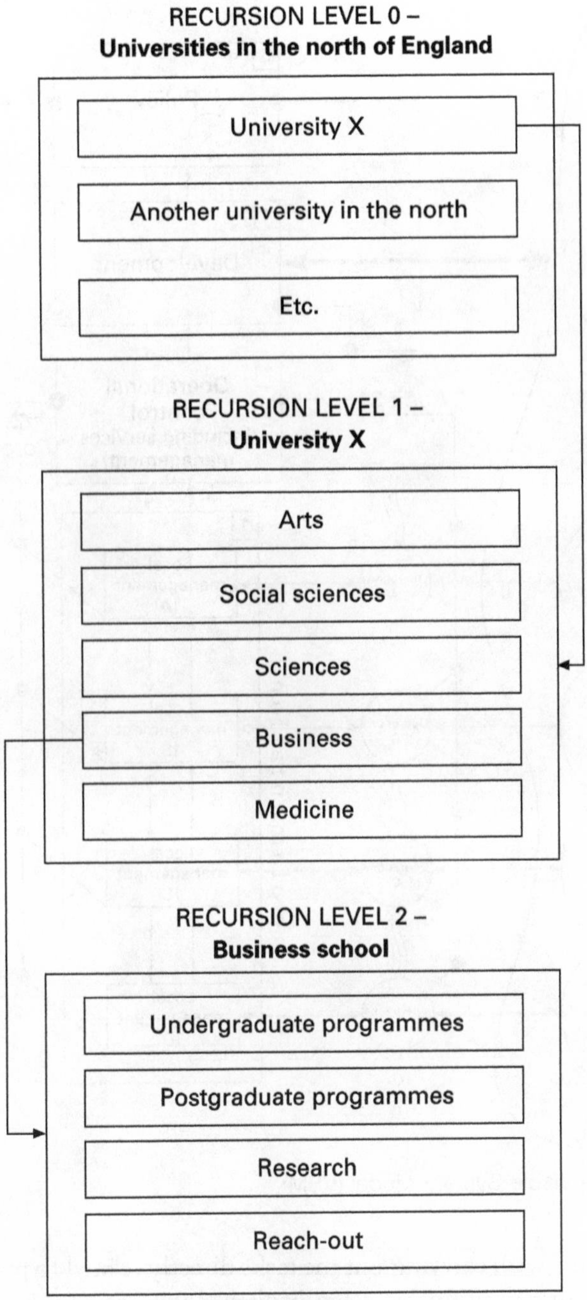

RECURSION LEVEL 0 –
Universities in the north of England

University X

Another university in the north

Etc.

RECURSION LEVEL 1 –
University X

Arts

Social sciences

Sciences

Business

Medicine

RECURSION LEVEL 2 –
Business school

Undergraduate programmes

Postgraduate programmes

Research

Reach-out

Figure 6.2 Triple recursion levels: an example.

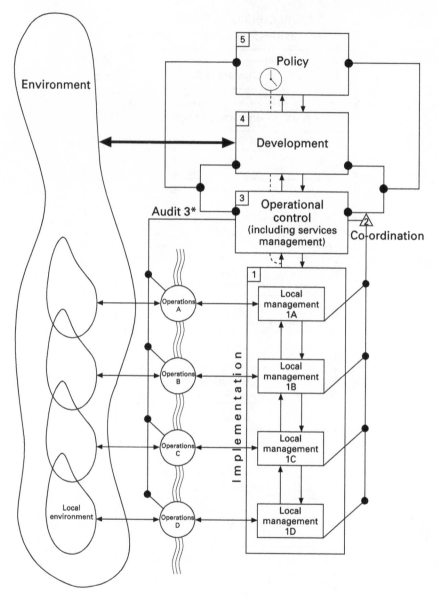

Figure 6.3   The Viable System Model (VSM).

implementation – with carrying out the tasks directly related to purposes. In Figure 6.3 the organization has been broken down into four operational elements, labelled A, B, C and D. Each of these has its own localized management 1A, 1B, 1C and 1D, and its own relations with the relevant part of the outside world. The elements may interact (shown by the wavy lines) in various ways, perhaps by passing on subassemblies, sharing facilities or competing for resources.

The System 1 parts, as we know, need to be as free as possible to deal with their environments. They too, therefore, must be designed according to the VSM, with their own policy, development, operational control, co-ordination and implementation functions. A 'blown-up' version of element B, with its localized management 1B and appropriate environmental relations, would resemble Figure 6.3 as a whole. In our university example, the business school is a black box to the vice-chancellor interested in his VSM model of the institution as a whole, but, by dropping a level of recursion, it can be examined in detail using the same model. The System 1 parts, then, are designed to be viable in their own right. They can respond to changes in their environments according to their own priorities. Localized management 1B, for example, agrees its goals with higher level management, interprets these for its own operations B, receives feedback information on performance and takes corrective action as necessary. The autonomy of the parts is the basis for spreading leadership and control throughout the whole system.

The only restrictions on the autonomy of the System 1 elements stem from the requirement that they continue to function as part of the whole organization. To this end they receive confirmation of their goals and objectives from System 5, refined into targets by System 3, down the vertical command channel, and are subject to co-ordination and audit by Systems 2 and 3*, respectively. They report back on performance to System 3.

It is easy to see the VSM as hierarchical and these restrictions on the freedom of the System 1 parts as 'constraints'. This is, however, a misrepresentation. The VSM really needs turning upside down so that it is clear that System 1 is the most important and that Systems 2–5, sometimes called the 'metasystem', merely facilitate the proper operation of System 1. Element B cannot realize its goals if it is destabilized by the actions of A, C or D – hence the need for co-ordination or System 2. There is no point in B continuing to pursue its existing goals, to take another example, if a massive change in the overall environment makes these irrelevant – hence the need for development driven by System 4. Systems 2–5, therefore, must be designed to be facilitative. The restrictions they impose need to resemble the laws of a democratic society. Laws against theft or fraud are seen as enabling not constraining. Danger arises when any of Systems 2–5 takes on a life of its own (becomes pathologically autopoietic!) and starts to get in the way of what System 1 needs to achieve as the operational arm of the organization's identity. Systems 2–5 must not become viable systems in their own right.

The autonomy of the System 1 elements is best protected, the VSM maintains, if management control is exercised by co-ordination and audit rather than authoritatively down the vertical command channel (see Figure 6.3). System 2 fulfils the co-ordination function. System 2 consists of the various rules and regulations that ensure the System 1 parts act cohesively and do not get in each other's way. It will also embed any legal requirements that must be obeyed. To continue with the university example, there are likely to be System 2 regulations relating to governance, finance, human resources and quality, among others. These prescribe ways of acting for the parts of Systems 1 and, if well formulated, should feel helpful rather than constraining to those who need to follow them. Other examples of System 2 in action would be a timetable in a school or production scheduling in a manufacturing concern. System 2 is there to ensure harmony between the elements of System 1. If Division A employed a member of staff on different terms and conditions than usually used in B, C and D, this could set up reverberations around the whole of System 1 and have a destabilizing impact.

System 3* is a servant of System 3, fulfilling an auditing role to ensure that targets specified by System 3 and rules and regulations promulgated by System 2 are being adhered to. This channel gives System 3 direct access, on a periodic basis, to the state of affairs in the operational elements. Through it, System 3 can check more immediately on performance, quality, conformance to financial regulations, maintenance, etc.

The role of System 3 proper is operational control of System 1 and services management (of functions such as human resources and finance). It has overall responsibility for the day-to-day running of the enterprise, trying its best to ensure that policy is implemented appropriately. It sits on the vertical command axis and must produce a co-ordinated plan and pass it down the line to System 1. It engages in a 'resource bargain' with the parts of System 1 during which targets are agreed together with the resources to achieve them. As soon as this is done it tries as far as possible (especially in the services area) to operate indirectly through co-ordination and audit. Occasionally, however, on the basis of information it receives from System 4, 3* or 2, it will need to employ more hierarchical control measures. It is after all in possession of information relevant to the whole organization while the System 1 parts have only local facts to go on. System 3 also has to report upward any information needed by the policy-determining System 5.

Systems 1, 2 and 3 make up what Beer calls the 'autonomic management' of the organization. They can maintain internal stability and optimize performance, within an established framework, without reference to higher management. Autonomic management does not however possess an overall view of the organization's environment, and it is therefore incapable of responding to threats and opportunities by reviewing corporate strategy. It does not possess the capacity for double-loop learning. This is why Systems 4 and 5 are necessary.

System 4, development, is the place in the organization where internal information received from System 3 is brought together with information about the organization's total environment and presented in a form that facilitates decision-making. Beer proposes it become the 'operations room' of the enterprise, a real 'environment of decision'. It follows that the primary function of System 4 must be to capture for the organization all relevant information about its total environment. If the organization is to match the variety of the environment it faces, it needs a model of that environment that enables predictions to be made about its likely future state. System 4 must provide this model and communicate information to System 3 if quick action is required or to System 5 if it has longer term implications. System 4 will also help the organization represent itself to its environment. In general, it is home to activities such as corporate planning, marketing, research and development, and public relations.

System 5, policy, is responsible for the direction of the whole enterprise. It formulates policy on the basis of the information received from System 4 and communicates this downward, to System 3, for implementation by the divisions. An essential task is balancing the often conflicting internal and external demands placed on the organization. Here it needs to adjudicate between System 3, representing the commitment of autonomic management to ongoing operations, and System 4, which with its links to the environment tends to be outward and future-oriented. System 5 has to ensure that the organization adapts to the external environment as and when necessary, but still maintains the benefits to be gained from internal stability.

System 5 must also articulate the identity and purposes of the whole system to the wider system of which it is part. In this role it is acting as the localized management of a particular element of the System 1 of that wider system.

Beer recommends that System 5 increase its variety by employing integrated teamwork and organizing itself as an elaborate, interactive assemblage of managers – a 'multinode'. Decision-making needs to be formalized and the effects of decisions monitored without threatening the freedom and flexibility of interaction in the multinode. System 5 may also on occasion seek to enhance its variety by recruiting experts or employing consultants.

Also crucial to the VSM is the proper functioning of the information flows it prescribes. Given the importance of negative feedback for control much of the information is about how different divisions, or the organization as a whole, are doing in relation to their goals. The information systems involved need to be designed to reduce the variety managers have to handle. They should convey only variances from planned performance to avoid managers becoming overwhelmed by irrelevancy. This is especially true if System 5 is to function effectively. Finally, Figure 6.3 shows a 'hatched line' information flow, leaving the normal System 1 to System 3 flow and speeding vital communications to System 5. This 'algedonic', or pleasure–pain, signal 'wakes up' (the alarm clock) System 5 to any potential disasters occurring lower down that it needs to be immediately aware of.

6.2.4 Methods

Three types of method have been developed that can help to operationalize organizational cybernetics. These are a set of 'guidelines' that can be followed to assist application of the VSM, an enumeration of 'frequent faults' found by VSM diagnosis and an approach to 'measures of performance' that Beer recommends using along with the VSM.

The guidelines are meant to facilitate development of new system designs or examination of existing designs. They can be divided into those relating to 'system identification' and those concerned with 'system diagnosis'.

(i) System identification

- Identify the purpose(s) to be pursued (using some appropriate participatory approach).
- Determine the relevant system for achieving the purpose(s) (this is called the 'system in focus' and is said to be at recursion level 1).
- Specify the system of which the system in focus is a part (wider systems, environments) (this is at recursion level 0).
- Specify the viable parts of System 1 of the system in focus ('unfolding complexity') – these are the parts that 'produce' the system in focus (they are at recursion level 2).

(ii) System diagnosis

Study System 1 of the system in focus:

- For each part of System 1 detail its environment, operations and localized management.
- Ensure that each part of System 1 has the capacity to be viable in its own right.
- Study what constraints are imposed upon the parts of System 1 by higher management.
- Ask how accountability is exercised for each part and what indicators of performance are used.
- Model System 1 according to the VSM diagram.

Study System 2 of the system in focus:

- List possible sources of disturbance or conflict in the organization.
- Identify the various System 2 elements that are needed to ensure harmonization and co-ordination.
- Ask how System 2 is perceived in the organization – as threatening or facilitating.

Study System 3 of the system in focus:

- List the System 3 activities of the system in focus.
- Ask how System 3 exercises authority – is this seen as autocratic or democratic in System 1 and how much freedom do System 1 elements possess?
- How good is System 3 at translating overall policy into operational plans?
- How is the 'resource bargain' with the parts of System 1 carried out?
- Who oversees the performance of the parts of System 1?
- What audit, or System 3*, enquiries into aspects of System 1 does System 3 conduct and are these appropriate?
- Are all control activities clearly facilitating the achievement of purpose?
- How is the performance of System 3 elements in enabling achievement of purpose measured?

Study System 4 of the system in focus:

- List all the System 4 activities of the system in focus.

- How far ahead do these activities consider?
- Do these activities guarantee adaptation to the future?
- Is System 4 monitoring what is happening in the environment and assessing trends?
- Is System 4 open to novelty?
- Does System 4 provide a management centre/operations room, bringing together external and internal information and providing an 'environment for decision'?
- Does System 4 adequately process, filter and distribute relevant information?
- Are all development activities clearly facilitating the achievement of purpose?
- How is the performance of System 4 elements in enabling achievement of purpose measured?

Study System 5 of the system in focus:

- Who is responsible for policy (e.g., on the 'board') and how do they act?
- Does System 5 provide a suitable identity and convey clear purposes for the system in focus?
- How does the 'ethos' set by System 5 affect the perception of System 4?
- How does the 'ethos' set by System 5 affect the relationship between System 3 and System 4 – is stability or change emphasized?
- Is System 5 organized to behave creatively?
- Does System 5 share an identity with System 1 or claim to be something different?

Finally, check that all information channels and control loops are properly designed.

A list of the 'frequent faults' discovered in organizations when the VSM is used can help to direct a manager's investigations into fruitful areas. The following are some of the most common faults in organizations as revealed by cybernetics (see Beer, 1984; Jackson, 2000):

- Mistakes in clarifying purposes and consequent recursion levels so, for example, an operational element crucial to overall success does not get the attention it deserves.
- Failure to grant autonomy to System 1 elements.
- Failure to ensure adequate localized management exists at the System 1 level.

- Systems 2, 3, 4 or 5 seeking to become viable in their own right (pathological autopoiesis) rather than serving the whole system by promoting implementation – leads to 'red tape'.
- Any of Systems 1–5 being absent or not working properly, but particularly –
  o System 2 is too weak, so co-ordination is jeopardized.
  o System 4 is too weak so System 5 'collapses' into System 3 and becomes overly concerned with day-to-day affairs.
  o System 5 does not represent the essential qualities of the whole system to the wider systems of which it is part.
- The information flows do not correspond to those believed necessary in any viable system.

Achievement in most organizations is measured in terms of money – the criterion of success being the extent to which profits are maximized. This is not however regarded as satisfactory by Beer. It ignores how well the organization is doing in terms of preparing for the future by investing in research and development, or in terms of more abstract resources like employee morale. It fails to reveal the cost-cutting manager who, in search of immediate profits, is damaging the organization's long-term future. Instead, Beer advises adopting three levels of achievement (actuality, capability and potentiality) that can be combined to give three indices (productivity, latency and performance) expressed in ordinary numbers. These can be used as comprehensive measures of performance in relation to all types of resource throughout the organization.

Defining more clearly the three levels of achievement:

- *actuality* is what we manage to do now, with existing resources, under existing constraints;
- *capability* is what we could achieve now, if we really worked at it, with existing resources and under existing constraints;
- *potentiality* is what we might be doing by developing our resources and removing constraints, although still operating within the bounds of what is already known to be feasible.

Then, the indices are:

- productivity: the ratio of actuality and capability;
- latency: the ratio of capability and potentiality;

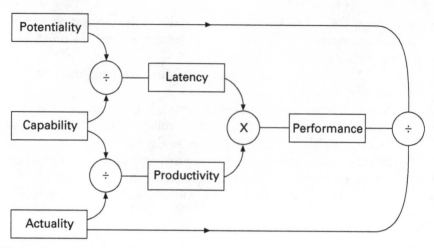

Figure 6.4 Measures of performance.

- performance: the ratio of actuality and potentiality and also the product of latency and productivity.

This is shown diagrammatically in Figure 6.4. These measures are able to detect the irresponsible cost-cutter. The cost-cutting manager will increase productivity not by increasing actual achievement but by lowering capability (e.g., by neglecting research and development and employee morale). This will show as an increase in productivity and, no doubt, this year's profits will rise. But the manager's latency index, under this scheme, will deteriorate. This should signal that a careful watch be kept on his or her overall perform-ance; future profits may be being threatened.

6.2.5 Recent developments

Organizational cybernetics can appear to managers as Utopian, rationalistic and overly prescriptive when presented to them by experts. Not surprisingly, therefore, recent developments have sought to 'soften' the approach. Espejo (in Espejo and Harnden, 1989) suggests a kind of combination of soft systems methodology and the VSM as a means of easing the implementa-tion problems often associated with organizational cybernetics.

More radically, other advocates of the approach have embraced what is called 'second-order cybernetics' – or the cybernetics of the observing system as opposed to the observed system. This shift, with its emphasis on subjectivity, mimics that already made by soft systems thinkers in systems thinking generally. Harnden (in Espejo and Harnden, 1989), for example, prefers to see the VSM not as a model trying to capture objective reality but as a focus for discussion about complex organizational issues among interested observers. Those readers who remember Chapter 3 will recognize that Harnden is trying to rescue the VSM from the functionalist paradigm for use according to the 'interpretive' rationale. There may be some benefits from such a move, but there are many losses. Beer (1974) trumpeted that Ashby's law of requisite variety was as important to managers as Einstein's law of relativity to physicists. It revealed something of the properties of complex systems and lost none of its force however long people conversed about its implications.

6.3 ORGANIZATIONAL CYBERNETICS IN ACTION

Beer's VSM has been much used both with single organizations and in grander scale applications. While there are many accounts of the former type of intervention in the literature, there are far fewer of the latter – Beer's work in Chile excepted. I am therefore grateful to Angela Espinosa for sharing with me the details of a recent VSM project in Colombia to create an ecoregional approach to sustainable development (see also Espinosa, 2002).

The Colombian Constitution of 1991 recognized a national environmental system (SINA) consisting of the Ministry of the Environment, a set of regional environmental corporations (CARs), and various environmental research institutes, including the Environmental Development Institute (IDEAM). SINA was seen as directly responsible for developing environmental policies, programmes and instruments that would lead to responsible environmental practices and the protection and regeneration of environmental resources at the local level. One of the main difficulties in the early years was the lack of co-ordination experienced at the level of the ecosystem, where the most critical problems needed action. The agencies charged with dealing with the problems were organized according to the existing political and administrative structures, whereas problems such as pollution and flooding require a co-ordinated approach based on an ecoregion. Another problem was a failure to follow through on the development of a National Environmental Information System (NEIS), which was to provide the data and models to support environmental management by SINA. This was despite several attempts, sponsored by agencies such as the International Development Bank, to design a centralized system to hold information on the main environmental issues as defined by academic disciplines – flora and fauna, water resources, forests, mineral resources, oceans, etc.

In 1999 the project described here began when the Ministry and IDEAM initiated a new approach to the NEIS using cybernetic thinking based on Beer's VSM. By 2001 a project team consisting of representatives from the Ministry, the CARs, IDEAM, other research institutes and other national institutions with an interest in the environment were using the VSM to radically reformulate their understanding of SINA and NEIS.

The identity of SINA was redefined as follows:

The National Environmental System [SINA] is a network of recurrent fluid interactions involving individuals, communities and institutions aimed at achieving a sustainable way of living and of interacting with each other and with nature.

Workshops have also been held at which agreements were reached about the levels of recursion in the system. The basic level of recursion, where environmental action happens, was seen as the community (individuals, families, local industries and organizations inhabiting a particular settlement) interacting with its natural environment. The organizational purpose at this level was seen as being sustainable development.

At the next higher level of recursion the parts of System 1 would be networks of communities with an interest in a particular subecoregion. They would need to interact to solve environmental problems stemming from, for example, a specific ecosystem like a river basin, a natural reservation or a forest region. A higher level of recursion, concerned with managing environmental issues shared by several subecoregions, was recognized as an ecoregion. At this level more than ten ecoregions were identified in Colombia. Finally, at a high level of recursion, there was the natural environment of the whole nation. Figure 6.5 represents these recursion levels.

With this analysis in place, it was possible to use the VSM to understand what had gone wrong with SINA and the NEIS, and to propose alternative organizational and structural arrangements. The starting point was to ensure that the parts of System 1 at each level of recursion (such as the communities and groups of communities) had the capacity to develop the practices and relationships necessary to achieve sustainable development (i.e., they could be autonomous). This meant that, for each level of recursion, Systems 2, 3, 4 and 5 would have to be put in place to support the System 1 parts. All the levels of recursion would also have to cohere as a whole capable of realizing sustainable development as a national priority. We can

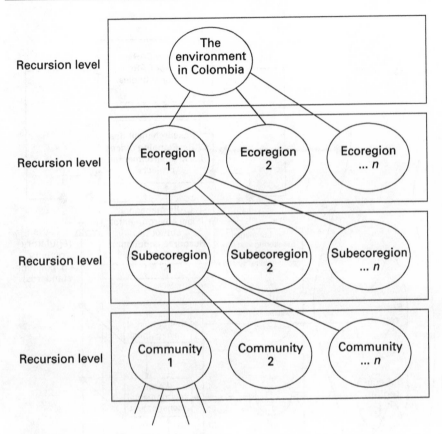

Figure 6.5 Recursion levels in SINA.

now consider, as illustrative examples, work under way at the level of the ecoregion, the community and aimed at the redesign of the NEIS.

Figure 6.6 can help us understand developments at the ecoregion level. It shows the VSM applied to SINA with an ecoregion as the system in focus at recursion level 1. Recursion level 0 is then the natural environment of Colombia and the operational System 1 elements (at recursion level 2) are the networks of communities concerned with environmental problems at the level of the subecoregion. The task for the project team was to assist in establishing a suitable metasystem (Systems 2, 3, 4 and 5) to manage and co-ordinate these networks of communities so that they could act on relevant environmental problems. Previous attempts had failed because the CARs, which might have done the job, were administratively related to existing governmental structures rather than to ecoregions and subecoregions. The

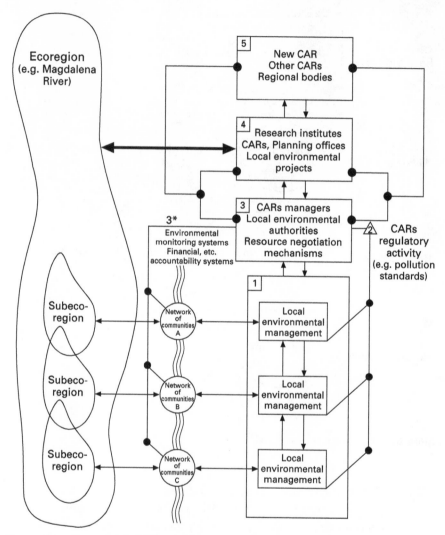

Figure 6.6 The viable system model: an ecoregion as the system in focus.

way forward, it seemed, was to redirect the CARs and get them to co-operate with other relevant agencies to produce the kind of metasystemic function required by the VSM diagnosis in order to deal with key environmental issues at the ecoregion level.

Aware of this, and determined to reorientate the CARs, the Ministry of Environment focused the main investment resources, from both national and international sources, on what they felt were important strategic ecoregions. The CARs, and other relevant institutions, had to put their effort into developing goals and programmes relevant to these ecoregions. In the process they learned co-operatively to overcome the divisions between them created by the existing governmental and administrative arrangements and, gradually, appropriate Systems 2, 3, 4 and 5 were established (see Figure 6.6) in some of the most strategic ecoregions in the country.

An example of how this happened was the co-ordination of projects on the Magdalena River. This is the second most important river in Colombia and provides water to dozens of communities, towns and cities. The health of this water source is critical for national development. There were significant problems of pollution that required co-ordinated management because no one would take on a commitment to clean the river unless they were convinced those upstream would do the same. A new CAR was established by the Ministry specifically to address the problems of the Magdalena River. System 2 was established through negotiations with other CARs from areas crossed by the river, which led to agreements on such matters as pollution standards. System 3 emerged from discussions between CAR managers and various local environmental authorities. It began to plan longer term policies and programmes to clean the river and to get agreement on clearer norms and sanctions if these were broken. Efforts began to pool resources to set up a proper System 4. This would need to collect and structure required knowledge on the main ecosystems bordering the river, as well as about the socioeconomic and cultural characteristics of the industries and neighbourhoods using and sometimes abusing it. The main challenge for System 5, in the medium term, was establishing a common culture of sustainable development among relevant regional bodies. This would require a significant educational effort to convince the appropriate people that it was necessary, especially as it could mean loss of short-term profit.

Of course, success at the level of the ecoregion and subecoregion depends critically on success at the community level of recursion. Everything ultimately rests on communities of individuals, families, local industries and organizations. Previous SINA efforts at this level had emphasized the establishment of mechanisms for controlling the use of resources, managing information and meeting legal requirements. The VSM diagnosis, however, focused on the need for communities to develop self-organizing skills in managing their local environments. Attention should be paid to sharing and improving local knowledge on environmental issues and their management, on employing local skills for environmental development, on conservation programmes and on utilizing local information to predict and respond to emergencies.

Success at all levels of recursion depended on rethinking the NEIS. The NEIS had previously concentrated on collecting information on the various relevant academic disciplines. If a local agency required information useful for dealing with high levels of pollution in a particular environment, it was unable to help. Following the VSM diagnosis it was recommended that it devote its attention toward information systems that would support decision-making relevant to the achievement of environmental goals at each level of recursion. Clear examples of such a reorientation have been some pilot projects, conducted for NEIS, in which CARs and the research institutes have sought to design shared information networks providing information on the type, current state of and critical issues surrounding the main environmental resources characterizing an ecoregion. To finish the job, it would be necessary to combine appropriate geographic information systems, databases and environmental indices in a manner suitable for supporting the main decision areas in the ecoregion.

Although the SINA project required considerable cybernetic expertise, it also recognized the need to cascade the VSM language downward. Long-term change in any organization cannot be achieved on the basis of remote, expert diagnosis by consultants and recommendations endorsed only by higher management. Participation at all levels is essential.

6.4 CRITIQUE OF ORGANIZATIONAL CYBERNETICS

Organizational cybernetics, as embodied in the VSM, offers a model of great generality that can be applied to all types of system and organization, and to systems at different levels in the same enterprise. It is able to do this because it concentrates on informing us about those aspects of organization that are essential to viability rather than on possible organizational structures as normally understood. The generality of the model certainly assists managers and management scientists in using it.

Those who have employed the model regard it as an extremely rich representation of organizations. I have argued elsewhere (Jackson, 2000) that the VSM integrates the findings of around 50 years of work in the academic discipline of organization theory. And it goes beyond organization theory by incorporating those findings in an applicable management tool that can be used to recommend very specific improvements in the design and functioning of organizations. The model is insightful in the way it treats organization and environment relations. The organization is seen as capable of influencing its environment as well as adapting to it. In essence, it needs to set up a sustainable balance with its milieu. It is sophisticated in the manner it understands the tension between stability and change (the System 3–System 4 interface), the vertical interdependence of different levels within an enterprise (through the notion of recursion), the horizontal interdependence of parts (integrated by Systems 2 and 3) and the spread of control throughout the system – so that decisions are taken and problems corrected as closely as possible to the point where they occur and senior management is freed to concentrate on strategic issues. The VSM also offers a particularly suitable starting point for the design of information systems in organizations because it emphasizes identification of the key operational elements and clarification of the role of the necessary facilitative functions.

As another point in its favour, the VSM offers a scientific justification for empowerment and democracy in organizations. The parts must be granted autonomy so that they can absorb some of the massive environmental variety that would otherwise overwhelm higher management levels. The VSM arrangements, particularly the emphasis on co-ordination and audit rather than hierarchical control, seek to ensure that the autonomy granted is the maximum possible subject only to the whole continuing to exist. Of course, for this freedom to be meaningful, the parts must also have a say in the overall purposes being pursued by the system. Beer recognizes this and insists that System 5 should embody the concerns of the workforce and managers, of customers and of the society that sustains the system, as well as looking after shareholders.

Any model is, necessarily, a partial representation of reality, and it is important to recognize the limitations of the VSM if we are to use it wisely. In essence, the VSM is about the design of organizations as adaptive, goal-seeking entities. It pinpoints various systemic/structural laws that must be observed if an enterprise is to be viable and succeed. Critics (e.g., Flood and Jackson, 1991; Jackson, 2000) argue, however, that the defining feature of social organizations is that their component parts are human beings who attribute meaning to their situations and act according to their own purposes. Effort should be concentrated, therefore, on managing processes of negotiation between different viewpoints and value positions. Although cybernetics pays lip service to notions of empowerment and democracy, it actually says little about how individuals can be motivated to perform and how participation and democracy can be arranged. In this respect 'team syntegrity', developed later in Beer's career (see Chapter 12), can be seen as complementary to the VSM.

Two further criticisms follow from the biases inherent in the VSM. The first states that although it may be the intention of the VSM to promote decentralization and autonomy, it actually offers to the powerful an extremely efficient means of increasing control and consolidating their own positions. In the wrong hands it becomes little more than a sophisticated management control device. This is because power relationships are endemic in organizations and we are accustomed to acquiescing in hierarchy. Beer (1985) acknowledges that power imbalances can disfigure use of the VSM but is unable to see any solution.

The second attacks the concept of 'good management' entailed by the VSM. Organizational cybernetics implies that good management is management that establishes requisite variety between itself and the operations managed, and between the organization as a whole and its environment. To those of another persuasion it seems clear that 'good management' is more about the meaning and significance of purposes for participants in an enterprise and whether the purposes themselves are good or bad.

Organizational cybernetics is about ensuring an organization is viable and so in a position to reach goals (efficacy) and about doing so without waste of resources (efficiency). It does not bother itself about whether the goals we are pursuing are the right ones in the sense that they are goals that we actually want to achieve (effectiveness). This stems from its innate functionalism. The VSM seeks to provide knowledge, based upon cybernetic principles, that supports regulation in the social domain. Its aim is to increase our ability to 'steer' organizations and other social systems. It is true that there are those who wish to 'capture' the VSM for other paradigms, but they need to ask whether it really is an appropriate tool with which to pursue interpretive and emancipatory ends, and what is lost in the process. For the VSM is an exceptionally sophisticated and powerful model used in the service of functionalism.

The model draws strength from its structuralist epistemology. It has been able to integrate some profound insights into a usable management tool that carries enormous explanatory power because it rests upon the science of cybernetics.

That strength is further enhanced by the combination of machine, organism and brain metaphors that the VSM employs. Autonomic management (Systems 1, 2, 3) ensures the optimum use of resources in carrying out transformation processes, while System 4 ensures adaptation to the environment and the institutionalization of learning. System 5 is charged with maintaining a balance between the 'inside and now' and the 'outside and then'. Being willing to draw upon these three metaphors enables cybernetics to employ the vast range of systems concepts to which they have given rise: black box, feedback, control, communication, variety, hierarchy, recursion, viability, autonomy, environment, autopoiesis, self-regulation, self-organization, learning, etc.

Critics, naturally enough, find that the culture, political system, psychic prison, instruments of domination and carnival metaphors are underplayed in cybernetics. They draw inspiration for their attacks on the approach from the interpretive, emancipatory and postmodern paradigms.

6.5 THE VALUE OF ORGANIZATIONAL CYBERNETICS TO MANAGERS

A little knowledge of the VSM can take managers a long way. And it can save them a lot of time – no need to read any more about organization theory; it is all here. That is not to say that once they become committed to the approach they do not need expert help. The VSM has many levels of sophistication and we have certainly not been able to touch on them all in this chapter. That said, let us outline the five main lessons that managers can learn from organizational cybernetics:

- It is essential to establish a clear identity for an organization, which embodies purposes achievable in the environment and is agreed and understood throughout the enterprise. If the environment changes, the organization will need to reinvent and reconfigure itself.
- The VSM offers an easy route to developing a shared understanding of organizational complexity and a precise language for discussing issues of organizational design and structure, stability and change, control and co-ordination, centralization and decentralization, etc.
- There is a solution to the perennial problem of centralization versus decentralization. The parts can be given autonomy and empowered without any threat to managerial control and organizational cohesion. Indeed, freedom and control are complementary rather than in opposition.
- Once an identity and purposes have been developed, the VSM enables essential business units and their necessary support services to be determined. It is a vehicle for design or diagnosis that tells managers

which structures and processes are essential and which can be dispensed with.

- Because the VSM spreads decision-making and control throughout the 'architecture' of the system it makes sense of the idea of leadership at all levels.

6.6 CONCLUSION

All managers, at one time or another, must have felt Stafford Beer's frustration and despair with organization charts as models of enterprises. Until Beer started to develop organizational cybernetics, however, there was nothing else available. We now have at our disposal the VSM. Just as organization charts embodied mechanistic thinking, the VSM captures what it is like to view organizations as organisms with a brain. This is an extremely powerful way of thinking, which managers should treasure and employ as an alternative to the conventional model. Since the VSM delivers that alternative in such a usable package, they have only themselves to blame if they do not do so.

REFERENCES

Ashby, W.R. (1956). *An Introduction to Cybernetics*. Methuen, London.

Beer, S. (1972). *Brain of the Firm*. Allen Lane, London (second edition, 1981, John Wiley & Sons, Chichester, UK).

Beer, S. (1974). *Designing Freedom*. CBC Publications, Toronto.

Beer, S. (1979). *The Heart of Enterprise*. John Wiley & Sons, Chichester, UK.

Beer, S. (1984). The viable system model: Its provenance, development, methodology and pathology. *Journal of the Operational Research Society*, **35**, 7–26.

Beer, S. (1985). *Diagnosing the System for Organizations*. John Wiley & Sons, Chichester, UK.

Espejo, R. and Harnden, R.J. (eds) (1989). *The Viable System Model: Interpretations and Applications of Stafford Beer's VSM*. John Wiley & Sons, Chichester, UK.

Espejo, R. and Schwaninger, M. (eds) (1993). *Organizational Fitness: Corporate Effectiveness through Management Cybernetics*. Campus Verlag, New York.

Espejo, R., Schuhmann, W., Schwaninger, M. and Bilello, U. (1996). *Organisational Transformation and Learning*. John Wiley & Sons, Chichester, UK.

Espinosa, A. (2002). *Proyecto Consolidación del Sistema de Información Ambiental Colombiano (SIAC)* (Working Paper, United Nations Development Program). United Nations, Bogotá, Colombia.

Flood, R.L. and Jackson, M.C. (1991). *Creative Problem Solving: Total Systems Intervention*. John Wiley & Sons, Chichester, UK.

Jackson, M.C. (2000). *Systems Approaches to Management*. Kluwer/Plenum, New York.

Maturana, H.R. and Varela, F.J. (1980). *Autopoiesis and Cognition: The Realization of the Living*. D. Reidel, Dordrecht, The Netherlands.

Complexity Theory 7

Although the specific path followed by the behaviour [of complex systems] ... is random and hence unpredictable in the long term, it always has an underlying pattern to it, a 'hidden' pattern ... That pattern is self-similarity, that is a constant degree of variation, consistent variability, regular irregularity ... a constant fractal dimension. Chaos is therefore order (a pattern) within disorder.

Stacey (1993)

7.1 INTRODUCTION

One of the most important popularizers of complexity theory, Gleick (1987), has argued that 20th century science will be remembered for three things: relativity, quantum mechanics and chaos. What all three share in common and signal is a revolutionary transformation in the nature of modern science. Scientists are required to abandon the mechanistic and deterministic assumptions underlying the Newtonian world view and to embrace a perspective that, in recognizing relationships and indeterminacy, is much more holistic in character.

Of the three scientific movements noted by Gleick, it is the study of chaos – in the form of complexity theory – that is having the most profound impact on thinking about management. Earlier models of organization can, from a complexity theory perspective, be seen as emphasizing order and regularity at the expense of the erratic and discontinuous. Complexity theory focuses attention on those aspects of organizational life that bother most managers most of the time – disorder, irregularity and randomness. It accepts instability, change and unpredictability and offers appropriate advice on how to act. Help is apparently at hand in areas where it was thought none was available.

7.2 DESCRIPTION OF COMPLEXITY THEORY

7.2.1 Historical development

The pioneer in the development of chaos theory is usually considered to be the meteorologist Edward Lorenz (see Gleick, 1987). Lorenz was working on the problem of long-range weather forecasting using a simple computer simulation based on just 12 equations. Intent on studying one particular weather sequence at greater length, and in a hurry, Lorenz re-entered the initial conditions, but using three rather than six decimal places. Given that the difference was only one part in a thousand, he assumed that the new run would exactly duplicate the old. To his amazement, however, the new weather pattern rapidly diverged from that shown in the previous run and within a few months all resemblance had been lost. Lorenz had discovered that tiny changes in a complex system's initial state can alter long-term behaviour very significantly. This sensitive dependence on initial conditions became known as the 'butterfly effect': on the basis that it suggested that the single flapping of a butterfly's wings today might, over time, alter a system to such an extent that it could lead to a storm occurring, or not occurring, somewhere else in the world.

Lorenz had discovered the non-linear relationships that are widespread in complex natural and social systems and that make prediction impossible. It was also clear to him, however, that there was a good deal of order underlying the chaos. After all, even if the weather is notoriously fickle in England, we do not suffer from severe drought, or monsoon, or frequent hurricanes. Lorenz began to experiment on a range of complex systems in an effort to understand the nature of the pattern that underlies unpredictability.

Lorenz published his results in a meteorological journal in 1963. The next decade or so was marked by individual scientists unearthing similar findings in a range of different disciplines. The behaviour of complex systems in mathematics, chemistry and biology was studied and found to be characterized by the emergence of unpredictability even though they appeared describable in terms of a few simple equations. In many cases, however, this unpredictability seemed to be governed by a considerable degree of order.

In the late 1970s the chaos and complexity theory movement began to take shape, defining itself as the science of the global nature of systems. For example, the Dynamical Systems Collective was formed, at Santa Cruz College in the USA, headed by the physicist Robert Stetson Shaw. The year 1984 saw the establishment of what has become the most famous centre for research into complexity theory. Known as the Santa Fe Institute, it brought together scientists from a range of disciplines, who have co-operated to build computer models of a variety of biological, ecological and economic systems.

By the time that the Santa Fe Institute was set up, the original term 'chaos theory' was giving way to the grander conception of 'complexity theory'. A strict interpretation of the scope of chaos theory sees it as limited to the mathematics of non-linear dynamic behaviour in natural systems, such as the weather system. Complexity theory, by contrast, is represented as being applicable to the behaviour over time of complex social as well as natural systems. Social systems are not just 'complex adaptive systems' bound by the fixed rules of interaction of their parts. Rather, they are 'complex evolving systems' that can change the rules of their development as they evolve over time.

Understood as embracing complex evolving systems as well as complex adaptive systems, new applications are constantly being found for complexity theory – in astronomy, geology, physiology, economics, computer art, music and, not least, in management.

7.2.2 Philosophy and theory

As we noted in the introduction, chaos and complexity theory is often represented as being part of a revolution in thinking that is having an impact on all scientific disciplines whether they study natural, human or social phenomena. The new paradigm that is emerging from this revolution (as charted by authors such as Capra, 1996; Jantsch, 1980; and Wheatley, 1992) is holistic in character. The parts of systems can only be understood, it seems, in terms of their relationships with each other and with the whole. The focus of attention, therefore, has to be on relationships (as, for example, in quantum mechanics). It is the pattern of relationships that determines what a system does.

The new paradigm also embraces a process view. Systems are constantly changing due to the interaction of their parts as they seek to process a continuous flow of matter, energy and information from their environments. They are therefore best understood as being in constant flux: as arenas of dynamic process from which stable structures are temporarily born. Order is an emergent property of disorder and it comes about through self-organizing processes operating from within the system itself.

The new thinking sees systems as in an intimate relationship and as constantly conducting exchanges with their environments. Furthermore, they do not simply adapt to their environments but coevolve with them. System and environment change in response to one another and evolve together. According to the Gaia hypothesis, for example, life on Earth has developed in mutual interaction with the world seen as a living system. They have become involved together in creating the conditions that support life.

The synthesis across disciplines, made possible by the widespread acceptance of the new paradigm, is best expressed in chaos and complexity theory. It is through this science that a number of the conjectures developed as a result of the 'systems revolution' have been refined into ideas and concepts rigorous enough to support a genuine 'general system theory', in von Bertalanffy's sense (see Chapter 1). There are perhaps six key theoretical notions in complexity theory : 'sensitive dependence on initial conditions', 'strange attractors', 'self-similarity', 'self-organization', the 'edge of chaos' and the 'fitness landscape'.

Lorenz had discovered that the way weather systems develop is extremely sensitive to minute changes in initial conditions. His later experiments on simpler systems, like a convection system and a waterwheel (see Gleick, 1987), confirmed this result. Other scientists, meanwhile, were replicating the finding in other disciplines, studying phenomena as diverse as biological populations and a dripping water faucet. It seems that the behaviour of systems of many types becomes completely unpredictable in the medium and long term.

Lorenz, however, the reader will recall, also postulated that there was a good deal of order underlying the apparent chaos. Weather systems with slightly differing initial conditions might not repeat the same behaviour over time, but they did demonstrate similar patterns. Again he was able to show that the sets of equations describing even simple systems often produced exactly the same result. The behaviour of his waterwheel, for example, when plotted on a graph, never repeated itself, but it did remain within the limits of a double spiral curve. It seemed, therefore, that although such systems were unpredictable they were 'attracted' to a particular pattern of behaviour. Lorenz called the image he had produced the 'Lorenz attractor'. It is shown (reproduced from Gleick, 1987) as Figure 7.1. Such 'attractors' are now called 'strange attractors'. They keep the trajectory followed by an otherwise unpredictable system within the bounds of a particular pattern, without ever requiring it to repeat itself exactly. It has been argued that all manner of natural systems, studied by physics, chemistry and biology, are governed by strange attractors.

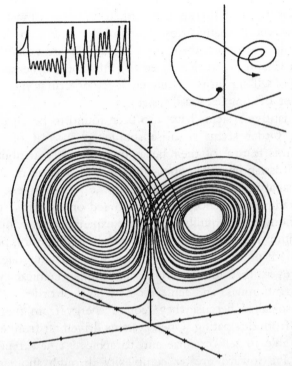

Figure 7.1 The Lorenz attractor. This magical image, resembling an owl's mask or butterfly's wings, became an emblem for the early explorers of chaos. It revealed the fine structure hidden within a disorderly stream of data. Traditionally, the changing values of any one variable could be displayed in a so-called time series (top). To show the changing relationship among three variables required a different technique. At any instant in time, the three variables fix the location of a point in three-dimensional space; as the system changes, the motion of the point represents the continuously changing variables. Because the system never exactly repeats itself, the trajectory never intersects itself. Instead, it loops around and around for ever. Motion on the attractor is abstract, but it conveys the flavour of the motion of the real system. For example, the crossover from one wing of the attractor to the other corresponds to a reversal in the direction of spin of the waterwheel or convecting fluid.

From Gleick (1987), reproduced by permission of the Random House Group.

Another characteristic of systems governed by strange attractors is that they exhibit self-similarity. If a graph of their behaviour is examined closely it will often be found to have an exact copy of itself inside on a different scale. The same property is observed when we look at the patterning of the parts of complex systems. The parts of the system are similar in shape to the whole. This type of structure is described as 'fractal'. Fractal structures have been observed in many fields of knowledge, and a special geometry has been established to study them. Simple examples are a cauliflower and a snowflake. In Chapter 6 we witnessed organizational cybernetics making use of the idea of self-similarity, at different levels of recursion, to understand the organization of complex social systems.

Complex adaptive systems have also been found to be capable of 'self-organization'. Order seems to arise spontaneously out of chaos. The discovery of this feature of their behaviour is usually attributed to Ilya Prigogine, a Russian chemist, who won the Nobel Prize in 1977 for his work on 'dissipative structures' (see Prigogine and Stengers, 1984). He argued that traditional science had concentrated on studying systems in a state of 'thermodynamic equilibrium' at the expense of those operating far from equilibrium. If a system is driven far from equilibrium, perhaps as a result of the effects of positive feedback loops, it may disintegrate. Prigogine showed, however, that under certain conditions chemical systems can pass through randomness and achieve a new level of order as 'dissipative structures' – so-called because they require energy from the outside to prevent them from dissipating. Open systems driven far from equilibrium appear to be able to self-organize and to achieve a new type of order. They can evolve toward greater complexity through spontaneous self-organization.

The 'edge of chaos' phenomenon was discovered independently by the physicist and mathematician Norman Packard, a member of the Dynamical Systems Collective, and Chris Langton, working on information systems at the University of Arizona (see Gleick, 1987). The edge of chaos is a narrow transition zone between order and chaos that is extremely conducive to the emergence of novel patterns of behaviour. A system driven to the edge of chaos is likely to exhibit the sort of spontaneous processes of self-organization witnessed by Prigogine in chemical systems. The edge of chaos notion has proved powerful in many different fields, including management and organization.

Kauffman, a medical scientist working at the Santa Fe Institute, was applying the notion to biology and evolution when he invented another important complexity theory concept: that of 'fitness landscapes'. Complexity theory holds, as we know, that systems coevolve with their environments. The environment of any system, of course, will contain numerous other systems engaged in the same process of coevolution. Kauffman (1995) envisages the overall environment as a heaving landscape, the behaviour of which is unpredictable from the point of view of any one system. The landscape, in shifting around, throws up peaks of different heights separated by valleys. A system has to try to navigate this landscape. If a system finds itself on a high peak, then it is highly evolved and can gaze contentedly at competitors. If it is in a fitness valley it is in a poor situation. Luck might drive it up a local peak, representing a rise in fitness, but it may still only be in the foothills compared with the high peaks it can now see in the distance. Furthermore, seeking to reach those distant peaks is treacherous both because it will have to cross a fitness valley and because of the ever-changing nature of the landscape. Even when the system attains a high peak it will need to be watchful because, as everyone else clambers onto it, their weight will force the peak down.

7.2.3 Methodology

Advocates of chaos and complexity theory insist that their approach demands a complete mind shift from managers if they want to secure business success. Managers have to accept that the long-term future of their organizations is inherently unknowable. Organizations and their environments are characterized by non-linear feedback loops, which make them sensitive to small differences in initial conditions and ensure that their behaviour is unpredictable. Long-term planning is therefore impossible. Indeed, long-term planning, and the rigid structures, precise task definitions and elaborate rules that often accompany it, is positively dangerous. It can 'fix' an organization in pursuit of a particular vision when an uncertain world requires flexible responses.

Managers are advised to accept and delight in chaos. The absence of a strict hierarchy and tight control does not mean that things will fall apart. Managers can trust in chaos and allow their organizations to evolve, remembering that continuous transformation and emergent order is a natural state of affairs. The burden of trying to plan, organize and control everything can be laid aside.

That said, all commentators also wish to give chaos a helping hand. It is from the recommendations of authors much as Morgan (1997), Stacey (1993, 1996) and Wheatley (1992), in this regard, that the outlines of a methodology for applying complexity theory ideas in practice can be discerned.

Figure 7.2, from Morgan (1997), suggests that there could be three stages to any such methodology. Stage 1 would consist of understanding the attractor pattern determining the current behaviour of the organization and the reasons why it is dominant. If the pattern is not desirable from the

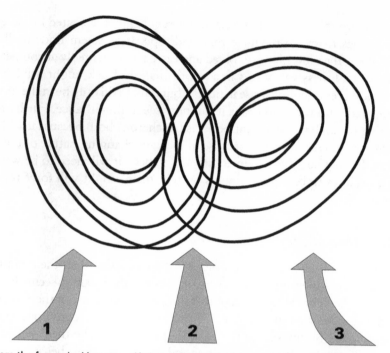

What are the forces locking an organization into its existing 'attractor' pattern? Structures? Hierarchies? Rules? Controls? Culture? Defensive routines? Power relations? Psychic traps? Is the 'attractor' appropriate? Should it be changed?

If change is required, how is the transition from one attractor to another to be achieved? How can small changes be used to create large effects?

What are the ground rules of the new attractor going to be? How can we manage through the 'edge of chaos' of Stage 2 while remaining open to self-organization?

Figure 7.2 Attractor patterns and organizational change.
From Morgan (1997), reproduced by permission of Sage Publications.

organization's point of view, then change must be brought about in order to ensure the system shifts to another pattern. Making the change is Stage 2. Stage 3 requires the new attractor pattern to be stabilized while, at the same time, ensuring that it does not lock the organization, in the long term, into routine forms of action.

The key to Stages 1 and 3, therefore, is to try to grasp 'pattern' at the deeper level, to unearth the order underlying chaos. If we can apprehend the pattern giving rise to complex dynamic behaviour, then we gain some insight into what is going on and we can start to make sensible decisions. This is made easier if we remember that such patterns are often constructed on the basis of simple fractal structures.

Apprehending patterns in complexity theory is similar to recognizing 'system archetypes' in Senge's 'fifth discipline' (see Chapter 5), although the process seems somewhat less sure. Stacey (1993) argues that success depends upon 'learning' and especially on honing our powers of intuition and reasoning by analogy. Wheatley (1992) looks for patterns of movement in the whole, focusing on qualities like rhythm, flow, direction and shape.

This may seem vague but, in fact, the use of intuition to gain understanding and to plan is something well understood by almost all of us. Peter Fryer, a consultant who uses complexity theory (see www.trojanmice.com), describes attending a strategic planning course run mainly for people working in the oil industry. The participants were asked to write on a card what they thought the price of oil would be in five years time. All put down pretty much the same price. They were then asked if they were willing to bet – cash, jewellery, any other valuables they had in their possession – on that price coming true. No one would. The tutor asked them to repeat the exercise, this time putting on the card a price they would be prepared to bet on. The answers were again very close to each other, but were completely different to the first price given. When asked why, they answered that the first price could be justified to the board of a company. In terms of trends, economic forecasts and political analyses, it was rational. The second answer could not be supported in this way, but it simply 'felt right'. They had more confidence in the answer that depended on their intuitive understanding of the complexities of the oil industry and its market.

Stages 1 and 3 require gaining an understanding of the relevant strange attractors. Stage 2 is about managing the shift between attractors. As do proponents of the 'fifth discipline', complexity theorists suggest identifying the points of maximum leverage so that small changes can be made that have the maximum impact. Peter Fryer calls these changes 'trojanmice'. Heavily flagged, large-scale, planned changes of the Trojan Horse variety usually fail because they are too big to be understood and owned by the workforce. The art in changing complex evolving systems is to recognize and implement those small, well-focused changes that have resonance with those concerned and that have significant, far-reaching effects.

Ultimately, however, the impact of any changes made by managers is unknowable, especially given the dynamic nature of the fitness landscapes in which organizations are, nowadays, usually embedded. Stage 2 must also involve, therefore, ensuring that organizations are quick enough on their feet to find the highest fitness peaks as the shape and structure of the landscape changes. Managers may not be able to predict and control organizations, but they can ensure their flexibility and responsiveness by propitiating favourable conditions for learning and self-organization.

Learning requires an empowered workforce operating under favourable group dynamics that allow new mental models to emerge – so that the learning can be 'double loop'. The existence of a strong, shared culture that stifles innovation must be avoided at all costs. Encouraging self-organization demands that we pay attention to structure. Wheatley (1992) conceptualizes this as a matter of 'relationships'. Because relationships are paramount in dynamic systems, different relationships evoke different potentialities from those involved. Experimenting by linking people, units and/or tasks in different ways can help ensure novelty. It is essential that structures do not inhibit relationships. The same is true if we want to encourage an organization to operate flexibly in its environment. Kauffman (1995) suggests that organizations should be broken up into networks of units that can act autonomously in their local environments, but are in continuous communication and interaction with each other.

Stacey (1996) uses the 'edge of chaos' concept to articulate the most detailed account of how learning and self-organization can be promoted in organizations. He notes the complexity theory conclusion that all complex adaptive systems can operate in one of three zones: a stable zone, an unstable zone and at the edge of chaos, a narrow transition zone between stability and instability. In the stable zone they ossify, in the unstable zone they disintegrate, but at the edge of chaos spontaneous processes of self-organization occur and innovative patterns of behaviour can emerge. This, therefore, seems to be the best place for organizations to be. At the edge of chaos, in a state of 'bounded instability', they behave like dissipative structures and display their full potential for creativity and innovation.

The edge of chaos is difficult to reach and sustain because it requires a kind of balance between the forces promoting stability in an organization and those continuously challenging the status quo. In Stacey's terms, it demands that an appropriate degree of tension exists between an organization's 'legitimate system' and its 'shadow system'.

The legitimate system consists of the dominant corporate culture and those structures, processes and power hierarchies that support it. It promotes 'ordinary management' in pursuit of the organization's objectives and is essential for ensuring the efficient delivery of products and services, and for containing conflict and anxiety. If it becomes too dominant, however, because the shadow system is not functioning properly, it can constrain all opposition, prevent questioning of objectives, kill double-loop learning and stop all change.

The shadow system of an organization consists of those informal aspects that harbour the potential for contradiction, conflict and change. It works well when it generates new ways of thinking that challenge the legitimate system and threatens, by bringing forth sufficient tension and crisis, to replace at least some parts of that system. If the shadow system becomes too dominant, however, because the legitimate system is unable to check the positive feedback loops produced by instability, anarchy can result. The shadow system sabotages pursuit of objectives, levels of anxiety rise among the workforce preventing creativity and double-loop learning, and the system enters the unstable zone and disintegrates.

The edge of chaos, the preferable state, demands therefore that creative tension be maintained between the legitimate and shadow systems. The legitimate system must provide clear guidelines, authorize appropriate structures and procedures, and contain anxiety among the personnel. At the same time, the shadow system must give rise to a diversity of perspectives. It is the source of innovation, contention and political struggle as different groups engage in dialogue and learning, and entertain alternatives to the status quo. If this creative tension is to fulfil its purpose, there will be occasions when the shadow system manages to undermine the legitimate system and forces it to change. The organization will then be able to perform its primary task in novel ways or to pursue entirely new primary tasks. Creativity has been unleashed, amplified to the organizational level and may allow the enterprise to climb higher up its fitness peak or even scale a new peak.

7.2.4 Methods

Stacey (1996) outlines five 'control parameters' that can be manipulated to ensure an organization remains at the edge of chaos. These are : 'information flow', 'degree of diversity', 'richness of connectivity', 'level of contained anxiety' and 'degree of power differential'. Inevitably, they suggest 'methods' that managers can employ in support of a commitment to complexity theory.

For an organization to achieve its potential, the increased information flow it will have to deal with must be managed through a combination of the formal and shadow system. If it overwhelms both, then the organization moves into an unstable state. The shadow system of an organization has to generate a sufficient degree of diversity to provoke learning, but not so much that it induces anarchy. Connections between parts of a system should be sufficient to produce variety, but not so great as to risk instability. They also need to be set at an appropriate strength so that while they add value they do not prevent new connections emerging. Anxiety is a necessity if creativity is to be encouraged, but at the same time the legitimate system has to contain it within certain parameters to prevent it becoming disabling. Power differentials are crucial if anxiety is to be contained within reasonable limits. On the other hand, if an organization is too authoritarian, then freedom of expression and creativity will be expunged.

Apart from what is hinted at in Stacey, few methods have been developed that are specifically attuned to assist with the application of complexity theory. Practitioners who want to employ the approach will need to look for appropriate methods among those originally produced to serve other systems approaches. A number of the techniques used by soft systems thinkers to promote 'learning' immediately spring to mind (see Chapters 8–10). We will nevertheless pick up more hints on application when we consider complexity theory in action in Section 7.3.

7.2.5 Recent developments

Stacey has long argued that complexity theory can provide a radical alternative to systems thinking, which he sees as irredeemably stuck within the stable equilibrium paradigm. In order to do this, however, he argues in more recent work (Stacey, 2000, 2003), complexity theorists need to finally throw off the 'dominant voice' that pervades thinking about management and organizations and that has inhibited them in mounting their radical challenge. That dominant voice, due to systems thinking, sees managers as standing outside organizational systems and trying to gain objective knowledge of how they function in order that they can better design and control them.

Stacey admits that he himself, in earlier writings, was one of those complexity theorists too much in thrall to the dominant systems way of thinking. He believed that organizations literally were complex adaptive systems, that they could be understood and that prescriptions about how they should be managed could be produced. He was simply, he now believes, restating the dominant discourse using the vocabulary of complexity theory.

The mind shift required, if complexity theory is to bring about its revolution, is away from thinking about organizations as systems and toward thinking about them as processes. Organizations should be seen as emerging from the relationships between their members. They result from self-organizing processes that are creative and unpredictable. Complexity theory needs to concentrate on paradox and on difference, spontaneity and diversity.

In the language of paradigms, Stacey wants to lead complexity theory away from functionalism and toward interpretivism and postmodernism. We shall consider this further in Section 7.4. Sufficient to note here that, rather than representing a break with systems thinking, this simply follows a path already well trodden by systems theorists.

7.3 COMPLEXITY THEORY IN ACTION

This case study explores the efforts made by Humberside Training and Enterprise Council under the leadership of its Managing Director (MD), Peter Fryer, to transform itself into a 'learning organization' by making use of complexity theory. The account is taken from material written by Frances Storr and Peter Fryer (and available on Peter Fryer's website at www.trojanmice.com), and from the findings of a PhD student of mine, Maria Ortegon (see Ortegon, 2002), who was invited to study the later stages of the process. Peter Fryer (in press) has recently provided a further account.

Training and Enterprise Councils (TECs) were established by government to promote local economic development by ensuring the provision of appropriate training and encouraging businesses to take advantage of the opportunities made available. In 1998 Humberside TEC had approximately 150 staff and a budget of around £30 million with which to reach its objectives.

Humberside TEC determined that it would achieve its purposes better if it could become a 'learning organization' and, during the second half of the 1990s, a number of initiatives were undertaken designed to bring this about. These included: the establishment of action learning groups; the introduction of 360° appraisal; experiments with soft systems thinking; and various other activities designed specifically to promote learning, such as the MD's 'serious thinking sessions' and the installation of an electronic bulletin board called CollabraShare.

During this period it became clear that what the TEC hoped to achieve, and much of what it was trying to do, was compatible with and could be better understood and facilitated using ideas from the emerging field of complexity theory. In 'Becoming a learning company', Storr explains that complexity theory demands a shift from a command-and-control style of management to one more suitable to organizations viewed as complex evolving systems. Complexity theory is a holistic rather than systematic approach and emphasizes creativity and change rather than stability. When organizations are pushed far from equilibrium, self-organizing processes occur naturally and they become capable of generating more variety and responding more flexibly to their environments. Sustaining this 'edge of chaos' state is essential because today's business environment is constantly changing as a result of decisions made by the tightly interconnected organizations inhabiting it. Using the 'fitness landscape' analogy, only flexible organizations are able to take adaptive walks to higher fitness points.

The TEC set out on the road to implementing complexity theory – although not in any tightly planned manner. Appropriate initiatives were introduced when they felt right rather than according to a linear trajectory. Crucial to the whole process were the leadership style adopted by the MD and a number of clearly identified organizational design principles.

The MD gave a clear lead in pushing the TEC to the edge of chaos. He described his own role as: explore the environment, share feedback, clear pathways, give oceans of support and bugger things up! At the same time, he sought to contain anxiety by stressing that mess and confusion were inevitable, even to be welcomed. In this vein, supportive messages were conveyed, such as 'the best ideas do not always come from the top', 'control is only an illusion' and 'people in the organization want to do a good job and will do so given the right support'.

The organizational design principles were articulated in such a way that people who were not interested in the technicalities of complexity theory could still nevertheless understand its essence and make use of its main ideas. In other words, they were the TEC's means of operationalizing the concepts of complexity theory. There were three principles: 'make connections', 'learn continuously' and 'make processes ongoing'.

If the TEC was to survive and thrive, it was seen as essential that it be highly interconnected both internally and externally. Strong networking allows information and knowledge to flow, breeds creativity and offers new opportunities for action. Various mechanisms were employed to encourage networking. Developments, such as moving to new premises and the 360° appraisal, were planned by cross-TEC groups. A new role was created with the remit to facilitate networking. Regular conferences and learning sessions were held for all staff. Informality and accessibility to managers at all levels, especially the MD, became the norm. Forms of dialogue, aimed at ensuring win–win rather than win–lose outcomes, were introduced to help overcome barriers to communication. The 'messages' conveyed to support 'making connections' were 'everyone can talk to everyone and should', 'everyone is responsible' and 'network extensively'.

The TEC needed to learn continuously if it was to improve its performance and be responsive to its coevolving and rapidly changing fitness landscape. Both single-loop and double-loop learning, involving a radical shift in world view, were essential. To ensure continuous learning, TEC staff needed to develop sophisticated thinking skills. They were encouraged to attend 'thinking skills modules' as well as the MD's 'serious thinking sessions'. The 'whole brain model' was introduced as a way of helping people to understand different modes of thinking. Staff completed a 'development activity sheet' each month, setting out what they had learned. These were read and followed-up by the MD. The messages conveyed to support 'learn continuously' were 'love mistakes to death', 'respond to the environment' 'learn by doing', 'be comfortable with the uncomfortable', and 'think out of the box'.

'Make processes ongoing' was meant to stress that the TEC was a self-organizing system and that structures and strategy should therefore follow rather than dictate what needed doing. To prosper in a continuously changing environment, learning, planning and evaluating had to be ongoing. This degree of flexibility and fluidity could only be obtained if controls were dropped and staff trusted to use their own judgement and exercise responsibility. TEC policies were changed to ensure they were related to outcomes rather than following procedures and that they were premised on the best people in the organization rather than the one or two who could not be trusted. Fixed working hours were abolished as long as the job got done. The expenses policy was simply to reimburse any reasonable expense incurred on TEC business. Any member of staff attending a meeting was granted the authority to commit the organization there and then. Staff were made responsible for their own appraisal under the 360° scheme. A favourite analogy used by Peter Fryer, to support the notion of 'make processes ongoing', likened rules and regulations to the stabilizers on a bicycle. They are useful when you are learning to ride, but a hindrance once you are able to cycle. Furthermore, the best way to teach someone to ride a bike is to provide supportive guidance, but then to let go when the time is right.

Storr and Fryer do not claim that a perfect result was achieved in the TEC on all the control parameters listed by Stacey as needing attention if the 'edge of chaos' state is to be reached and sustained. They conclude that at any one time certain parts of the organization exhibited chaos while others were much more stable. Nevertheless, the informal system was engaged to handle information; 'valuing the difference' became embedded in people's thinking; explicit attention was given to connectivity; staff were assisted in dealing with high levels of anxiety; and hierarchy was combined with giving people self-responsibility. As a result the whole system was robust enough to tolerate a creative mixture of stability and instability. External auditors rated the performance of Humberside TEC against its objectives very highly indeed.

Maria Ortegon, as a participant–observer during the later stages of the complexity programme, was able to judge the impact of the changes made. In her view, thanks to the language used in setting out the organization design principles, the main ideas of complexity theory were relatively easily absorbed in the TEC. People worked out the implications of the new concepts for themselves. Terms such as self-organization and the edge of chaos became part of the jargon used by staff to understand their situation. In this way the essentials of complexity theory were assimilated into the culture of the organization and began to change values and actions as people found alternative ways of doing things.

Observing one self-managed team of around 30 consultants, within the 'investors in people' directorate, Ortegon saw initial uncertainty develop into increasing confidence. People began to enjoy working in this way, collective decisions were taken, commitment was gained and creativity was enhanced. The team began to learn how to learn and to think more strategically about their role in the organization.

For those who witnessed the introduction of complexity theory to Humberside TEC, two questions continue to loom large. The first is whether the TEC, as a medium-sized organization with a high degree of interconnectivity, provided a rather favourable environment for testing the ideas of complexity theory. The second is whether the paradox of using command and control to get rid of command and control can ever be overcome.

7.4 CRITIQUE OF COMPLEXITY THEORY

Complexity theory would have a huge claim on the attention of managers if it could be demonstrated that the laws it reckons to have discovered, operating in physical and biological systems, apply equally to the complex evolving systems that managers have to deal with. If this were so, they could use the knowledge gained to manipulate and control organizations so that they 'thrive and strive'. Through the control parameters they could ensure that their enterprises operated at the edge of chaos. Once this happy state was attained, the legitimate system would enable managers to plan for and control short-term performance. It would never be possible to plan for the long term, but an organization operating at the edge of chaos would self-organize and throw up patterns of behaviour that managers could intuitively understand, even if they could not predict in detail what was going to happen. Moreover, they could encourage creativity and learning in such a way as to give the organization the best chance of recognizing those patterns that could be detected and responding to whatever unpredictable events the fitness landscape conjured up.

The first problem with this strong claim, according to Rosenhead (1998), is that chaos and complexity theory still has much to do, as a science, to establish its scope and validity in the domain of natural systems. There is some evidence of its power, but other results rest more on suggestive computer simulations rather than on empirical observations. In the social domain there is a complete lack of solid evidence that complexity theory holds and that adopting its prescriptions will produce the benefits claimed. Given its state of immaturity as a field of research, we should be careful of complexity theory even as a source of well-defined analogies that managers can employ.

There is a more fundamental problem with applying complexity theory to management, which has to do with the difference between natural and social systems. Physical systems, like the weather, are governed by a limited number of deterministic laws. In these circumstances it is possible to see how strange attractors arise. Social systems, however, are influenced by innumerable variables and probabilistic elements abound. Strange attractors do not seem to manifest themselves. In particular, Rosenhead (1998) argues, because of the self-consciousness and free will exhibited by humans, the behaviour of social systems cannot be explained in the same way. Humans think and learn, act according to their own purposes and are capable of reacting against and disproving any law that is said to apply to their behaviour.

Even if the strong claim cannot be justified, complexity theory might still deserve the attention of managers as an illuminating metaphor – throwing light on those aspects of the organizational world ignored by traditional theory because they seem too 'difficult', chaotic, unpredictable and controversial. Rosenhead sees the metaphor to which complexity theory gives rise as particularly useful because it challenges the classical view that consensus in organizations is a good thing. It suggests that shared vision can lead to groupthink, which prevents valuable alternative opinions being expressed. It suggests that organizational politics need to be fostered as a means of ensuring the creativity and learning necessary for organizational survival.

If this is true, it needs to be recognized that there are downsides to the metaphor as well. For the most part, complexity theorists believe that, even in social systems, there is enough order underlying chaos to enable them to provide advice to managers on how to improve their organizations. Science tells them that organizations must be manoeuvred to the edge of chaos and how this can be achieved. To that extent, managers who embrace complexity theory believe that they have access to some specialist knowledge denied to other stakeholders. There is a justification for authoritarian action hidden in this.

And what does complexity theory seek to achieve? It denies that managers can use the techniques of planning to pursue purposes. At best they can act to increase the ability of their organizations to survive, adapt and reach higher fitness peaks. The market environment seems to be the determinant of all things. As with organizational cybernetics, 'good' management tends to be reduced to improving efficiency and efficacy, to doing things right. Effectiveness, or doing the right things, is recognized as important by complexity theory, but not directly assisted by it. The idea of choosing purposes and using organizations as rational vehicles of, say, achieving social progress is not easily conceptualized in its language. Rosenhead (1998) suggests that complexity theory is so popular at present because it offers intellectual succour to the political argument that there is no alternative to the market for ordering our social affairs.

Given its origins in the natural sciences, the emphasis on finding order underpinning chaos and the representation of the edge of chaos as a desirable state, it is not surprising that complexity theory finds itself most at home in the functionalist paradigm (see Jackson, 2000). The great majority of writers on complexity theory interpret it this way and discuss the apparent insights that it can offer managers about how to drive their organizations to the edge of chaos. Stacey's more recent work (e.g., 2000, 2003), as we saw, is an exception. He wants to reinvent complexity theory by using its concepts in the service of interpretivism and postmodernism. Here lies a problem for complexity theory. If it remains theoretically underdeveloped, confused even, then its ideas can easily be captured by any paradigm. We end up with functionalist, interpretive, emancipatory and postmodern versions of complexity theory emphasizing, respectively, order beneath chaos, learning, self-organization and unpredictability. Stacey sometimes seems to approve of this, regarding complexity theory as ordering a variety of compatible insights in one paradigm. The problem is that there is not just one paradigm at work. We have four competing paradigms interpreting complexity theory in radically different ways. The whole thing falls apart.

The only coherent future for complexity theory in management, I would argue, lies in the functionalist paradigm. It is comfortable playing around with a mix of machine, organism, brain, and flux and transformation metaphors and giving them its own twist through notions such as legitimate system, strange attractors, self-organization, edge of chaos and the fitness landscape. Although there is reference to culture and politics this is under-played by comparison, and these metaphors play a dependent role in assisting organizations to arrive at the edge of chaos. The functionalist paradigm is the natural home for complexity theory, and it can play a significant role there in revitalizing functionalism by introducing a set of original and insightful ideas and concepts. Beyond functionalism it will be unable to compete with other forms of systems thinking (explored under Types B, C and D) that have a much longer history of exploring and developing alternative paradigms.

7.5 THE VALUE OF COMPLEXITY THEORY TO MANAGERS

In picking out five lessons that managers can easily learn from complexity theory, I take a lead from Peter Fryer (see www.trojanmice.com) who used the approach to manage Humberside TEC and now employs it in his consultancy practice. Peter Fryer's lessons derive from comparing the complexity theory approach to the traditional approach to management. Traditional management theory advises managers what to do in order to achieve goals in an optimum way. It teaches them how to organize the parts of an enterprise into a coherent structure. It seeks conformity from employees and puts in place detailed control procedures to ensure that this is realized. By contrast, complexity theory teaches that:

- The most important thing that managers can do is change their way of thinking, abandoning mechanism and determinism, and learning to appreciate and cope with relationships, dynamism and unpredictability.
- Organizations coevolve with their environments, and therefore managing relationships with the environment is crucial. This means being prepared to respond to the environment, adapting as necessary but also being ready to grasp opportunities as they present themselves.

- The best managers are able to intuitively grasp the patterns that are driving the behaviour of their organizations and the environments they are confronting. They look for patterns in the whole and seek small changes that can have the maximum impact on unfavourable patterns.
- The most successful organizations do not try to control everything. To an extent managers can trust in chaos and allow the processes operating at the edge of chaos to bring new order through self-organization.
- So that organizations have the best chance of understanding those patterns that do exist and responding to the unpredictable, managers should encourage learning, diversity and a variety of opinion.

7.6 CONCLUSION

Complexity theory, as applied to management in a variety of contexts, is very fashionable these days. Its advocates sometimes claim that it represents an advance on systems thinking. This is nonsense. With its emphasis on holism, emergence, interdependence and relationships, complexity theory is definitely a systems approach. Indeed, previous work in the systems field, on informal groups, group working, autonomous work groups, double-loop learning, organizations as information processing systems, open systems and 'turbulent field' environments, seems to cover much of the territory that complexity theory wants to claim as its own. Nevertheless, it has introduced a set of original concepts that help to enrich the functionalist form of systems thinking.

To find systems ideas used in radically new ways, however, we need to study systems approaches that have developed in and are now inextricably linked to alternative sociological paradigms. That is what we shall do under Types B, C and D in the rest of this part of the book.

REFERENCES

Capra, F. (1996). *The Web of Life: A New Synthesis of Mind and Matter*. Flamingo, London.

Fryer, P. (in press). Complexity – A case study: Humberside Training and Enterprise Council. In: D. Kernick (ed.), *Complexity and Health Care Organisation*. Radcliffe Medical Press, London.

Gleick, J. (1987). *Chaos: The Making of a New Science*. Abacus, London.

Jackson, M.C. (2000). *Systems Approaches to Management*. Kluwer/Plenum, New York.

Jantsch, E. (1980). *The Self-Organising Universe: Scientific and Human Implications of the Emerging Paradigm of Evolution*. Pergamon Press, Oxford.

Kauffman, S. (1995). *At Home in the Universe*. Oxford University Press, New York.

Morgan, G. (1997). *Images of Organisation*. Sage Publications, London.

Ortegon, M. (2002). An exploration of chaos and complexity theory in management from a critical systems thinking perspective. PhD. thesis, University of Lincoln.

Prigogine, I. and Stengers, I. (1984). *Order out of Chaos: Man's New Dialogue with Nature*. Bantam Books, New York.

Rosenhead, J. (1998). *Complexity Theory and Management Practice* (LSE Working Paper 98.25). London School of Economics, London.

Stacey, R.D. (1993). *Strategic Management and Organizational Dynamics*. Pitman, London.

Stacey, R.D. (1996). *Complexity and Creativity in Organizations*. Berret-Kohler, San Francisco.

Stacey, R.D. (2000). *Complexity and Management: Fad or Radical Challenge to Systems Thinking?* Routledge, London.

Stacey, R.D. (2003), *Strategic Management and Organisational Dynamics* (4th edn). Prentice Hall, Harlow.

Storr, F. and Fryer, P. (www.trojanmice.com).

Wheatley, M.J. (1992). *Leadership and the New Science: Learning about Organization from an Orderly Universe*. Berret-Kohler, San Francisco.

Type B

Exploring Purposes

Here we detail three systems approaches that aim to assist managers improve the way in which they decide what purposes their enterprises should pursue and achieve a measure of agreement around those purposes. These approaches are strategic assumption surfacing and testing, interactive planning and soft systems methodology. They were developed because of the failure of functionalist systems approaches, especially hard systems thinking, to pay sufficient attention to the existence of differing values, beliefs, philosophies and interests in a world exhibiting increasing pluralism. Agreement on purposes could no longer be taken for granted. The three approaches emphasize effective problem resolution based on the clarification of purposes and the formulation of elegant solutions that can command stakeholder commitment. In sociological terms they are interpretive in character, orientated toward achieving greater mutual understanding between different interested parties so that better regulation of the enterprise can be obtained. The approaches differ from one another in the manner in which they seek to progress in dealing with pluralism along the horizontal axis of the System Of Systems Methodologies (SOSM) (see Chapter 2). These differences are reflected in the ways they draw variously on the culture and political systems metaphors and in their willingness to pay attention to other images of organization.

Strategic Assumption Surfacing and Testing

8

The systems approach begins when first you see the world through the eyes of another.

Churchman (1968)

8.1 INTRODUCTION

Surveying the field of management science in the late 1970s, Mason and Mitroff (1981) concluded that the methodologies and tools then available could only be successful if used on relatively simple problems. This was selling managers short because most of the policy, planning and decision-making problems they had to deal with were 'messes': ill-structured problem situations made up of highly interdependent problems. Mason and Mitroff determined to design an approach specifically to deal with messes or, as they preferred to describe them, 'wicked problems'. The result was Strategic Assumption Surfacing and Testing (SAST).

SAST, therefore, is a systems methodology that is meant to be employed when managers and their advisers are confronted by wicked problems. These are characterized by being interconnected and complicated further by lack of clarity about purposes, conflict, uncertainty about the environment and societal constraints. In tackling wicked problems, problem structuring assumes greater importance than problem-solving using conventional techniques. If problem formulation is ignored or badly handled, managers may end up solving, very thoroughly and precisely, the wrong problem.

8.2 DESCRIPTION OF STRATEGIC ASSUMPTION SURFACING AND TESTING (SAST)

8.2.1 Historical development

The reader will recall from Chapter 4 the names of Ackoff and Churchman, who were among the most influential pioneers of operations research (OR) in the postwar period in the USA. During the 1960s and 1970s both became increasingly disillusioned with OR and turned their considerable talents to the development of what is now known as soft systems thinking. We consider Churchman's later work in this chapter (the primary influence on Mason and Mitroff) and Ackoff's in the next.

Churchman's disillusionment (see 1979a) stemmed from what he saw as the betrayal of the original intention of OR. In his view it set out to be a holistic, interdisciplinary, experimental science addressed to problems in social systems. It had ended up obsessed with perfecting mathematical tools and techniques of relevance only to a narrow range of tactical problems. As a result, Churchman established his own educational programme in 'social systems design', at Berkeley, which was an attempt to keep alive the original vision he had for OR. This programme influenced Mason and Mitroff and many others, including Ulrich whose 'critical systems heuristics' is considered in Chapter 11.

One effect of Churchman's antipathy to the way he saw OR going was that social systems design, and the same can be said of the systems approaches of his disciples, came to resemble nothing more closely than conventional OR turned on its head. These opposite characteristics would, borrowing from Rosenhead (1987), include:

- a satisficing rather than optimizing rationale;
- an acceptance of conflict over goals;
- different objectives measured in their own terms;
- the employment of transparent methods that clarify conflict and facilitate negotiation;
- the use of analysis to support judgement with no aspiration to replace it;
- the treatment of human elements as active subjects;
- problem formulation on the basis of a bottom-up process;
- decisions taken as far down the hierarchy as there is expertise to resolve them;
- the acceptance of uncertainty as an inherent characteristic of the future and a consequent emphasis on keeping options open.

8.2.2   Philosophy and theory

In formulating his social systems design, Churchman (1968, 1971) drew on the whole of the Western philosophical tradition – although this was filtered through his understanding of American pragmatism and especially the work of E.A. Singer. The most pithy account of the conclusions he reached is to be found in the four aphorisms that close his book *The Systems Approach* (1968). We shall take each of these in turn and expand on its meaning.

> *The systems approach begins when first you see the world through the eyes of another.*

Here we learn lessons from Kant and Hegel. We are reminded that whatever world view, or in German *Weltanschauung* (W), we hold is inevitably based on certain taken-for-granted, a priori assumptions (Kant). Following Hegel, we also need to recognize that there are many possible, alternative Ws constructed on different sets of taken-for-granted assumptions. Systems designers, therefore, must accept that completely different evaluations of social systems, their purposes and their performance will inevitably exist. The only way we can get near to a view of the whole system is to look at it from as many perspectives as possible. Subjectivity should be embraced by the systems approach.

> *The systems approach goes on to discovering that every world view is terribly restricted.*

This aphorism has profound implications for our understanding of objectivity in systems thinking. In the hard, system dynamic, cybernetic and complexity theory traditions, objectivity is seen to depend on how well the model constructed predicts and, preferably, explains the behaviour of the system of concern. Churchman is arguing that a model can only capture one very restricted version of the nature of a social system. It follows that a different understanding of objectivity is necessary – one that includes subjectivity rather than trying to exclude it. Only by 'sweeping in' different subjectivities, through stakeholder participation, can the restricted nature of any one W be overcome.

A related point, noted by Churchman, is that although particular world views are terribly restricted they are also usually very resistant to change. Certainly, they cannot be seriously challenged just by exposing them to apparently contrary 'facts', which they will simply interpret to fit their own assumptions. What we need to do, therefore, is to get at the foundations of Ws by examining them systemically.

Churchman recommends employing a dialectical approach to objectivity, which he derives from Hegel. Faced by a set of proposals emanating from one particular, inevitably restricted W, we first need to understand the nature of that world view – why it makes the proposals meaningful. This first W (or *thesis*) should then be challenged by another 'deadly enemy' W, based on entirely different assumptions that give rise to alternative proposals (*antithesis*). Whatever facts are available can then be considered in the light of both world views. This should help to bring about a richer (i.e., more objective) appreciation of the situation, expressing elements of both positions but going beyond them as well (*synthesis*).

Churchman argues that it is the role of systems designers to challenge the mental models of powerful decision-makers so that they are brought to act according to the purposes of 'clients' or 'customers', the people supposed to benefit from the systems they participate in.

There are no experts in the systems approach.

This refers to adherents of any particular branch of science who might claim special expertise in resolving a problem situation. They all offer partial viewpoints and need to be co-ordinated in a systemic process of inquiry. It applies most strongly, however, to systems thinkers themselves. Systems designers, because they seek to address systems as wholes, may become arrogant in the face of opposition from apparently sectional interests. They need to listen carefully to all 'enemies' of the systems approach (such as religion, politics, ethics and aesthetics) since these enemies reflect the very failure of the systems approach to be comprehensive – to draw the boundary wide enough (see Churchman, 1979b). Churchman insists that when it comes to matters of aims and objectives (and appropriate means), which inevitably involve ethical considerations and moral judgements, there can be no experts.

The systems approach is not a bad idea.

The attempt to take on the whole system remains a worthwhile ideal even if it cannot be realized in practice. The systems designer says Churchman, echoing Singer, must pursue his or her profession in the 'heroic mood'. Increasing human purposefulness and participation in systems design is a never-ending process. There is a need to help bring about a consensus around a particular perspective so that decisions can be taken and action occur. Before this world view can solidify into the status quo, however, it should itself be subject to attack from forceful alternative perspectives. The process of generating learning through the dialectical method is never ending.

The radical reorientation in the systems approach demanded by Churchman's philosophy comes through in a story of the engagement of his research group with NASA during the period of the Apollo space programme. NASA wanted an evaluation of the innovative, hard systems methods it was using to manage the project. Churchman's group (see 1979b) drew the boundary much wider and began asking challenging questions about the purpose of the Apollo programme, which from *their* systems perspective did not obviously contribute to the betterment of the human species. Reviewing the performance of Churchman's group, NASA awarded it the highest marks for interdisciplinarity and the lowest for relevance to their mission.

Mason and Mitroff (1981) have adopted all of Churchman's philosophy and given it their own, slightly more mundane twist.

They accept the interconnectedness associated with all wicked problems and the implication that they must therefore be tackled holistically. This demands the participation of all involved and affected parties in the process of problem resolution. Each of these will bring his or her own perspective on the problem situation and interpret the facts from the point of view of that perspective.

The problem with conventional planning and problem-solving, according to Mason and Mitroff, is that it fails to recognize the value that can be obtained from entertaining different world views. Most organizations fail to deal properly with wicked problems because they find it difficult to challenge accepted ways of doing things. Policy options that diverge from current practice are not given serious consideration. An approach to planning and problem resolving is needed that ensures that alternatives are fully considered. This requires the generation of radically different policies, based on alternative world views, because data alone, which can always be interpreted in terms of existing theory, will not lead an organization to change its preferred ways of doing things. An organization only really begins to learn when its most cherished assumptions are challenged by counterassumptions. Assumptions underpinning existing policies and procedures should therefore be unearthed and alternatives put forward based on counterassumptions. A variety of policy perspectives, each interpreting the data available in its own way, can then be evaluated systemically. Furthermore, because problem situations are dynamic, this type of organizational learning needs to be ongoing.

Mason and Mitroff recognize that tensions will inevitably arise during the process of continuously challenging assumptions – not least because its success depends, initially at least, on different groups being strongly committed to particular policy options. However, they regard it as naive to believe that wicked problems can be tackled in the absence of such tensions. Organizations are arenas of conflict between groups holding to and expressing alternative world views. This offers great potential for developing and examining alternative strategies; but, the manner in which this is done needs to be carefully managed. SAST attempts to surface conflicts and to direct them productively as the only way eventually of achieving a productive synthesis of perspectives. It is in the design of this methodology that Mason and Mitroff have shown real originality.

8.2.3 Methodology

Four principles are highlighted by Mason and Mitroff (1981) as underpinning the SAST methodology:

- participative – based on the belief that different stakeholders should be involved, because the knowledge and resources required to resolve wicked problems and implement solutions will be spread among different parts and levels in an organization and different groups outside the organization;
- adversarial – based on the belief that different stakeholders perceive wicked problems very differently and that judgements about how to tackle such problems are best made after full consideration of opposing perspectives;
- integrative – based on the belief that the different options thrown up by the participative and adversarial principles must eventually be brought together again in a higher order synthesis, so that an action plan can be produced and implemented;
- managerial mind supporting – based on the belief that managers exposed to different assumptions that highlight the complex nature of wicked problems will gain a deeper insight into the difficulties facing an organization and appropriate strategies that will enable it to move forward.

It may not be obvious that an approach can be both adversarial and integrative. That it can was brought strongly home to me while conducting an intervention in a printing company that was in the process of adopting a quality management programme (see Jackson, 1989). In that firm there was an apparent consensus around the need for a particular type of quality programme. In fact, this consensus was founded on very different interpretations of the key concepts underpinning the programme. Only through a process of adversarial debate could these very significant differences be highlighted and the ground prepared for a more soundly based consensus built on common understanding.

The four principles are employed throughout the stages of the SAST methodology. The following account is drawn from a variety of sources (Mason and Mitroff, 1981; Mason, 1969; Mitroff et al. 1977; Mitroff et al., 1979) and recognizes the approach as having four main stages:

- group formation;
- assumption surfacing;
- dialectical debate;
- synthesis.

We shall consider these in turn.

As wide a cross section of individuals as possible who have an interest in the policy or problem being investigated should be involved in the SAST process. They are first carefully divided into groups. Within each group the aim is to maximize convergence of perspectives so as to minimize interpersonal conflict and to achieve constructive group processes. Between groups the aim is to maximize divergence of perspectives so as to get the most out of all the groups in their totality by taking advantage of their differences. A number of techniques can be used to accomplish this – grouping according to functional area, organizational level or time orientation (short- or long-term perspective), or on the basis of personality type and vested interest, or advocates of particular strategies. Each group should have or develop a preferred strategy or solution, and each group's viewpoint should be clearly challenged by at least one other group.

The aim of the second, assumption surfacing, stage is to help each group uncover and analyse the key assumptions on which its preferred strategy or solution rests. It is important to provide a supportive environment and good facilitation so that people can be as imaginative and creative as possible. Three techniques are recommended to help with this stage and they are dealt with in Subsection 8.2.4.

The groups are then brought together and encouraged to enter into a dialectical debate. A spokesperson for each group will present the best possible case for its preferred strategy or solution, being careful to identify the key assumptions on which it is based. During this presentation other groups are only allowed to ask questions of clarification. It is important that each group understands each other's viewpoint and assumptions before debating and challenging them. Only after each group has presented its case clearly does open, dialectical debate begin. The debate may be guided by asking the following questions:

- How are the assumptions of the groups different?
- Which stakeholders feature most strongly in giving rise to the significant assumptions made by each group?
- Do groups rate assumptions differently (e.g., as to their importance for the success of a strategy)?
- What assumptions of the other groups does each group find the most troubling with respect to its own proposals?

After the debate has proceeded for a time, each group should consider whether it now wishes to modify its assumptions. This process of 'assumption modification' should continue for as long as progress is being made.

The aim of the synthesis stage is to achieve a compromise on assumptions from which a new, higher level of strategy or solution can be derived. Assumptions continue to be negotiated and modified, and a list of agreed assumptions is drawn up. If this list is sufficiently long an implied strategy can be worked out. This new strategy should bridge the gap between the different strategies of the groups and go beyond them as well. If no synthesis can be achieved, points of disagreement are noted and research undertaken to resolve the remaining differences. Any strategy adopted will be very fully understood and the assumptions on which it is based can be evaluated as it is put into effect.

8.2.4 Methods

The three methods most closely associated with SAST are stakeholder analysis, assumption specification and assumption rating. They all serve the assumption surfacing stage of the methodology.

Mason and Mitroff believe that a strategy or solution can be thought of as a set of assumptions about the current and future behaviour of an organization's stakeholders. In surfacing the assumptions underlying a particular strategy or solution, therefore, it is useful to decide who the relevant stakeholders are taken to be. Stakeholder analysis recommends that each group putting forward a strategy be asked to identify the key individuals, parties or groups on which the success or failure of their preferred strategy would depend were it adopted. These are the people who have a 'stake' in the strategy. The process can be helped by asking questions like:

- Who is affected by the strategy?
- Who has an interest in it?
- Who can affect its adoption or implementation?
- Who cares about it?

Stakeholder analysis was used to help decide whether to undertake substantial capital expenditure on a swimming pool for the social club of a hospital in the Middle East (see Flood, 1995). In this example, it yielded the following list of stakeholders:

- Western nurses;
- developing countries' male staff;
- Arab families;
- matron;
- residential medical staff;
- government liaison staff;
- recruiters;
- swimming pool manufacturers;
- financial controller;
- hospital administrator;
- support services manager;
- hotels in the city;
- religious fundamentalist groups.

The second technique is assumption specification. This asks each group to list what assumptions it is making about each of the stakeholders identified in believing that its preferred strategy will succeed. Two or three assumptions should be unearthed for each stakeholder. These are therefore the assumptions on which the success of the group's preferred strategy or solution depends.

Assumption rating, our third method, requires each group to rank each of the assumptions it is making according to two criteria:

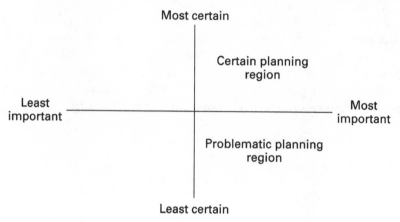

Figure 8.1 Assumption rating chart.

- How important is this assumption in terms of its influence on the success or failure of the strategy?
- How certain are we about the likelihood of occurrence or the truth of the statement of events contained in the assumption?

The results are recorded on a chart such as that shown in Figure 8.1. Because of their lack of importance those assumptions falling on the extreme left of the chart are of little significance for effective planning or problem resolving. Those falling in the top right (certain planning region) are important, but it is those in the lower right-hand quadrant (problematic planning region) that are most critical. Because of their significance but our uncertainty about them, they deserve close attention.

8.2.5   Recent developments

A more recent development has seen Mitroff and Linstone (1993) seeking to integrate elements of SAST with Linstone's 'multidimensional' systems thinking. Linstone recommends examining any problem situation through three lenses: the traditional, Technical (T) perspective, an Organizational (or societal) perspective (O) and a Personal (or individual) perspective (P). These three lenses offer radically different world views that can be taken advantage of in SAST. The combined Mitroff and Linstone approach is labelled 'unbounded systems thinking'.

It is also worth mentioning again the influence that Churchman's writings have had on emancipatory systems thinking, particularly on Ulrich's 'critical systems heuristics'. In many respects the work of Churchman, and similarly that of Mason and Mitroff, can be seen as obsessed with how the 'boundaries' are drawn around a system of interest. What assumptions lead us to draw the boundaries in a particular place? What difference would it make to draw the boundaries in another way? How can we challenge the way the boundaries are currently drawn? This easily leads on, as we will see in Chapter 11, to the emancipatory systems question of who is advantaged and who disadvantaged by particular boundary judgements.

8.3 STRATEGIC ASSUMPTION SURFACING AND TESTING (SAST) IN ACTION

Good examples of the use of SAST can be found in Mason and Mitroff (1981), Ellis (2002), Flood (1995) and Jackson (2000). This case study is taken from an intervention I was involved in with the Humberside Co-operative Development Agency (CDA) (see also Flood and Jackson, 1991).

The CDA was established to serve its region by fostering, encouraging, developing and promoting industrial and commercial activity through the formation of co-operative enterprises – enterprises owned by the people who work in them and usually also managed by those same people. The particular focus of the SAST exercise was a disagreement in the CDA over the relative merits of 'top-down' as opposed to 'bottom-up' co-operative development work. The top-down approach, which involves identifying business opportunities and then recruiting individuals to form workers' co-operatives in these fields, is usually viewed with great distrust in co-operative circles. The preferred approach is bottom-up, essentially encouraging and assisting groups already thinking about starting co-operatives in particular areas of work. The description of this exercise follows the four stages of the SAST methodology.

Within the CDA the idea of trying a top-down strategy had some support, although there was also vehement opposition from other development workers. The development workers were therefore divided into two groups, one consisting of those with some sympathy for the top-down approach and the other of those opposed. The opposed group was asked to make the best case it could against top-down. It was felt that this, rather than asking them directly to make the case for bottom-up, would lead to the most fruitful debate.

The separated groups then went through the assumption surfacing phase, using the stakeholder analysis, assumption specification and

Table 8.1 Stakeholders listed in the study for the Humberside Co-operative Development Agency.

Group 1 (for top-down)	Group 2 (against top-down)
The development workers	The development workers
The unemployed	Potential clients
Local authorities	The ideologically motivated
Business improvement schemes	Local authorities
Existing co-operatives	Department of Trade and Industry
Funding bodies	Existing co-operatives
Other CDAs	People already in work
Marketing agencies	
Trade unions	
General public	
Other businesses	

assumption rating techniques. The groups came up with widely different lists of stakeholders, obviously influenced by initial perceptions about which individuals or groups might or might not support the case for the top-down strategy. The stakeholders listed by each group are shown in Table 8.1.

The lists of stakeholders were combined and each group was asked, following the logic of assumption specification, what it was assuming about each stakeholder in believing that its arguments for or against the top-down strategy were correct. This facilitated the emergence of numerous assumptions supporting/against the top-down strategy. These were ranked as to their importance and certainty by each group and the results recorded on assumption rating charts. Table 8.2 contains lists of those assumptions rated most significant by the two groups (i.e., those appearing in the right-hand quadrants of Figure 8.1). The particular stakeholder generating each assumption is noted in parentheses.

The groups were then brought back together to engage in dialectical debate. During the presentations it became clear that the groups were emphasizing assumptions derived from consideration of different stakeholders as the main props for their arguments. Group 1 (for top-down) drew heavily on the stakeholders 'funding bodies' (increase in credibility, ensures continuous support, carries out expectations) and 'unemployed' (provides employment, gives unemployed a solution in a package). Group 2 (against top-down) concentrated on assumptions generated by the stakeholders

Table 8.2 Significant assumptions concerning the stakeholders listed in Table 8.1.

Group 1 (for top-down)	Group 2 (against top-down)
Another way to set up workers' co-operatives (potential clients)	Mixed feelings of the development workers toward the strategy (development workers)
Increases the CDA's credibility in job creation (funding bodies)	Lack of group cohesion among the cooperators (potential clients)
Ensures continuous support to the CDA (funding bodies)	Lack of willingness to co-operate among the co-operators (potential clients)
Carries out the expectations of the funding bodies (funding bodies)	Getting people who are not motivated (the unemployed)
Strengthens the co-operative sector (existing co-operatives)	Less development workers' time on helping existing co-operatives (existing co-operatives)
Provides employment (the unemployed)	Lack of knowledge of business opportunities hinders 'top-down' (development workers)
Provides the unemployed with a solution in a package (the unemployed)	Lack of experience of the development workers in this area of activity (development workers)
A more effective way of starting worker's co-operatives (development workers)	Lack of commitment to business idea among the new co-operators (potential clients)
Establishes a successful precedent (other CDAs)	Against principle of self-determination (ideologically motivated)
Increases numbers working in co-operatives (existing co-operatives)	Could be criticized as a waste of development workers' time (funding bodies)
Increase in industrial democracy (trade unions)	Very dangerous if failed (funding bodies)
	Suspicions of other co-operatives, fear of hierarchy and getting co-operatives a bad name (existing co-operatives)
	Too risky a venture for them (funding bodies)
	No previous association of co-operative members (potential clients)
	May have nothing in common with other co-operators (potential clients)

'development workers' (mixed feelings, lack of knowledge about business opportunities, lack of experience in the area), 'potential clients' (lack of group cohesion, lack of willingness to co-operate, lack of commitment to business idea, etc.) and 'existing co-operatives' (less development workers' time for them, suspicion). This analysis helped clarify for the participants the nature and basis of the arguments for and against top-down and contributed to a very productive debate.

As debate continued, other interesting results emerged. The two groups interpreted the reaction of the stakeholder 'funding bodies' from entirely different perspectives. Group 1 insisted that top-down would assist the CDA's credibility in job creation and fulfil the expectations of funders, so ensuring continued support. Group 2 believed that top-down might be seen as a waste of development workers' time on risky ventures and this dangerous experiment could lose the CDA credibility with the funders if it failed. On the issue of whether top-down promoted industrial democracy, Group 1 argued that more people in workers' co-operatives would inevitably bring this effect; Group 2 argued that the very idea of top-down took choice away from the individuals concerned; and Group 1 argued back again that many of these were unemployed and had few choices anyway, so work in a co-operative could only increase their options.

The most troubling assumptions of the other side for Group 1 (for top-down) were the divisions among the development workers themselves and the possible lack of commitment from those brought together in a top-down scheme. Group 2 (against top-down) worried that, if no top-down work took place, a genuine opportunity to set up more co-operatives would be wasted and chances to improve the lot of the unemployed and to gain credibility with funders would be missed.

Following the dialectical debate attempts were made at assumption negotiation and modification, but it proved impossible to arrive at any overall synthesis. Consensus was however reached on particular matters, such as the need to seek out sources of information about business opportunities, to research other top-down experiences elsewhere and to carry out some experiments with a modified top-down approach.

The intervention using SAST in the Humberside CDA was useful in assisting creativity, in helping to clarify where differences of opinion lay and in generating a very full and rich discussion. Overall synthesis proved impossible to achieve, but agreement around specific issues was obtained and this brought benefits. The inclusion of the items mentioned above in an action plan would not have been possible without the changes in perception and culture brought about through the use of SAST.

8.4 CRITIQUE OF STRATEGIC ASSUMPTION SURFACING AND TESTING (SAST)

There is little empirical evidence in favour of the superiority of SAST over more conventional planning approaches. Where tests have been carried out the results have been ambiguous (see Jackson, 1989). This does not surprise Mason and Mitroff (1981) who remind critics that SAST was designed to assist with 'wicked problems'. In the context of wicked problems the concern is with clarifying purposes and finding elegant ways forward, rather than with producing the 'best' solution that can be compared with solutions derived from other methodologies. We are drawn back therefore, as with all soft systems thinking, to the philosophy of the approach and the way that philosophy is operationalized in the methodology as the only possible guarantees for the benefits said to be associated with using SAST. Mason and Mitroff recognize this well enough and search for guarantees in aspects such as participation, the provision of challenging assumptions, and the controlled conflict encouraged.

In a thought experiment, Mason (1969) seeks to highlight SAST's advantages by comparing it with the 'expert' and 'devil's advocate' approaches to planning.

In the expert approach, organizations set up special planning departments or obtain the services of outside experts and require them to produce a plan based on the best available evidence. However, the planners' or experts' own world views and strategic assumptions often remain hidden. Moreover, experts usually provide plans from a limited perspective and ignore the wide range of additional perspectives that policy-makers and managers might usefully take into account. The lack of transparency over assumptions and the failure to test assumptions leaves the decision-makers handicapped at crucial stages of the formulation and implementation process.

The devil's advocate approach does allow the surfacing and testing of some assumptions when the planners present their proposals for scrutiny by senior management. However, this approach often encourages top management to be hypercritical, with the added problem that, if they are too destructive, the suggested plan disintegrates with no alternative to replace it. In these circumstances, planners may be tempted to produce 'safe' plans to protect themselves from severe criticism. Again, with the devil's advocate approach the chance is lost to develop alternative plans constructed on the basis of different world views.

Mason argues that the dialectical philosophy embedded in SAST overcomes the weaknesses of the other two methods. Critics (see Jackson, 2000) have largely been willing to accept the coherence of that philosophy and its value when translated into problem management. At the same time they insist that it limits the domain of applicability of SAST.

Mason and Mitroff designed SAST for use with wicked problems. In doing so they appear to assume that formulating such problems is synonymous with tackling them. There seems to be an unwarranted, for some, assumption that once problems arising from the existence of different world views have been dissolved, then all the hard work is done. This appears to skip over the daunting tasks associated with organizing large-scale complex systems – those matters that system dynamics, organizational cybernetics and complexity theory concern themselves with.

Other critics point out that SAST depends for its success on the willingness of participants to have their assumptions exposed. This is fine in situations where some basic compatibility of values and interests exists and compromise is possible. There will be many circumstances, however, where there are barriers to the extension of the participative principle, and in such instances many of the benefits of SAST will be lost. The 'powerful' have the need to be convinced that it is of value to them to reveal their strategic assumptions. In 'coercive' contexts this is unlikely to be the case and any employment of SAST will get distorted and provide benefit only to those who already hold power in the organization.

It is clear, with SAST, that we are dealing with a completely different animal to the 'functionalist' systems approaches reviewed as Type A. In the language of Chapter 2, SAST is seeking to develop systems thinking along the horizontal dimension of the System Of Systems Methodologies (SOSM). It is an approach primarily concerned with philosophies, perceptions, values, beliefs and interests. It focuses managers' attention on diverse world views, multiple perspectives and different assumptions, and seeks to achieve a much greater degree of mutual understanding. To this end, SAST works well – handling pluralism effectively first by sustaining and making use of it to generate creative discussion and then managing its resolution in a new synthesis. SAST is a successful example of a soft systems methodology.

We noted in Subsection 8.2.1 that SAST could be represented as being conventional OR turned on its head. This, of course, indicates that it operates from a completely different paradigm. SAST is clearly an 'interpretive' systems approach that embraces subjectivity rather than the 'objectivism' that underpins those systems methodologies wedded to functionalism. The shift in paradigm arises from following Churchman's philosophy. For Churchman, systems and whether they work or not are in the mind of the observer, not in the 'real world'. A model captures only one possible perception of the nature of a system. To gain an appreciation of the whole we have to engage with multiple subjectivities. And the results of a systems study can only receive their guarantee from the maximum participation of different stakeholders, holding to various Ws, in the design process. 'Objectivity', it turns out, can only emerge from open debate among holders of many different perspectives.

This shift in paradigm allows a new set of metaphors to come forward. The machine, organism and brain metaphors fade into the background to be replaced by those of 'culture' and 'political system'. These marry with and gain enhanced meaning from systems concepts, such as purpose, stakeholder, world view, boundary, dialectical debate and synthesis, to produce a powerful methodology orientated to pluralist problem contexts. SAST is well equipped to assist in structuring the exploration of different perceptions and values, and to help in bringing about a synthesis, or at least accommodation, among participants so that action can be taken.

To those who do not share SAST's commitment to the interpretive paradigm, and the culture and political system metaphors, it is an easy approach to criticize. Functionalists bemoan the lack of attention given to efficient processes and well-designed organizational structures, as their favoured machine, organism and brain metaphors are pushed aside. Emancipatory systems thinkers, employing the 'psychic prison' and 'instruments of domination' images of organization, believe it is impossible in most circumstances to achieve the participative and adversarial debate necessary for the proper application of SAST. Integration is achieved in coercive contexts, they argue, by power and domination rather than through consensual agreement. Because it lacks an emancipatory dimension (in this respect it fails to follow the implications of Churchman's systems thinking), SAST becomes little more than a kind of multigroup brainstorming, that tinkers with the ideological status quo in ways which further benefit the powerful. Its journey along the horizontal dimension of the SOSM takes SAST far enough to encounter pluralist contexts but not far enough to recognize coercive situations.

8.5 THE VALUE OF STRATEGIC ASSUMPTION SURFACING AND TESTING (SAST) TO MANAGERS

We are committed to setting down five lessons that managers can learn from each systems approach. Having gained an appreciation of SAST, it is reasonable to suggest that the following list captures the main learning it has to impart:

- SAST demonstrates that systems thinking can be employed to help managers arrive at decisions about the purposes they should pursue based on a higher order synthesis of stakeholder objectives. Systems thinking is not simply technical – it can promote effectiveness and elegance as well as efficiency and efficacy.
- The use of dialectical debate helps managers overcome the tyranny of 'either–or' – proposals and counterproposals seen as exclusive alternatives. There is the possibility of the 'and': combining two opposites as part of a new and grander synthesis.
- In the right circumstances SAST is a methodology that can encourage and orientate a participative style of problem management. The involvement of many stakeholders brings a large spread of opinion to bear on a problem situation and eases the implementation of proposed courses of action.
- It is often argued that the best and most creative debate occurs when there is strong opposition to a preferred set of proposals. The problem is that tensions arise. SAST shows that an approach can be both adversarial and integrative. The understanding gained by participants of the assumptions underlying favoured options, and of the deeply held convictions of other parties, prepares the ground for a more soundly based consensus.
- The methods associated with SAST – stakeholder analysis, assumption specification and assumption rating – are profoundly 'managerial mind supporting'. They are excellent means of feeding a comprehensive debate on planning or problem resolution and throw up many previously unconsidered issues.

8.6 CONCLUSION

As we saw in Chapter 2, during the 1960s and early 1970s systems thinking had begun to lose its way. OR and management science had become obsessed with perfecting mathematical solutions to a small range of tactical problems. Meanwhile, most of the pressing problems managers faced were of the ill-structured variety, strategic in nature and set in social systems. SAST was specifically developed by Mason and Mitroff to deal with ill-structured problems of significance to senior managers of organizations. As we have seen, it has much to offer. It is well grounded on Churchman's systems philosophy, which in practice it does much to promote. It has helped to revitalize systems thinking.

SAST is one of three soft systems approaches that we will consider in this book. In looking at the work of Ackoff and Checkland in the next two chapters we shall gain a deeper appreciation of what it is like to pursue systems thinking and practice from an interpretive perspective – and in the process enrich still further our understanding of what SAST seeks to achieve.

REFERENCES

Churchman, C.W. (1968). *The Systems Approach*. Dell Publishing, New York.

Churchman, C.W. (1971). *The Design of Inquiring Systems*. Basic Books, New York.

Churchman, C.W. (1979a). Paradise regained: A hope for the future of systems design education. In: B.A. Bayraktar, H. Muller-Merbach, J.E. Roberts and M.G. Simpson (eds), *Education in Systems Science* (pp. 17–22). Taylor & Francis, London.

Churchman, C.W. (1979b). *The Systems Approach and Its Enemies*. Basic Books, New York.

Ellis, K. (2002). Toward a systemic theory of organisational change. PhD thesis, City University, London.

Flood, R.L. (1995). *Solving Problem Solving*. John Wiley & Sons, Chichester, UK.

Flood, R.L. and Jackson, M.C. (1991). *Creative Problem Solving: Total Systems Intervention*. John Wiley & Sons, Chichester, UK.

Jackson, M.C. (1989). Assumptional analysis: An elucidation and appraisal for systems practitioners. *Systems Practice*, **2**, 11–28.

Jackson, M.C. (2000). *Systems Approaches to Management*. Kluwer/Plenum, New York.

Mason, R.O. (1969). A dialectical approach to strategic planning. *Management Science*, **15**, B403–414.

Mason, R.O. and Mitroff, I.I. (1981). *Challenging Strategic Planning Assumptions*. John Wiley & Sons, Chichester, UK.

Mitroff, I.I., Barabba, C.P. and Kilmann, R.H. (1977). The application of behavioral and philosophical techniques to strategic planning: A case study of a large federal agency. *Management Science*, **24**, 44–58.

Mitroff, I.I., Emshoff, J.R. and Kilmann, R.H. (1979). Assumption analysis: A methodology for strategic problem-solving. *Management Science*, **25**, 583–593.

Mitroff, I.I. and Linstone, H.A. (1993). *The Unbounded Mind*. Oxford University Press, New York.

Rosenhead, J. (1987). From management science to workers' science. In: M.C. Jackson and P. Keys (eds), *New Directions in Management Science* (pp. 109–131). Gower, Aldershot, UK.

Interactive Planning   9

If you read the newspapers and are still satisfied with the state of the world, put this book down; it is not for you. My objective is not to convert those who are satisfied – even though I believe they need conversion – but to give those who are dissatisfied cause for hope and something to do about it.

Ackoff (1974)

9.1 INTRODUCTION

It is a tribute to his continual inventiveness and to the power and originality of his insights that Russell Ackoff, who formulated 'interactive planning', still bestrides the world of the management sciences more than 50 years after he first came to prominence.

In that time he has inspired several new directions in the discipline: as when his research gave birth to 'social systems science' and 'community operational research'. His personal interventions have helped to develop the management sciences in various countries. And he has had a significant impact on areas of work as diverse as Operational Research (OR), corporate planning, applied social science, management information systems and management education.

Interactive planning is of particular relevance to us in this book because it was specifically designed to cope with the 'messes' that arise from the increased complexity, change and diversity that managers have to confront in the modern era (see the Preface). Ackoff (1974) argues that about the time of the Second World War the 'machine age' associated with the industrial revolution began to give way to the 'systems age'. The systems age is characterized by increasingly rapid change, by interdependence and by complex purposeful systems. It demands that much greater emphasis is placed on learning and adaptation if any kind of stability is to be achieved. This, in turn, requires a radical reorientation of world view. Machine-age thinking, based on analysis, reductionism, a search for cause–effect relations and determinism, must be complemented by systems-age thinking, which proceeds by synthesis and expansionism, tries to grasp producer–product relations and admits to the existence of free will and choice. Those who would manage organizations in the systems age, and those who would intervene to improve social systems, need a different kind of planning that reflects this new thinking – interactive planning.

9.2   DESCRIPTION OF INTERACTIVE PLANNING

9.2.1   Historical development

Ackoff's graduate work was done in the philosophy of science under the tutelage of C. West Churchman who, we saw in the last chapter, was much influenced by the American pragmatist tradition and especially the writings of E.A. Singer. Ackoff, originally trained as an architect, was a very practical philosopher. Indeed, he recounts (Ackoff, 1999a) that he was dismissed from his first professorial appointment in philosophy because he wanted to create a centre for applied philosophy and dared to put on a conference on philosophy and city planning.

Ackoff's commitment to philosophically grounded practice led him to change his academic affiliation to OR. In Chapter 4 we saw how, with Churchman, he became one of the most influential pioneers of OR in the postwar period in the USA.

The same commitment led Ackoff out of OR again when he judged that it had become wedded to its mathematical models ('mathematical masturbation' as he described it) and lost touch with the real issues that concern managers. In his view (Ackoff, 1981) those who continue to work in the vein of hard systems thinking, with its emphasis on optimization and objectivity, inevitably opt out of tackling the important issues of the systems age. To cling to optimization in a world of multiple values and rapid change is to lose your grip on reality. The emphasis has to be on adapting and learning. Objectivity in the conventional sense is also a myth. Purposeful behaviour cannot be value-free.

Disillusioned with OR, Ackoff (1974, 1981) set out to develop a more all-encompassing systems approach, giving the name 'social systems sciences' (S^3) to the educational and consultancy activities he initiated at the

University of Pennsylvania. Interactive planning is the main vehicle for putting S^3 into effect.

9.2.2 Philosophy and theory

Ackoff's (1974) general philosophical orientation endorses that of Churchman, and he has contributed to the new understanding of 'objectivity' that is embraced in soft systems thinking. For him, the conventional view that objectivity results from constructing value-free models that are then verified or falsified against some real world 'out there' is misguided. Objectivity in social systems science can only be approached through the interaction of groups of individuals with diverse values. It can be approximated by science seen as a system, but not by individual scientists. It is 'value full', not value-free.

These conclusions lead to some distinctive Ackovian themes. One is that planning and design must be based on wide participation and involvement. Another is that improvement needs to be sought on the basis of the client's own criteria. It may well be that the analyst's model of reality differs markedly from that of the client. Nevertheless, if you want to serve that client you are better off granting rationality to him or her than rationality to yourself as the analyst. A linked idea is that people must be allowed to plan for themselves. People's own ideals and values must be paramount in the planning process; although operationalizing that process may require assistance from professional planners. This sidesteps one of the major paradoxes of conventional planning, how to quantify quality of life, since this only strikes if you are trying to plan for somebody else.

Ackoff's philosophy acquires a more precise meaning when we see it applied to the management of organizations in the 'systems age'. Those who manage corporations in the modern era, he argues (Ackoff, 1981), need to alter the way they think about them. In the past it has been usual to regard corporations either as machines serving the purposes of their creators or owners, or as organisms serving their own purposes. Today, organizations must be viewed as social systems serving three sets of purposes: their own, those of their parts and those of the wider systems of which they are part. It follows that corporations have responsibilities to themselves (control problem), to their parts (humanization problem) and to those wider systems (environmentalization problem). Managers should seek to serve purposes at all these three levels, developing their organization's various stakeholders and removing any apparent conflict between them. If this is achieved, internal and external stakeholders will continue to pursue their interests through the organization and ensure that it remains viable and effective.

Ackoff has devised a new approach to planning, which he believes reflects the nature of the systems age and responds to the three sets of purposes. It is called 'interactive planning' and brings his philosophy to bear on systems of interdependent problems, or messes, set in social systems. It is best understood if it is compared with three other ideal types of planning: reactivist, inactivist and preactivist.

Reactivist planners want to return to some 'golden age' they believe existed in the past. They treat problems in a piecemeal fashion and fail to grasp current realities. Inactivists want to keep things as they are. They too treat problems separately as they muddle through, trying to avoid real change. Their approach is to satisfice as they try to resolve day-to-day difficulties. Preactivist planners are future-orientated and seek to predict what is going to happen in order that they can prepare for it. Their aim is optimization on the basis of forecasting techniques and quantitative models that allow problems to be solved. To Ackoff this 'predict and prepare' approach is illogical since if the future was so determined that we could accurately predict it, there would also be nothing we could do about changing it.

Ackoff's preferred approach is interactive planning (see Ackoff, 1974, 1981, 1999a, 1999b). Interactivists do not want to return to the past, keep things as they are or accept some inevitable future. They take into account the past, the present and predictions about the future, but use these only as partial inputs into a methodology of planning aimed at designing a desirable future and inventing ways of bringing it about. Interactivists believe that the future can be affected by what the stakeholders of an organization do now – especially if they are motivated to reach out for ideals. In the process problems simply 'dissolve' because the system and/or environment giving rise to them is changed so radically.

Ackoff recounts how severe inventory and customer satisfaction problems plagued General Electric's Appliance Division because of uncertainty about how many left-hinged and right-hinged refrigerators to build. The problem failed to respond to either resolving (salesmen-generated forecasts) or solving (statistically based forecasts) approaches. It was eventually dissolved by designing refrigerators with doors that could be mounted on either side and thus could be made to open either way. As well as eliminating the inventory mix problem, this proved an attractive marketing feature as customers were not faced with the possibility of having to replace their fridge when they moved.

We have noted the depth and breadth of Ackoff's influence in the management sciences. An important explanation is the inspiring vision he presents for the discipline, deriving from his philosophy and theory. The job of the systems practitioner is no longer just to build mathematical models in order to enable key decision-makers to 'predict and prepare' their enterprises for an inevitable future. Rather, it is to assist all the stakeholders to design a desirable future for themselves and to invent the means of realizing it.

While carrying out development work with leaders of the Mantua ghetto in Philadelphia, Ackoff was delighted to find many of the lessons he was trying to impart to management scientists captured in the motto of the Mantua Community Planners: 'plan or be planned for'. These sentiments, in turn, bring to mind the words of the English poet William Blake (1815):

> *I must Create a System, or be enslaved by another Man's;*
> *I will not Reason and Compare: my business is to Create.*

It is indeed the case that the spirit of Blake's words is well captured in Russell Ackoff's work. He has shown why they are apposite to systems thinking and why they are just as relevant, probably more relevant, to the systems age as to the time when Blake wrote them. Ackoff's achievement goes beyond this, however. For in his book *Creating the Corporate Future*, subtitled 'plan or be planned for', he sets out a detailed methodology that can actively be used by stakeholders to plan and pursue a desirable future.

9.2.3 Methodology

Three principles underpin the methodology of interactive planning (Ackoff, 1981, 1999b). The first is the *participative* principle. If possible all stakeholders should participate in the various phases of the planning process. This is the only way of ensuring 'objectivity'. It also secures the main benefit of planning – the involvement of members of the organization in the process. This is more important than the actual plan produced. It is by being involved in the process that stakeholders come to understand the role they can play in the organization. It follows, of course, that no one can plan for anyone else. The role of professional planners is not to do the planning, but to help others plan for themselves.

The second principle is that of *continuity*. Because values change and unexpected events occur, plans need to be constantly revised.

The third is the *holistic* principle. Because of the importance of the inter-actions between the parts of a system, we should plan simultaneously and interdependently for as many parts and levels of the organization as possible.

With these principles in mind we can now consider the five phases of the interactive planning methodology itself:

- formulating the mess;
- ends planning;
- means planning;
- resource planning;
- implementation and control.

These phases may be started in any order and none of the phases, let alone the whole set, should ever be regarded as completed. They constitute a systemic process.

Formulating the 'mess' involves determining the future an organization would be in if it were to continue its current plans, policies and practices, and if its environment changed only in ways that it expected. It demonstrates that every organization needs to adapt. Three types of study are necessary:

- systems analysis – giving a detailed picture of the organization, what it does, its stakeholders and relationships with its environment;
- obstruction analysis – setting out any obstacles to corporate development;
- reference projections – extrapolating on the organization's present performance in order to predict future performance if nothing is done and trends in the environment continue in entirely predictable ways.

Synthesizing the results of these three types of study yields a 'reference scenario', which is a formulation of the mess in which the organization currently finds itself. It reveals the seeds of self-destruction inherent in its current policies, practices, plans and external expectations.

Phase 2, ends planning, is about 'where to go' and involves specifying the purposes to be pursued in terms of ideals, objectives and goals. It has five steps. First, a mission statement is prepared. This should outline the organization's ultimate ends (its 'ideals'), incorporate the organization's responsibilities to its environment and stakeholders, and aim to generate widespread commitment. Second, planners should help the stakeholders to prepare a comprehensive list of the desired properties stakeholders agree should be built into the system. Third, an 'idealized design' of the organization should be prepared. The fourth step requires formulation of the closest approximation to this design that is believed to be attainable. Finally, the gaps between the approximation and the current state of the system should be identified.

Idealized design is both the unique and most essential feature of Ackoff's approach. It should capture the vision that the stakeholders have for the organization. An idealized design is the design for the enterprise that the stakeholders would replace the existing system with today, if they were free to do so. The idea that the system of concern was destroyed 'last night', no longer exists and can be designed afresh today, is meant to generate maximum creativity among those involved.

It is recommended that idealized design should be repeated twice – once to produce a 'bounded' design, assuming no changes in the wider system, and once to produce an 'unbounded' design, assuming that changes in the containing system can be made. In Ackoff's view, designers will find that most organizations can be considerably improved just within the context of the bounded design. This is because the barriers to change are usually in the decision-makers' own minds and in the organization itself.

To ensure that creativity is not hindered during idealized design only three constraints on the design are admissible. First, it must be technologically feasible, and not a work of science fiction. It can be based on likely technological developments, but not, for example, on telepathy. Second, it must be operationally viable: capable of working and surviving if it were implemented in what would be its environment now. Third, the design must be capable of being continuously improved. The aim of idealized design is not to produce a fixed 'Utopia', but an 'ideal-seeking system' that will be in constant flux as it responds to changing values, new knowledge and information, and buffeting from external forces. Beyond these three constraints everything is open. Constraints of a political, financial or similar kind are not allowed to restrict the creativity of the design.

An idealized design should cover all aspects of an organization and Ackoff (1999b) provides the following as a typical list:

- Products and services to be offered.
- Markets to be served.
- Distribution system.
- Organizational structure.
- Internal financial structure.

- Management style.
- Internal functions, such as –
  - purchasing;
  - manufacturing;
  - maintenance;
  - engineering;
  - marketing and sales;
  - research and development;
  - finance;
  - accounting;
  - human resources;
  - buildings and grounds;
  - communications, internal and external;
  - legal;
  - planning;
  - organizational development;
  - computing and data processing.
- Administrative services (e.g., mail and duplicating).
- Facilities.
- Industry, government and community affairs.

The remaining three phases of interactive planning are aimed at the realization of the idealized design, at closing the gaps that have been identified in the final step of that process.

Means planning is concerned with 'how to get there'. Policies and procedures are generated and examined to decide whether they are capable of helping to close the gap between the desired future, the idealized design and the future the organization is currently locked into according to the reference scenario. Creativity is needed to discover appropriate means of bringing the organization toward the desirable future invented by its stakeholders. Alternative means must be carefully evaluated and a selection made.

Resource planning involves working out 'what's needed to get there'. Five types of resource should be taken into account:

- money;
- plant and equipment (capital goods);
- people;
- materials, supplies, energy and services (consumables);
- data, information, knowledge, understanding and wisdom.

Each of the chosen means will require appropriate resources. It must be determined how much of each resource is wanted, when it is wanted and how it can be obtained if not already held. It almost always turns out that there is an excess or a shortage in terms of the initial means plan. This, in turn, leads to a planning cycle in which either a productive use of excesses is found or they have to be disposed of, or shortages have to be overcome or plans changed.

Implementation and control is about 'doing it' and learning from what happens. Procedures must be established for ensuring that all the decisions made hitherto are carried out. Who is to do what, when, where and how is decided. Once implementation is achieved the results need to be monitored to ensure that plans are being realized. The outcome is fed back into the planning process so that learning is possible and improvements can be devised.

9.2.4 Methods

Readers of Ackoff's books and articles will find him using many methods, tools and techniques in support of the interactive planning process. Here we concentrate on four models that he believes should be employed to help shift from a 'mechanistic' or 'organismic' to a social–systemic form of organization; and so are essential to the establishment and success of interactive planning. In considering these four models – of a 'democratic hierarchy', a 'learning and adaptation support system', an 'internal market economy' and a 'multidimensional organizational structure' – we also need to bear in mind Ackoff's injunction that transformational leadership is essential in putting them into effect.

The need for a democratic hierarchy, or 'circular organization', arises: from the fact that managers are best employed focusing on the interactions of the parts rather than on controlling the parts directly; from the rising level of educational attainment among the workforce; and from dissatisfaction, in democratic societies, with working in organizations structured along Stalinist lines (Ackoff, 1999b). The proposed democratic organization strongly supports the participative principle that underpins interactive planning.

In a circular organization every manager within the organization is provided with a 'board'. At the top level this will involve external stakeholders as well. Each manager's board should minimally consist of the manager whose board it is, the immediate superior of this manager and the immediate subordinates of this manager. This design is shown in Figure 9.1 (from

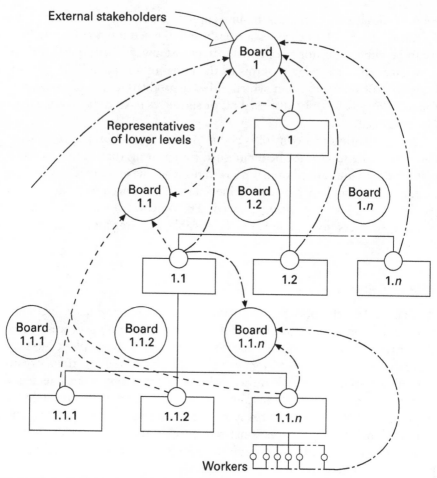

Figure 9.1 A circular organization.
From Ackoff (1999a), reproduced by permission of John Wiley & Sons.

Ackoff, 1999a). The functions of the board are defined as planning for the unit whose board it is, policy for that unit, co-ordination, integration, quality of work life, performance improvement and approval (if necessary, dismissal) of the head of unit. Although this arrangement may seem un-wieldy and time-consuming, Ackoff's experience is that the benefits in terms of synergy and motivation are very considerable.

The model of a learning and adaptation support system should be used in constructing the 'ideal-seeking system' that carries the idealized design. It contains five essential functions (Ackoff, 1999a, b):

- identification and formulation of threats, opportunities and problems;
- decision-making – determining what to do about these;
- implementation;
- control – monitoring performance and modifying actions;
- acquisition or generation, and distribution of the information necessary to carry out other functions.

This model is built on an array of feedback controls and takes account of the work of Argyris and Schön on organizational learning, especially the importance of double-loop learning. It also insists that an organization monitor errors of omission as well as errors of commission. Errors of omission, which occur when something is not done that should have been done, are usually ignored in bureaucracies that tend to be much more interested in punishing people who do things.

Ackoff (1999b) has found that many organizational problems involve 'internal finance'. These can be dissolved if the typical centrally planned and controlled corporate economy is replaced with an internal market economy. Every unit within an organization, including the executive office, must become a profit centre or a cost centre for which some profit centre is responsible. It should then be permitted to purchase goods and services from any internal and external supplier it chooses and sell its output to any buyer it wishes. Higher authorities can override these decisions, but if they do so are required to compensate the unit for any loss of income or increased costs that arise due to the intervention.

A multidimensional organizational structure (Ackoff, 1999b) is recommended because it increases flexibility and eliminates the need for continual restructuring. Organizations divide their labour in three ways and, in so doing, create three types of unit:

- functionally defined units whose output is primarily consumed internally;
- production- or service-defined units whose output is primarily consumed externally;
- market- or user-defined units defined by type or location of customers.

Restructuring occurs when the relative importance of the three ways of dividing labour changes and the system adjusts the level in the hierarchy at which different types of unit are manifested. Ackoff argues that time and effort can be saved if units of each type are placed permanently at every level. Reorganization can then be replaced by reallocating resources.

9.2.5   Recent developments

In recent times Ackoff (1999a) has felt obliged to use his considerable intellect to denounce the 'panaceas, fads and quick fixes' with which managers are assailed and to which they are, unfortunately, prone. He shows that such approaches as quality management, business process re-engineering and the balanced scorecard are always likely to fail because they are fundamentally antisystemic. They treat the whole as an aggregation of parts that can be improved independently of one another. As systems thinking explains, this often does not lead to any improvement in the performance of the whole because it is the interactions between the parts that are fundamental and need managing.

Another recent development is the establishment of the Ackoff Center for Advancement of Systems Approaches (ACASA) at the University of Pennsylvania. This is significant because Ackoff has often had problems integrating the entrepreneurial and practice-orientated units he has pioneered in normal university structures. It provides a base from which the Ackovian form of systems thinking can be further refined and applied to the many organizational, societal and world problems to which it is relevant.

9.3   INTERACTIVE PLANNING IN ACTION

The account that follows picks some highlights from an interactive planning project conducted in the DuPont Specialty Chemicals Safety, Health and Environment (SHE) Function. Further details can be found in Leeman (2002), who was central throughout. Ackoff was involved at various points as an advisor and has endorsed the project as a good example by including a version in *Re-creating the Corporation* (1999b). My account is drawn from these two sources. During the period that the work was ongoing (1995–1998) DuPont was undergoing major corporate-wide transformation and downsizing. The circumstances were not necessarily favourable, therefore, for a successful application of interactive planning.

Throughout its long history, in the chemical production industry, DuPont has prided itself on the attention it pays to the health and safety of its employees. More recently, it has evinced similar concern about its impact on the environment. The year 1994 saw a further step forward in all these areas when its SHE policy was revised and released as 'The DuPont Commitment – Safety, Health and the Environment'. From this commitment, the corporation derived a new slogan, 'The Goal is ZERO'. Its business units were to aim for zero injuries and illnesses, zero wastes and emissions, and zero environmental, process and transportation accidents and incidents. In the Specialty Chemicals business unit it was recognized that this meant the SHE function would need to go about its work in a radically different fashion.

Leeman realized that bringing about such a transformation would require a methodology that allowed purposes to be rethought and new goals systemically pursued, and that encouraged widespread participation. Following a chance meeting with Ackoff and an analysis using the System Of Systems Methodologies (SOSM) (see Chapter 2), it became apparent that interactive planning would be suitable.

Mess formulation was curtailed as Ackoff pointed out that DuPont was already a leader in needed, occupational health and environmental protection, and the real effort, therefore, should go into improving its leadership position by gaining competitive advantage by further developing the excellence of its SHE function. Nevertheless, a brief systems analysis was conducted to ensure that SHE professionals were fully acquainted with Specialty Chemicals' businesses. And a brief obstruction analysis helped to reveal certain weaknesses in the way SHE performed its current role. It was structured in a centralized–hierarchical manner with a regulative rather than facilitative orientation. As a result its expertise was not integrated into business decision-making. SHE professionals were caught in a situation of having to perform a multitude of mundane tasks and operating in a reactive mode to crises. Knowledge management was poor.

Ends planning, featuring idealized design, was divided into two parts. First, a group of consumers of SHE information and knowledge was invited to specify the properties of an ideal SHE system. Second, a designer group was asked to redesign the SHE system according to those specifications.

The consumer group consisted of individuals from Specialty Chemicals chosen on the basis of six criteria:

- they use SHE information;
- they are responsible for its implementation;
- they are capable of specifying what they need from a SHE system;
- they represented diversity in thought and in gender and race;
- they are capable of thinking 'out of the box';
- they understand the need for SHE and its role in the business.

A number of SHE professionals were irritated by the role given to the consumer group, believing that only they had the expertise to contribute sensibly to the redesign of SHE.

A first session concentrated on identifying positive and negative outputs from the current SHE system. Some of Senge's ideas (see Chapter 5) helped the group to recognize the main structural problem as being the failure of the SHE function to connect to the business needs of the Strategic Business Units (SBUs). The next step was to specify the properties for an ideal SHE system based on the presumption that the existing system had been destroyed the night before and the new system could be designed unhindered by traditional constraints. The consumer group identified 58 specifications for the ideal system; later narrowed to 19 and categorized in 9 major arenas.

The designer group was then put together, consisting of an even number of SHE professionals and other managers from within Specialty Chemicals with detailed knowledge of SHE. The group was tasked with designing an ideal SHE system, to replace the one destroyed the previous night, using all the specifications from the consumer group and being sure to *dissolve* all the negative outputs that had been identified.

The process began with the identification of nine stakeholders crucial to SHE's success: customers; employees; representatives from plant sites; business functions; government agencies; SBUs; local communities; the DuPont Company; and the corporate SHE function. The expectations of each of these groups with regard to the SHE system were considered. John Pourdehnad, from ACASA, then suggested following a version of idealized design that required three iterations of four major steps:

- creating a mission statement;
- identifying the functions of the SHE system;
- formulating the processes for doing the SHE work;
- organizing the SHE structure to do the SHE work.

The final version of the mission statement read as follows:

A seamless SHE system that integrates, enables, and installs the core DuPont SHE competency to successfully make chemicals, win in business, and sustain our communities.

Paying attention to stakeholder expectations, the designer group then identified the key functions that the redesigned SHE system needed to offer. The eventual list was:

- performance auditing and analysis;
- related project front-end loading guidance;

- training and education;
- personnel development;
- knowledge and learning;
- risk assessment and recommendations;
- federal, state and local regulatory advocacy;
- community interactions;
- methodology and technology development;
- management and decision-making (planning);
- core competency management;
- information management.

For each function the group then designed the necessary work processes for getting the work done. Finally, an organizational structure was proposed for SHE that provided for appropriate relationships between units and flows of responsibility, authority, communications and resources, in order to deliver the functions to the businesses. At the end of the three iterations the designer group was convinced that their idealized design would meet stakeholder expectations, match consumer specifications and dissolve all the output issues. The SHE ideal system is shown compared with the SHE current state, in terms of mission, function, process and structure, in Table 9.1.

The next phase of interactive planning, means planning, involves determining how the gaps between the idealized design and the current state are going to be filled. The team chosen for this task consisted of SHE professionals from within Specialty Chemicals, most of whom had also been in the designer group. The critical gaps identified were as follows:

- current SHE system does not adjust to changing needs;
- SHE professionals do not have time to deliver the 'high value' functions – prevention versus intervention;
- we currently do not deliver many of the ideal state primary functions;
- we do not know where the 'required inputs' reside;
- SHE is focused on operations, not on increasing the business competitive advantage.

For each of these, ways of closing the gap were proposed. For example, 'SHE is focused on operations ...' could be addressed by:

- clearly defined connections between SHE and business leaders;
- clearly defined and supported SHE functions for business teams and customers;
- make SHE part of the SBU staff to increase status.

Leeman emphasizes the efforts needed during this phase to keep the team focused, integrated and committed, and to ensure continued high-level management support.

The resource plan, aimed at identifying and providing the resources necessary to bridge the gaps and realize the idealized design, was then put in place. This consisted of personnel planning, financial planning, facilities and equipment planning, and materials, suppliers and services planning. In personnel planning, for example, the need to hire a full-time project manager and new facilitator, and to set up eight SHE knowledge networks, a core team and a steering team were identified.

Implementation concerns who is going to do what, when, where and how. It was achieved successfully by paying particular attention to 'the human factor', 'the organizational factor' and 'the commitment factor', and by ensuring that controls over implementation were designed that allowed tracking of progress.

At the end of the interactive planning project in DuPont, it was possible to identify the following clear benefits:

- a step-change improvement in SHE performance, shown by the most significant improvement in operational SHE performance metrics in its history;
- SHE work was aligned with business goals and objectives to such an extent that relationships between SHE professionals and people in the business were transformed into a partnership;
- SHE began to be perceived as a value-adding profit centre rather than a 'cost-of-doing-business' unit, and its services became highly valued by the wider organization and recognized as a powerful differentiator by external customers;
- organizational learning flourished among SHE professionals who were enabled to do more higher value-adding work, while their knowledge was made available to all to aid decision-making and routine SHE tasks were carried out by line employees;
- a wider range of creative and less expensive solutions to SHE issues and problems were explored and implemented.

Table 9.1 Safety, Health and Environment (SHE) fundamental changes.

SHE current state	SHE ideal state
Mission	*Mission*
1. Compliance-driven	1. Stakeholder-driven
2. Reactive/Intervention	2. Proactive/Prevention
3. Not aligned with business	3. Fully integrated within the business
4. Cost of doing business	4. Revenue enhancer/Value adder
Function	*Function*
1. SHE is operations support	1. SHE is business, operations and customer support
2. Regulation tracking and interpretation	2. Regulation knowledge: • shaping regulations • quick access to regulation interpretations • shaping business plans
3. SHE training	3. SHE education
4. Data/Information generation	4. Knowledge/Understanding generation
Process	*Process*
1. Policing through auditing	1. Risk assessment and loss prevention
2. Government report preparation	2. Automated/Electronic reporting
3. Manual data collection/documentation	3. Automated data collection/documentation
4. Classroom training	4. Online learn–teach–learn SHE system
Structure	*Structure*
1. SHE is 'centralized'	1. SHE is leveraged and distributed
2. 'Stovepiped'	2. SHE is on cross-functional business teams
3. Hierarchical	3. 'Lowerarchical'
4. SHE personnel confined to plant	4. SHE personnel on transunit teams
5. Line accountable for safety	5. Business and line accountable for SHE
6. SHE reports to operations	6. SHE reports to vice-president/general manager

Leeman is convinced that the project's success was due to the principles of participation, continuity and holism embraced and operationalized through interactive planning. The idealized design process was essential for unleashing creativity, and participation ensured that energy and commitment levels were maintained during the hard work of implementation.

9.4 CRITIQUE OF INTERACTIVE PLANNING

Ackoff's development of interactive planning, with its commitment to dissolving problems by designing a desirable future and inventing ways of bringing it about, has taken him a long way from some of his erstwhile colleagues stuck in the predict-and-prepare paradigm of hard systems thinking. In the systems age, he believes, it has become necessary to shift the emphasis of management science toward exploring purposes and institutionalizing agreed ideals, objectives and goals in a manner that allows for continuous learning and adaptation. Idealized design seeks to harness the diverse purposes of different stakeholders by focusing their attention away from petty differences onto the ends they would all like to see their organization pursue. Participation at the different stages of the planning process allows stakeholders to incorporate their aesthetic values in the idealized design and the means necessary to realize it. Doing the right things (effectiveness) according to the values of stakeholders and in ways that are pleasing to them (elegance) are central to Ackoff's approach.

Ackoff has demonstrated the usefulness of interactive planning as a practical systems approach in hundreds of projects with organizations of all types in the USA and elsewhere. Much of its success is due, he believes (Ackoff, 1999a), to the fact that it is based on an appropriate kind of systems model. In explaining this, he argues that there are four different types of system. 'Deterministic' systems have no purposes and neither do their parts (although they can serve the purposes of other purposeful systems). 'Animated' systems have purposes of their own, but their parts do not. 'Social' systems have purposes of their own, contain purposeful parts and are usually parts of larger purposeful systems. 'Ecological' systems contain interacting mechanistic, organismic and social systems, but unlike social systems have no purposes of their own. They serve the purposes of the biological and social systems that are their parts. Problems arise if a model appropriate to one type of system is applied to a system of a different type.

Ackoff builds interactive planning, as we have seen, on the back of a purposeful systems model. This is appropriate to organizations, he believes, because social systems are purposeful systems containing other purposeful systems and are part of wider purposeful systems. Interactive planning seeks to galvanize stakeholders, upholding various purposes, in pursuit of a vision of what their organizations might be like. It conducts a process that can generate consensus, mobilize stakeholders and reveal to them that only their own limited imaginations prevent them from getting the future they most desire right here, right now. Those who apply deterministic or animate models to social systems may sometimes bring benefits, over a short period of time, but in the longer run they will get less desirable results because these models omit to consider what is essential about social systems.

It needs remembering, though, that while Ackoff distances himself from deterministic and animate models, and builds interactive planning on a more sophisticated view of the nature of organizations, he is still willing to make use of what the earlier thinking had to offer in support of his own pre-ferred S^3. Systems age thinking complements rather than replaces machine age thinking and, for example, Ackoff's model of a 'learning and adaptation support system', recommended for use in support of interactive planning, has much in common with Beer's neurocybernetic 'viable system model'.

Critics of Ackoff (see Jackson, 1982, 1983, 2000; Flood and Jackson, 1991) concentrate on what they see as a bias in the particular social systems model that he endorses. There has always been a tension in social theory between those who emphasize the consensual and those who concentrate on the conflictual aspects of social systems. To his critics, the nature of interactive planning suggests that Ackoff's orientation is toward consensus. He seems to believe that there is a basic community of interests among stakeholders, which will make them willing to enter into interactive planning and to participate freely and openly in idealized design. It appears that there are no fundamental conflicts of interest between and within system, wider system and subsystem that cannot be dissolved by appealing to this basic community of interests.

It is further argued that it is only because Ackoff believes in a basically con-sensual social world that he is able to lay such store by participation as a remedy for so many organizational ills. Participation is essential to interactive planning because it guarantees the 'objectivity' of the results and because it generates creativity and commitment, and ensures implementation. Critics point to various barriers to full and effective participation. The powerful may not be willing to enter into a debate about an idealized design that would result in them losing their influence and prestige. Even if interactive planning can be got under way, we cannot expect that all the stakeholders will be able to participate equally. They will enter the process with widely divergent economic, political and international resources. The less fortunate will be disadvantaged and the debate will be exceptionally constrained.

All this seems obvious to those who argue that conflict is endemic in social and organizational systems and that incompatibility of interests is common. Such critics see Ackoff as operating at the ideological level to smooth over subjective differences of opinion. In their view, however, permanent resolution of conflicts between stakeholders needs to be in terms of objective and not merely subjective interests, and may require a revolution in the whole social structure.

Ackoff (1982, pers. commun. 2003) argues back that in every case in which conflicting parties have been willing to meet him, face to face, he has been able to find a solution to the conflict. If participation proves to be an issue, it is possible to work at gradually increasing the involvement of less privileged stakeholders and assisting them when they do get involved. What do the critics expect? It is surely better to work with stakeholders to see what changes are possible in the circumstances prevailing than to wait for ever for the arrival of a Utopia in which no inequalities exist. Furthermore, if he comes across genuinely irresolvable conflicts and cannot bring the parties together, Ackoff is quite prepared to work with the willing (usually disadvantaged) party to help them get what they want and what he feels is just. He will not work for clients whose values he cannot endorse.

The critics respond that Ackoff underestimates the frequency of irresolvable conflicts because he does not seek to challenge his sponsors' interests. By getting the disadvantaged to believe they have interests in common with the powerful he is locking them further into 'false-consciousness' and depriving them of the ability to represent properly their real interests.

In the exchanges between Ackoff and his critics we are witnessing a war between sociological paradigms. In breaking with hard systems thinking and establishing S^3, Ackoff was moving from a functionalist rationale, emphasizing making systems work more efficiently, to an interpretive rationale emphasizing the need for mutually agreed purposes among stakeholders. To critics of an emancipatory persuasion, however, both these positions remain 'regulative'. What Ackoff is missing is an understanding of the forms of power and domination that distort social systems and that can only be overcome by radical change. In terms of the SOSM, Ackoff explores the 'participants dimension' far enough to take account of pluralism, but not far enough to be able to recognize coercion.

Metaphor analysis provides further insight. Ackoff is not happy with looking at corporations, in the systems age, as though they are machines or organisms. His purposeful systems view brings the culture and political system metaphors to the fore. The problem, for emancipatory theorists, is that this still leaves out of account the metaphors that they most value – organizations as psychic prisons and as instruments of domination.

Ackoff's work is powerful because it addresses a wide variety of organizational issues as revealed by a number of important metaphors. It responds to the idea that organizations depend on a political coalition of stakeholders sharing something of a common culture, as well as recognizing that they should be designed to promote learning, like brains. The machine and organism models are seen as useful too – in a dependent role and in the right circumstances. Recognition of the different insights provided by this range of metaphors gives Ackoff access to almost the full dictionary of significant systems ideas and concepts. And the process is not finished. Jamshid Gharajedaghi (1999), a disciple of Ackoff's, has sought to interpret chaos and complexity theory in an interactive planning framework. Ackoff (1999b) has taken to talking of his 'multidimensional organizational structure' as a fractal design. What if anything Ackoff misses seeing, in terms of emancipatory and postmodern concerns, can be judged from a review of the approaches described under Types C and D in this part of the book.

9.5 THE VALUE OF INTERACTIVE PLANNING TO MANAGERS

The advantages for managers of adopting interactive planning are said to be many, and these are well documented in Ackoff's work. The five most frequently cited and evidenced are the following:

- The approach facilitates the participation of all stakeholders in the planning process and therefore secures the main benefit of planning, continuous engagement in the process itself and not the production of some final document.
- Allowing stakeholders to be dominant in the planning process and to incorporate their own aesthetic values into planning relieves professional planners of the impossible task of measuring 'quality' on behalf of others.
- Idealized design releases large amounts of suppressed creativity and harnesses it to organizational and personal development.
- Interactive planning expands participants' conception of what is possible

and reveals that the biggest obstructions to achieving the future we most desire are often self-imposed constraints.
- The participative principle helps generate consensus and commitment, and eases the implementation of the outcomes of planning.

9.6 CONCLUSION

Interactive planning was developed by Ackoff to assist stakeholders design a desirable future for themselves, their organization and the environment it inhabits, and to help them invent ways of bringing that future about. This is a powerful vision of the role of management science and explains in large part why Ackoff's work has had such a colossal impact on the OR and systems communities.

Examined in detail, and in terms of what it is really able to deliver, interactive planning does not disappoint. It is arguable, however, that no approach can be comprehensive enough to achieve what Ackoff wants from interactive planning and that, in representing itself as being comprehensive, it inevitably disguises its own particular biases. Creative holism or critical systems thinking, as we will see in Part III, shares the vision, but tries to pursue it in a rather different way.

REFERENCES

Ackoff, R.L. (1974). *Redesigning the Future*. John Wiley & Sons, New York.
Ackoff, R.L. (1981). *Creating the Corporate Future*. John Wiley & Sons, New York.
Ackoff, R.L. (1982). On the hard headedness and soft heartedness of M.C. Jackson. *Journal of Applied Systems Analysis*, **9**, 31–33.
Ackoff, R.L. (1999a). *Ackoff's Best: His Classic Writings on Management*. John Wiley & Sons, New York.
Ackoff, R.L. (1999b). *Re-creating the Corporation: A Design of Organizations for the 21st Century*. Oxford University Press, New York.
Blake, W. (1815). *Jerusalem* (Chapter 1).
Flood, R.L. and Jackson, M.C. (1991). *Creative Problem Solving: Total Systems Intervention*. John Wiley & Sons, Chichester, UK.
Gharajedaghi, J. (1999). *Systems Thinking: Managing Chaos and Complexity*. Butterworth-Heinemann, Boston.

Jackson, M.C. (1982). The nature of soft systems thinking: The work of Churchman, Ackoff and Checkland. *Journal of Applied Systems Analysis* **9**, 17–28.

Jackson, M.C. (1983). The nature of soft systems thinking: Comments on the three replies. *Journal of Applied Systems Analysis*, **10**, 109–113.

Jackson, M.C. (2000). *Systems Approaches to Management*. Kluwer/Plenum, New York.

Leeman, J.E. (2002). Applying interactive planning at DuPont. *Systems Practice and Action Research*, **15**, 85–109.

Soft Systems Methodology   10

Here we need to remember that what in the end turns out to be feasible will itself be affected by the learning generated by the project itself: human situations are never static.

Checkland and Scholes (1990)

10.1 INTRODUCTION

Peter Checkland, the founder of Soft Systems Methodology (SSM), studied chemistry and did research on spectroscopy at Oxford before spending 15 years with ICI, initially as a technical officer later as a group manager. As his managerial responsibilities increased in ICI, he began to look for assistance to the literature of management science, then dominated by 'hard systems thinking'. He was shocked and disappointed to find that much of what he read was completely irrelevant to his job. Management science was in thrall to the 'goal-seeking' paradigm exemplified in the work of the Nobel Prize winner Herbert Simon. Checkland regarded this as an inadequate formulation in terms of the actual practice of management, which he later came to describe, following Geoffrey Vickers, as much more about 'relationship maintaining'.

A growing fascination with such matters, together with an interest in the application of systems ideas, led Checkland to leave ICI and to join the first 'systems' department in the UK: the Department of Systems Engineering established at Lancaster University, with a grant from ICI, by Professor Gwilym Jenkins. There, in 1969, he began the research from which SSM emerged.

SSM is a methodology, setting out principles for the use of methods, that enables intervention in ill-structured problem situations where relationship maintaining is at least as important as goal-seeking and answering questions about 'what' we should do as significant as determining 'how' to do it. The success of SSM has been central to the soft systems revolution which has liberated systems thinking from the intellectual straightjacket in which it was locked and, at the same time, has made it much more relevant to managers. Today, SSM is used by both academics and practitioners, is important in a number of applied disciplines (e.g., 'information systems') and has spread its influence to many countries outside the UK.

10.2 DESCRIPTION OF SOFT SYSTEMS METHODOLOGY (SSM)

10.2.1 Historical development

The systems approach used in the newly established department at Lancaster University was inevitably Jenkins' systems engineering, as described in Chapter 4. This demanded well-structured problems and clearly defined objectives and measures of performance; it was a typical hard systems methodology. Jenkins was determined, however, that systems engineering should not stagnate, which it was likely to do if its study became purely 'academic', and so he initiated an action research programme in which the approach was 'tested' in real organizations outside the University. A virtuous circle of interaction between ideas and experience became possible and was fully exploited in later years by Checkland and his coworkers at Lancaster.

The research strategy adopted by Checkland when he arrived at Lancaster was to try to use Jenkins' systems engineering approach to tackle management problems and to learn from the results. During the course of this action research the methodology had to be radically changed to make it appropriate for dealing with the greater complexity and ambiguity of the managerial as opposed to the engineering context. What eventually emerged after considerable project work and reflection on the experience gained was an entirely different kind of approach – Checkland's SSM (see Checkland, 1981, 1999).

In the first full account of this methodology, Checkland (1976) describes three of the most significant early project experiences that led to the break from systems engineering and the formulation of SSM. In all three it was clear that serious problems existed in the organizations of interest, but the clients simply could not say what they were in precise terms. Each of the problem situations was vague and unstructured. One of the projects, in a textile firm, gave rise to at least a dozen candidates for the role of 'the problem'. Generalizing from these three projects, Checkland was able to specify how SSM needed to differentiate itself from hard approaches.

First, in confronting 'softer' problems the analysis phase of a methodology should not be pursued in systems terms. In the absence of agreed goals and objectives, or an obvious hierarchy of systems to be engineered, using systems ideas too early can lead to a distortion of the problem situation and to jumping to premature conclusions. Analysis, in soft systems approaches, should consist of building up the richest possible picture of the problem situation rather than trying to capture it in systems models.

Second, given that it is not obvious which if any system needs to be engineered, it is more appropriate from the analysis to define a range of systems possibly relevant to improving the problem situation, each expressing a particular world view (or *Weltanschauung*). These notional systems can be named in 'root definitions' and developed more fully in 'conceptual models'. The use of SSM will therefore lead to the construction of a number of models to be compared with the real world, rather than just one as in hard methodologies.

These models represent 'human activity systems', and Checkland came to recognize their delineation as one of the most important breakthroughs in the development of SSM. Previous systems thinkers had sought to model physical systems, designed systems, even social systems, but they had not treated purposeful human activity systemically. A human activity system is a model of a notional system containing the activities people need to undertake in order to pursue a particular purpose.

Finally, while the models produced by hard approaches are meant to be models of the real world or blueprints for design, human activity system models are contributions to a debate about change. They explicitly set out what activities are necessary to achieve a purpose meaningful from a particular point of view. On the basis of such models, participants in the problem situation aim to learn their way to what changes are systemically desirable and culturally feasible. The models are thus epistemological devices used to find out about the real world.

The action research programme that was established at Lancaster and yielded these early successes has been continued in many hundreds of projects since. Figure 10.1 shows the essence of the process as described by Checkland and Holwell (1998). The researcher first seeks out a real-world problem situation relevant to his or her research interests. He then negotiates entry into that area of concern (A) declaring in advance the framework of ideas (philosophy, theories, etc.) and methodology he will use in trying to bring about improvements. He takes part in action in the situation and reflects on

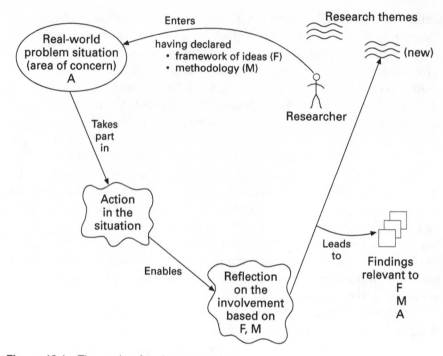

Figure 10.1 The cycle of action research.

From Checkland and Holwell (1998), reproduced by permission of John Wiley & Sons.

what happens using the framework of ideas (F) and methodology (M). This yields findings relevant to F, M and A, and possibly some new research themes.

The articulation and pursuit of this action research programme ensured that lessons could be learned from experience and incorporated in SSM, that reflection could take place on the philosophical underpinnings of the methodology, and refinements could be made to supportive methods and techniques. The developments that have occurred can be traced through the series of books Checkland has written on SSM: *Systems Thinking, Systems Practice* (1981); *Soft Systems Methodology in Action* (with Scholes) (1990); *Information, Systems and Information Systems* (with Holwell) (1998); and *Systems Thinking, Systems Practice* (including a 30-year retrospective) (1999).

10.2.2   Philosophy and theory

In reflecting on the shift in philosophical perspective necessary to establish SSM, Checkland (1983) has suggested that whereas hard systems approaches are based on a paradigm of optimization, his own methodology embraces a paradigm of learning.

Hard approaches assume the world contains systems the performance of which can be optimized by following systematic procedures. These procedures involve establishing clear objectives and then using generalizable models, based on systems logic, to enable prediction and control of the real-world systems of concern so that the objectives are realized with maximum efficiency and efficacy. Unfortunately for hard systems thinking, logic is usually much less significant in terms of what happens in organizations than is the history, culture and politics of the situation.

Recognizing this, SSM takes reality to be problematical and ceases to worry about modelling it systemically. Instead, it seeks to work with different perceptions of reality, facilitating a systemic process of learning in which different viewpoints are examined and discussed in a manner that can lead to purposeful action in pursuit of improvement. Participants use a systemic methodology to learn what changes are feasible and desirable given the peculiarities of their problem situation. Checkland puts this concisely in stating that SSM shifts 'systemicity from the world to the process of enquiry into the world.'

At the theoretical level what is being announced is a complete break with the functionalism that, until the 1980s, dominated the systems approach. The implied social theory of hard systems thinking, for example, is clearly functionalism. It is objectivist and regulative in orientation. Checkland rightly argues that the social theory implicit in SSM is interpretive rather than functionalist. In his methodology, systems are seen as the mental constructs of observers of the world. Different descriptions of reality, based on different world views, are embodied in 'root definitions'. These root definitions are turned into conceptual models that are explicitly one-sided representations of reality expressing a particular *Weltanschauung*. A debate is then structured around the implications of these different perceptions of the way things could be. This is resonant of the interpretive sociology of Weber rather than the functionalism of Durkheim, and of the phenomenology of Husserl and Schutz rather than the positivism of Comte.

As a final attempt to elucidate the philosophy and theory underpinning SSM, it is worth outlining the concept of 'organization' that Checkland and Holwell (1998) see as implied by the approach. SSM treats the notion of 'organization' as extremely problematical. It only arises because of the readiness of people, members and non-members alike, to talk and act as though they were engaging with a collective entity capable of purposeful action in its own right. On this basis, there may emerge a degree of agreement on purposes, social processes to pursue those purposes, and criteria for evaluating performance. This, in turn, may lead to the definition of organizational 'roles' and the establishment of norms and values. Despite the willingness of individuals to conform in this way, there will be many different conceptualizations of the nature and aims of the 'organization', premised on the values and interests of individuals and subgroups, apart from any 'official' version of its purpose. People constantly seek to renegotiate their roles, norms and values, and are capable of displaying considerable 'cussedness and irrationality' in the face of official goals. Because the different values and interests will rarely coincide exactly, the 'organization' depends for its existence on the establishment of temporary 'accommodations' between individuals and subgroups. These also provide the basis for any action to bring about change.

The concept of 'organization' set out by Checkland and Holwell suggests, following Vickers (1965, 1970), that management is much more about managing a richly unfolding set of relationships than it is about taking rational decisions to achieve goals. This, of course, is exactly what SSM seeks to do. Checkland and Holwell argue that the hundreds of successful action research projects conducted using SSM speak for the superiority of their concept over the traditional, machine model of organization.

10.2.3   Methodology

Although Checkland no longer favours it, the representation of SSM as a seven-stage cyclic, learning system, which appeared in 1981 in *Systems Thinking, Systems Practice*, is still frequently used today. It is shown in Figure 10.2.

In the first stage a sense of unease felt by individuals leads to the identification of a problem situation that demands attention. The second stage requires that this problem situation is expressed, not in systems terms but in the form of a rich picture. The aim is to gain and disseminate creative understanding of the problem situation. The early guidelines emphasized the need for a 'neutral' rich picture constructed by gathering information about the structures and processes at work, and the relationship between the two – the 'climate'. Later, it became clear that a good way of doing the expression stage was to take the idea of rich pictures literally and to draw pictorial, cartoon-like representations of the problem situation that highlight significant and contentious aspects in a manner likely to lead to original thinking at stage 3 of SSM. The rich picture technique is one of the most successful and frequently used of the methods that have come to be asso-

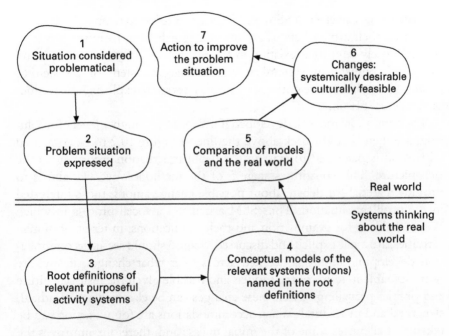

Figure 10.2 The learning cycle of Soft Systems Methodology (SSM).

ciated with SSM and, as with other such methods, is explained in Subsection 10.2.4.

It is now time for some 'below the line' (see Figure 10.2) systems thinking to be undertaken. In stage 3 some relevant human activity systems, potentially offering insight into the problem situation, are selected and from these 'root definitions' are built. A root definition should be well formulated to capture the essence of the relevant system and, to ensure that it is, should pay attention to the factors brought to mind by CATWOE (Customers, Actors, Transformation process, World view, Owners and Environmental constraints). As the W indicates, each root definition reflects a different way of conceiving the problem situation. Checkland (1987) provides the example of a prison, which it can be helpful to consider as a punishment system, a rehabilitation system, a system to deter, a system to protect society and as a 'university of crime'. In stage 4 these root definitions are used to construct conceptual models. Conceptual models consist initially of seven or so activities, each with a significant verb, structured in a logical sequence and representing those minimum activities that are necessary to achieve the transformation enshrined in the root definition. They are perhaps the key artefact in SSM and Checkland refers to them as 'holons' to emphasize their artificial status and to distinguish them from the 'systems' people loosely refer to as existing in the real world. Thus, for example, no prison *is* 'a punishment system' or 'a rehabilitation system' or 'a system to protect society'; these are notional concepts relevant to exploring the realities of any actual prison.

The conceptual models, developed if necessary to a higher level of resolution, are then brought back above the line in Figure 10.2 to be compared with what is perceived to exist in the problem situation according to the rich picture. This constitutes stage 5 of the methodology. The aim is to provide material for debate about possible change among those interested in the problem situation. Thus SSM articulates a social process in which Ws are held up for examination and their implications, in terms of human activities, are made explicit and discussed. Stage 6 should see an accommodation developing among concerned actors over what changes, if any, are both desirable in terms of the models and feasible given the history, culture and politics prevailing. Often these changes can be classified as attitudinal, structural and procedural. When accommodations are found, action can be taken that alleviates some of the initial unease and, therefore, improves the problem situation.

The conclusion of the methodological cycle is more likely to lead to the emergence of another, different problem situation than it is to provide a long-standing 'solution'. Ending a systems study is therefore, for Checkland, an arbitrary act. Problem resolving should be seen as a never-ending process in which participants' attitudes and perceptions are continually explored, tested and changed, and they come to entertain new conceptions of desirability and feasibility.

An important point to note, and one that is clear from Figure 10.2, is that SSM is doubly systemic. It uses 'human activity system' models in stages 4 and 5 as part of an *overall* systemic learning process.

As experience of using SSM accumulated, Checkland began to find the original seven-stage representation too limiting. It had always been stressed that the learning cycle could be commenced at any stage and that SSM should be used flexibly and iteratively, but the seven-stage model still seemed to contribute to a systematic (rather than systemic) understanding of the process and one, moreover, in which use of the methodology appeared cut off from the ordinary day-to-day activities of the organization. In an attempt to overcome this, and to demonstrate that SSM in use requires constant attention to and reflection on cultural aspects of the situation of concern, a new representation of the methodology was developed. This

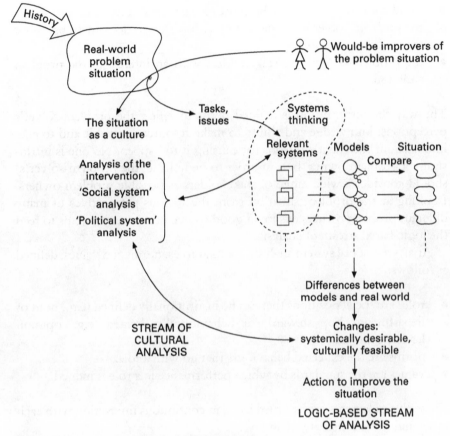

Figure 10.3 The two-strands version of SSM.
From Checkland and Scholes (1990), reproduced by permission of John Wiley & Sons.

'two-strands model', which first appeared in Checkland and Scholes' *Soft Systems Methodology in Action* (1990), is shown in Figure 10.3.

The two-strands model of SSM gives equal attention to a 'stream of cultural analysis' as to the logic-based stream of analysis that had tended to dominate the seven-stage version. SSM after all takes, as its task, management of the 'myths and meanings' that are so central to the functioning of organizations because they are the means by which individuals make sense of their situations. The enhanced cultural analysis takes the form of three types of inquiry, referred to as Analyses 1, 2 and 3.

Analysis 1 considers the intervention itself and the roles of client, problem-solver and problem-owners, defined as follows:

- the client is the person(s) who causes the systems study to take place;
- the problem-solver is the person(s) who wishes to do something about the problem situation;
- the problem-owners are stakeholders with an interest in the problem situation.

The way the intervention is defined needs to reflect the problem-solver's perceptions, knowledge and ability to make resources available and to take into account the client's reasons for causing it to happen. No one is intrinsically a problem owner, but, in order to be holistic, the problem-solver(s) should consider a wide range of stakeholders as possible problem owners. Looking at the problem situation from the various perspectives of many different problem owners ensures a good source of relevant systems to feed the logic-based stream of analysis.

Analysis 2, social system analysis, looks at roles, norms and values, defined as follows:

- roles are social positions that can be institutionally defined (e.g., head of department, shop steward) or behaviourally defined (e.g., opinion leader, confidante);
- norms are the expected behaviours that go with a role;
- values are the standards by which performance in a role is judged.

These three elements are assumed to be in continuous interaction with each other and to be constantly changing.

Analysis 3 examines the politics of the problem situation and how power is obtained and used. This can be overt or covert and rests on various 'commodities' that bring influence in an organization, such as command over resources, professional skills, talent and personality.

Analyses 1, 2 and 3 are not done once and then stored for reference in a systems study. It is essential that they are continually updated and developed as the intervention progresses. Often it is helpful to incorporate them into an initial rich picture, which is then revisited and reworked. Recognition of the cultural and political aspects of a problem situation, and the way they are changing, can massively assist in the logic-based stream of analysis. It can guide the choice of insightful relevant systems, help an analyst secure more open discussion and inform the process of arriving at recommendations for feasible changes.

Before leaving soft systems methodology itself, it needs to be emphasized that the process of using it should be participative. It is desirable that as many interested parties as possible come to 'own' the study and the changes it recommends, by being involved in using the methodology. Only in this way will participants learn their way to new conceptions of what is feasible as their perceptions and attitudes are tested and modified. Changes that could not be conceived of before the intervention began, because of the history and culture of the situation, may then seem obvious by the time it is finished.

10.2.4 Methods

Given the importance of participation for the success of SSM interventions, it is surprising that Checkland and his coworkers have not given more attention to how it might be promoted and facilitated. This is especially the case when we consider the effort that has gone into refining certain other methods associated with the methodology. Here we consider four of the best known tools: rich pictures, root definitions, conceptual models and 'comparison'. The first assists with the cultural stream of analysis, the second and third with the logic-based stream, and the fourth provides the link between the two.

Rich pictures are actual drawings that allow the various features of a problem situation, as it is perceived, to be set down pictorially for all to see. There are no rules for drawing rich pictures and, while some are quite formalized, others are very cartoon-like in nature. Much depends on the skill and purposes of the person(s) doing the drawing. The idea that it is useful to look at a problem situation in terms of structures, processes and climate may help, and Analyses 1, 2 and 3 should certainly feed into the rich picture(s). Otherwise, it is obvious that rich pictures are selective and that it is an art to know which issues, conflicts and other problematic and interesting aspects to accentuate. If done well, rich pictures can assist creativity, express the interrelationships in a problem situation better than linear prose, allow the easy sharing of ideas between those involved in an intervention, catalyse discussion and act as an excellent memory aid. Figure 10.4 is a rich picture produced by Superintendent P.J. Gaisford (1989) during a soft systems study of female street prostitution in central London.

From the representation of the problem situation in the rich picture and drawing especially on what the problem owners regard as important, various 'relevant systems' can be chosen for further analysis. Relevant systems should offer insight into the problem situation and begin to suggest actions for improving it. They are the bridge to the rigour of the logic-based stream of analysis.

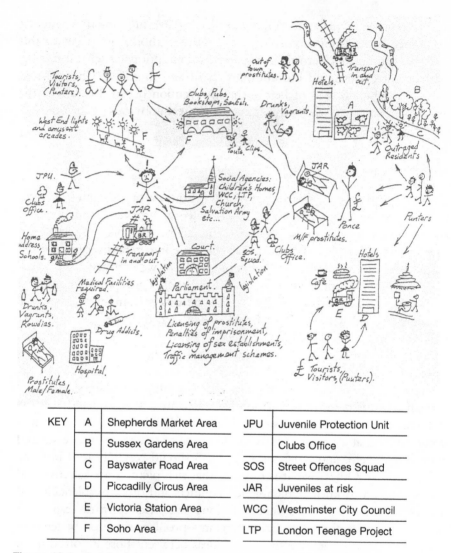

KEY	A	Shepherds Market Area	JPU	Juvenile Protection Unit
	B	Sussex Gardens Area		Clubs Office
	C	Bayswater Road Area	SOS	Street Offences Squad
	D	Piccadilly Circus Area	JAR	Juveniles at risk
	E	Victoria Station Area	WCC	Westminster City Council
	F	Soho Area	LTP	London Teenage Project

Figure 10.4 A rich picture.

From Flood and Carson (1988), reproduced by permission of Plenum Press.

Each relevant system is expanded into a 'root definition', which is a concise statement of what that (notional) system is in its most fundamental form. Since this root definition is the basis for a model of purposeful human activity, it needs to have at its core a transformation (T) process in which some input is changed into a new state or form, which then becomes the output. It must also specify the *Weltanschauung* (W) that makes the transformation meaningful in terms of the context. A well-formulated root definition – one that can give rise to a useful conceptual model – is also likely to pay attention to who can stop the transformation from happening, who is to do it, who is to benefit or suffer from it, and what environmental constraints limit the actions and activities.

We now have six elements that a root definition should make reference to unless justification can be provided for omitting any of them. These are captured in the mnemonic CATWOE as follows:

C   'customers' – the beneficiaries or victims of the transformation process;
A   'actors' – those who would undertake the transformation process;
T   'transformation' – the conversion of input to output;
W   'world view' – the world view that makes this transformation meaningful;
O   'owners' – those who could stop the transformation;
E   'environmental constraints' – elements outside the system that are taken as given.

In a study for the Information and Library Services Department (ILSD) in ICI Organics (discussed in Checkland and Scholes, 1990), Checkland produced the following root definition of the role of 'enabling systems', which continues to be influential in SSM:

An ICI-owned and staffed system to operate wealth-generating operations supported by enabling support systems which tailor their support through development of particular relationships with the main operations

C   ICI
A   ICI people
T   need for supported wealth generation – need met via a structure of main operations and enabling support
W   a belief that this structure will generate wealth
O   ICI
E   structure of the main operations plus support; ICI ethos.

Root definitions are used to explore the possibilities available for change in the problem situation given its history, culture and politics. To ensure the exploration is thorough, or 'holistic', it is always necessary to consider a number of different root definitions. It is also useful to take forward two types of root definition: 'primary task' and 'issue-based'. Primary task root definitions tend to refer to officially declared tasks in the organization and to give rise to models that map existing organizational structures. Issue-based models refer to current matters of concern, perhaps the need to be more innovative or to resolve a conflictual situation, that cross established boundaries.

Finally, Checkland and Scholes (1990) suggest that it can help to conceive the core transformation in a root definition as 'a system to do P by Q in order to contribute to achieving R'. This ensures that 'what to do', 'how to do it' and 'why do it' are captured and draws attention to concerns at the system, subsystem and wider system levels.

A root definition is a precise account of what a relevant system is. Once it has been formulated satisfactorily, a 'conceptual model' can be built from it that sets out the activities that must be undertaken in order to carry out the transformation and fulfil the other requirements of the root definition. Conceptual models are not models of anything in the real world; they are purposeful 'holons' constructed with the aim of facilitating structured debate about the problem situation and any changes to it that might be desirable. They should therefore be developed from their relevant root definitions alone, without reference to reality.

A conceptual model is produced by thinking through and writing down the minimum number of activities that seem necessary to carry out the transformation in the way defined in the root definition. Since they are 'human activity systems' they will consist of verb statements describing actual activities that humans can undertake. They will normally, at the first stage of their development, consist of a handful, usually around seven activities. These are logically ordered in terms of their interactions, showing how they depend on one another. A common feature is to have a number of verbs in one subholon concerned with operations and another set of activities that are responsible for monitoring and control. Proper monitoring and control depends minimally on specifying criteria for efficiency ('amount of output divided by amount of resources used'), efficacy ('do the means work?') and effectiveness ('is the transformation meeting the longer term aim?'). Checkland suggests that other criteria setting out measures for 'ethicality' and 'elegance' can be added.

The conceptual model derived by Checkland from the earlier root definition and CATWOE analysis is presented in Figure 10.5. Basic models of this type, containing seven or so verbs, can if necessary be expanded to higher levels of resolution by taking any activity within them as the source of a new root definition and accompanying conceptual model.

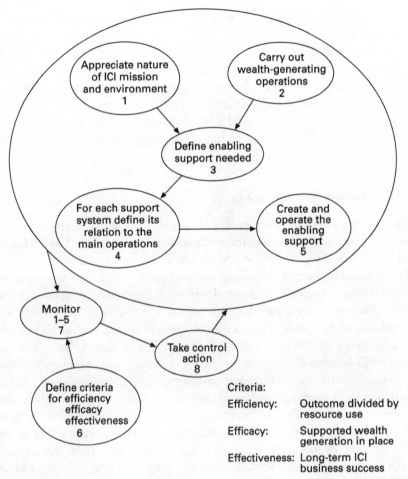

Figure 10.5 A conceptual model derived from the root definition presented earlier.

As we know, in order to generate debate about possible changes that might be made in the problem situation, it is necessary to make a 'comparison' between the conceptual models and what is perceived to exist there, often expressed in rich pictures. Checkland (1981) mentions four ways in which this might be carried out:

- informal discussion of the main differences between the models of what might be and what seems to be the case now;
- a more formal questioning of the main differences, which involves filling out a matrix that asks for each activity such questions as: does it exist or

not in the real situation?, how is it done?, how is it judged?, any other comments?

- scenario writing based on notionally operating the human activity system, in the mind or on paper, to see how it is expected to behave into the future – this might be compared with how an actual system appeared to work in the past in similar circumstances;
- trying to model the real world using the same structure employed in the conceptual model in order to highlight any significant differences that might provoke discussion.

10.2.5   Recent developments

Although not a recent development in terms of its initial formulation (in Checkland and Scholes, 1990), the distinction between Mode 1 and Mode 2 SSM is still being worked on, especially the exact nature of Mode 2.

Checkland argues that because of the experiences with systems engineering and the need to concentrate on developing an alternative approach that is more successful with problems of managing, much of early SSM was methodology-orientated. The methodology was introduced as an external recipe to drive an intervention in a structured and sometimes sequential manner. This is now defined as Mode 1 usage. As experience grew, however, those using SSM began to internalize the methodology. When this happens, it allows them to remain much more situation-driven and problem-orientated. The methodology ceases to dominate what is done and becomes instead the basis for reflecting on what is happening in the everyday flux of occurrences. It is used flexibly and only occasionally breaks the surface to interact with ongoing ideas and events. This is Mode 2 SSM.

Although Mode 1 and Mode 2 are 'ideal types', and any SSM study is likely to include elements of both, it seems clear that Mode 2 is more easily incorporated by managers in their daily working lives. Managers are absorbed by the concerns and pressures of their immediate environments. They act and react according to their personalities, knowledge, instincts, values, etc. and are unlikely, on an everyday basis, to operate according to the rules of a methodology. Inevitably, they are situation-driven. Occasionally, however, they may wish to step outside the hurly-burly of ongoing events to make sense of what is happening (perhaps using rich pictures) or to apply some structured, systems thinking to proposals for change (perhaps using root definitions and conceptual models). In these circumstances, if SSM's procedures and methods have been sufficiently internalized, a manager or group of managers can refer to the approach to help them think through the situation they are experiencing and the possibilities it opens up.

A more obvious 'recent development' is the attention now given by Checkland and his collaborators to the use of SSM in the specific field of 'information systems'. A third Checkland book *Information, Systems and Information Systems* (1998), written with Holwell, signals this new emphasis. The volume is an ambitious attempt to initiate 'conceptual cleansing' in the Information Systems (IS) area. This involves trying to bring intellectual clarity to confusions about concepts such as 'data', 'information' and 'knowledge', and replacing the outdated model of the organization as a machine, which has traditionally been used to underpin work in information systems, with one that more adequately matches actual experience. This alternative model must emphasize values and meanings, and the processes that obtain as purposeful action is formulated. Once such action has been decided and agreed it becomes possible to see what information needs exist among those involved and to provide appropriate ISs to support action. SSM is seen as the perfect vehicle to guide the development of ISs that truly meet users' needs. To illustrate this further, I have chosen an IS study as our example in the next subsection.

10.3 SOFT SYSTEMS METHODOLOGY (SSM) IN ACTION

This SSM intervention was conducted by Checkland and Holwell for an Information Department (ID) located in the central research and development laboratories of a multinational science-based group. ID had just over 100 staff and was linked to a library employing a further 25. It consisted of four sections; three concerned with technical aspects of IT and telecommunications and one with the organization of ID itself and IS rather than IT issues. The role of ID was to serve the Research and Development laboratories (R&D), ensuring they were up to date with relevant knowledge and that the new knowledge they generated was appropriately managed and made available to those who needed and were entitled to it. R&D was itself divided into four sections: products research, process research, engineering research and general administration (of which ID was a part).

The 'Reorganization Project', as it was known (see Checkland and Holwell, 1998), was led by Eva, a member of staff seconded from that part of ID (call it IDI) concerned with its organization and the more general information systems issues. The project was a response to the feeling that the service offered by the IS/IT professionals to R&D needed rethinking. Its justification was the rate of technical change overtaking IT, and it was supposed to answer questions such as 'what are the presentation requirements for information transfer?', 'what are the costs of information access, storage and quality?' and 'at what rate will changes occur within the laboratories?' SSM was called on because it was felt a more holistic approach to this broad 'information support problem' would bring benefits.

In entering the problem situation, Checkland and Holwell noted that, although the project had been set up by the head of ID, its recommendations were supposed to be limited to the activities of IDI. It seemed inevitable that the project would impact on the whole of ID and its relationships with R&D. Perhaps the head of ID was worried about possible resistance to change from the other section heads within ID and about the reaction of clients in R&D. This was just one of the historical, cultural and political factors they faced. Others were a lack of high regard for the work of ID and the difficulty of justifying expenditure on any aspect of R&D when the returns are indeterminate and often far into the future.

The 'problem situation expressed' stage took the form of workshops involving Checkland and Holwell, Eva, other staff from ID and around 20 clients of ID from R&D. A rich picture, reproduced as Figure 10.6, was developed, and this helped to bring about a shared understanding of ID's support function and to identify some important roles and processes worthy of further investigation. Another problem-structuring device used was a conceptual model derived by taking the ID's official mission statement as a root definition. This had the added benefit of familiarizing participants with some of the most important techniques associated with SSM.

The logic-based stream of analysis was carried forward in two one-day workshops at which researchers and ID professionals were present. They began with the head of ID and Eva explaining the Reorganization Project, which, increasingly, was becoming associated with achieving greater 'client orientation' and with determining how relationships between ID and R&D should develop going forward. Then some models, previously tried out on researchers, were presented for discussion and modification in small groups. These were about the role of R&D in the company in the particular circumstances it faced. One example, and the root definition from which it came, is presented in Figure 10.7.

Later in the sessions small groups were again used, this time to discuss R&D–ID interaction. In the first workshop, for example, attention was focused on those activities in the models that either were or could be supported by ID. The groups were then asked to consider, for each activity that might be supported, whether ID should do it, provide expertise relevant

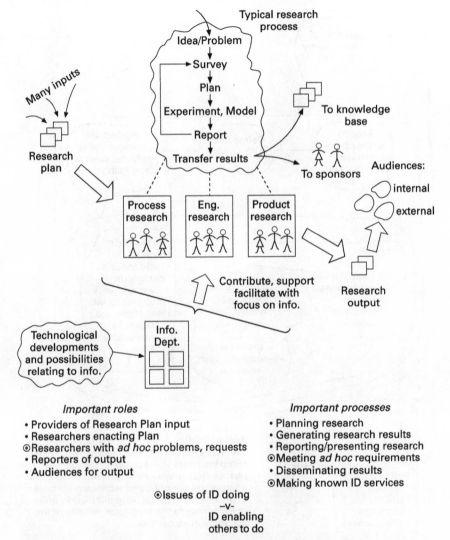

Figure 10.6 An initial picturing of the problem situation in the research laboratories.
From Checkland and Holwell (1998), reproduced by permission of John Wiley & Sons.

to it, offer appropriate education and training, or help manage it. Figure 10.8 reproduces one of the models used to assist the debates. It is an expanded version of activity 7 in the earlier model (Figure 10.7), with the thick arrows indicating activities to which ID could contribute support.

The learning from the two workshops was condensed into reports that highlighted a number of matters – such as whether ID should be more

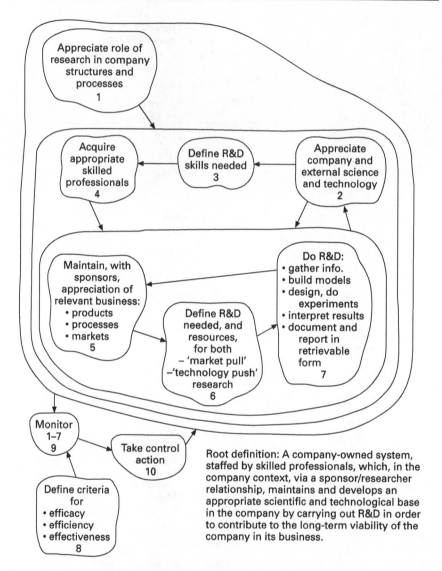

Figure 10.7   An activity model relevant to carrying out R&D in the company.
From Checkland and Holwell (1998), reproduced by permission of John Wiley & Sons.

responsive or proactive. The most significant issue, however, was the need to improve mutual understanding and contact between ID and R&D. Unless this happened there was no chance of ID succeeding in its aim of becoming more client-centred. A conceptual model was therefore produced, setting out what activities would be necessary to ensure that ongoing dialogue

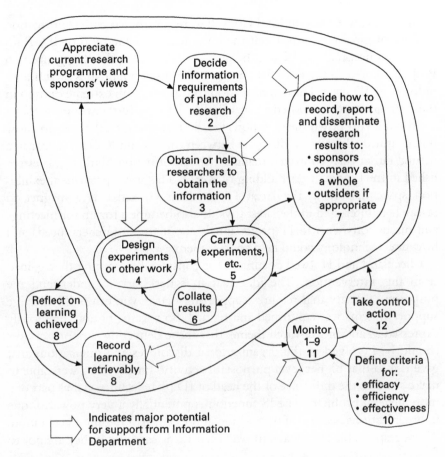

Figure 10.8 An activity model that expands activity 7 of Figure 10.7.

From Checkland and Holwell (1998), reproduced by permission of John Wiley & Sons.

between ID and R&D became institutionalized. Eva then argued for the Reorganization Project to continue: first, by making changes in IDI and then by spreading change to the whole of R&D in a manner that would realize productive ID–R&D relationships.

It is worth noting at this point that the 'stream of cultural analysis' was proceeding alongside the logic-based stream throughout the project. It took the form of a very informal use of Analyses 1, 2 and 3. The cultural shift of ID toward a more client-driven perspective was monitored. Discussions at the workshops helped surface hidden agendas and possible political constraints on progress. There was growing realization that, despite its turbulent environment, things changed pretty slowly in this company. Now, Checkland and Holwell were confronted with confirmation of their original concerns about the nervousness of the head of ID. Both the new conceptual model and the plan for continuing the Reorganization Project pointed to the need for change beyond the boundaries of IDI and, indeed, the ID itself. His determination to proceed with extreme caution in these circumstances imposed a considerable delay on further progress.

About a year down the line, however, an idea emerged that was to allow the institutionalization of dialogue between the ID and R&D to occur in a natural rather than contrived manner. An 'Information Market' was established in the headquarters building of R&D. This was a permanent exhibition space displaying the latest IT products. It acted as a magnet to researchers interested in the latest toys. It also became a forum for meetings and discussions with IS/IT professionals about the researchers' needs and how new technology could help address them.

Checkland and Holwell document the considerable learning they gained from this intervention. The idea that it is necessary to understand the purposeful activity that requires supporting before you can build effective support systems was confirmed and refined. So was the notion, previously expressed as an SSM research theme, that those delivering support services should be involved in the organizational discourses and interactions that give rise to that higher level purposeful activity. Finally, they were able to make sense of the diffidence of the head of ID by reflecting on it as part of a more general problem. The IS function is potentially a very powerful one in organizations because of its position at the centre of meaning generation. Those responsible for it have to play their cards carefully if they are not to be seen as a threat.

10.4   CRITIQUE OF SOFT SYSTEMS METHODOLOGY (SSM)

At the beginning of his endeavour to establish a systems methodology more appropriate to the problem situations faced by managers, Checkland (1976) declared his intention to take systems thinking beyond the abstractions of general system theory and the constraints of the specialized techniques then dominating such approaches as operational research. The story of SSM reveals the success of this enterprise.

Contemporary SSM is based on some clearly defined activities that guide the process of intervention in ill-structured problem situations. Subsuming the cultural stream of analysis into each of the elements, Checkland (1999) recognizes four essential activities:

- finding out about a problem situation, including culturally/politically;
- formulating some relevant purposeful activity models;
- debating the situation, using the models, seeking from that debate both –
  - changes that would improve the situation and that are regarded as both desirable and (culturally) feasible; and
  - the accommodations between conflicting interests that will enable action to improve to be taken;
- taking action in the situation to bring about improvement.

At the same time as it sets out these principles of methodology, SSM does not constrain method use. It is capable of providing a different response in each situation depending on the user and the nature of the situation. Mode 2 SSM, as we saw, requires the methodology to be flexible enough to supply its assistance when placed in a secondary position to the demands of the problem situation. Although it has some extremely powerful methods (rich pictures, root definitions, conceptual models, etc.) associated with it, SSM does not require that they all be used, or that they are used in the same way, in each intervention. It is this flexibility that ensures its relevance in so many managerial situations.

Another reason why SSM is so widely applicable is that the cyclic learning process it seeks to articulate builds naturally on the complex social processes, including processes of management, that occur in organizations. As we know, organizations for Checkland are made up of individuals possessing different evaluations of the situation they are in. Their evaluations will overlap to some extent, but there will usually be sufficient difference among world views to give rise to issues that have to be managed. The aim of SSM is to structure a debate that will lead, if not to the creation of shared perceptions, at least to an accommodation between different viewpoints and interests so that desirable change can be implemented. Managers trying to improve things in organizations have to worry about the present situation, try to get some handle on it, postulate alternative ways forward and seek accommodations that allow change to happen. With all of these, SSM can help. There is nothing in SSM, therefore, that should seem unnatural to managers. Indeed, once they have participated in a few SSM studies, managers should be able to internalize the methodology in a manner that will enable them to use it in their everyday work. The soft systems thinker is aware of this and is as concerned to give the approach away as to provide a set of recommendations for action.

The main criticism of SSM (see Jackson, 1982, 1983, 2000) is that it has a limited domain of applicability and fails to recognize it. Checkland is happy to criticize hard systems thinking in this respect, but cannot, seemingly, see the relevance of the same critical point to his own approach. SSM is well suited to pluralist situations where there is a need to create some shared appreciation among stakeholders about what action needs taking to bring about improvement. If the problem situation is one in which organizational design of complex systems is required or in which significant conflict and coercion figures, then SSM is much less obviously the most suitable approach.

To hard systems thinkers and those concerned with building complex adaptive systems, SSM offers a limited perspective on why problem situations occur. For example, the idea that there are cybernetic laws that must be obeyed when all complex systems are being organized is not taken seriously in the soft systems thinking of Checkland. He sees hard or system dynamic or cybernetic approaches as usable only in the 'special case' when world views have coalesced to such an extent that there is consensus about what system to design. It is soft systems thinking that must be employed in the vast majority of cases where these special circumstances do not pertain. 'Harder' systems thinkers regard this as anathema. They believe it is possible to provide knowledge that can guide action in large areas of social and organizational life. Within these domains it is the rationality of their approaches, as witnessed by their ability to increase prediction and control, that must hold sway. What is the best queuing system for a supermarket or what would be an efficient and efficacious information systems design for a multinational company are, for them, more matters of expertise than of intersubjective agreement.

For a different reason, emancipatory systems thinkers also regard SSM as having a limited domain of applicability. They argue that SSM veers too closely to a consensus world view that plays down fundamental conflicts of interest and promotes the belief that they can be papered over through a debate structured around conceptual models. The alternative sociological position, that deep-seated conflict is endemic and the social world is characterized by asymmetry of power, does not seem to be given proper attention by Checkland. This leads (as with Ackoff) to an exaggerated commitment to participation as the appropriate and apparently sufficient mechanism for achieving mutual understanding on purposes.

Participation is of considerable importance in SSM, especially at stages 5 and 6 when comparisons between conceptual models and what is perceived to exist in the real world are being made, and feasible and desirable changes agreed. Checkland, however, does not address the issue of how far the participation should run or offer ground rules for what is to count as 'genuine' participation. In the absence of such rules any debate that takes place can be constrained and distorted because particular individuals or agendas are excluded, because of hierarchy and the threat of sanctions, because of the unequal intellectual resources or powerful ideologies that hold sway. It is all too easy for those with power and influence to dominate the discussions and to have their own priorities reflected in the outcome. To the critics, therefore, SSM cannot be properly employed in the many circumstances where participation is severely constrained and power determines the outcome of the debate.

Checkland (1982) argues back that, rather than just asserting the existence of dominating power relationships and other constraining features of social reality, critics could test their hypotheses using SSM. It is open to them to propose radical root definitions. Since SSM is a learning system it can, at the very least, help them find out about whatever constraints do exist. This would augment Analysis 3, which explores power and politics to the degree that it is useful to do so. Given that SSM encourages *Weltanschauungen* to change it might, given the chance, assist radicals to shift attitudes and events in ways that will enable them to realize their aspirations. In the end, as Checkland puts it (pers. commun. 2003), SSM cannot guarantee the overthrow of 'tyrants'; no mere methodology – which is only some words on paper – can do that. It will depend on the user and the situation how 'regulative' or 'emancipatory' SSM proves to be in any particular case (Checkland, pers. commun. 2003).

In trying to get some handle on these arguments at the theoretical level, the first thing to notice is the apparent 'isolationism' of Checkland's work on SSM. Mingers (2000) claims that he cannot find a single example from Checkland's writings where any other methodology is used alongside SSM. He points out as well how self-contained the SSM cycle of learning has become. New problem situations prompt a search of earlier Lancaster experiences for related projects rather than a review of other relevant, easily available and well-known literature.

Checkland (pers. commun. 2003) responds that he was not seeking to conduct an academic review of different systems approaches, but to find out through experience better ways of coping with real-world problem situations, starting with the basic systems ideas he had inherited. Fair enough, but it is clear that SSM has benefited much from being theoretically informed; early on by the work of Churchman and Vickers, later by the interpretive philosophical and sociological theories of Husserl and Weber, and by various social theory classifications. Checkland is the most theoretically pure of the soft systems thinkers because he recognized the theoretical

direction in which his thinking was heading, made this explicit and, in constructing SSM, consciously employed interpretive theoretical foundations.
If one looks back at the account of the interpretive paradigm provided in
Chapter 3, it is difficult to conceive how any systems methodology could
be truer to it than that of Checkland.

Self-consciously embracing an unadulterated interpretive position brings
many advantages to Checkland. It enables him to theorize thoroughly the
nature of his break with hard systems thinking and to identify some
'tensions' between hard and soft positions that remain in Churchman's and
Ackoff's work. Because he is clear about the theory he employs, relevant
research themes can be identified and explored in a recoverable way using a
well-defined methodology that is constructed according to the dictates of
the theory. Methods can be used and tested in a theoretically informed
manner. Checkland is able to extract the greatest possible benefit from the
culture and politics metaphors and the systems concepts (client, problem-
solver, problem-owners, appreciative systems, *Weltanschauung*, purposeful
systems, learning, etc.) that are most clearly linked to the interpretive
paradigm.

Such a wholehearted adherence to interpretive thinking, however, appears
to blind Checkland to the allure of other paradigms and their associated
systems approaches. This makes SSM a tempting target for critics who
adopt and value other theoretical positions.

Functionalist systems thinkers get frustrated with the subjectivism of
SSM and its failure, as they see it, to provide knowledge about how to
design complex adaptive systems. They are dismayed that the prescriptions
they derive from the machine, organism, brain, and flux and transformation
metaphors are ignored. They believe that there is something real about the
various models produced by experts in management science and organization theory that managers must take seriously. To Checkland such models
may merit a place at the debating table and prove useful in specific circumstances, but they certainly cannot provide any objective truth about how
organizations should be designed and managed.

Critics of an emancipatory persuasion attack the 'regulative' orientation
they see SSM inheriting from the interpretive paradigm. They view the
social world as full of conflict of real interest, coercion and contradiction,
and believe that the failure of interpretive thinkers, such as Checkland, to
address this directly means that their methodologies become distorted in
use and are ineffective in achieving significant change for the better. Much
of the argument, as we saw, is about the nature of the accommodations

that SSM is able to bring about and on which agreements about change are founded. The critics argue that the methodology, if it is to have any emancipatory potential, must pay attention to the possibility that 'systematically distorted communication' can jeopardize the emergence of genuine shared purposes. SSM suggests nothing can be done about this and thus too easily facilitates a social process in which the essential elements of the status quo are reproduced – perhaps on a firmer footing since differences of opinion will have been temporarily smoothed over. Methodologies cannot of themselves overthrow 'tyrants', but they can be more helpful to those seeking their overthrow.

The reason SSM ignores constraints on discussion, according to Mingers (1984), comes back to its subjectivism. It is condemned by this to act only at the level of ideas; seeking to change things by changing people's world views. It cannot recognize that it is difficult to change world views without first doing something about the structures – organizational, political and economic – that give rise to world views and determine their influence. A sophisticated social theory, embracing the psychic prison and instruments of domination metaphors, is necessary in order to 'unmask' ideologies and provide an understanding of how emancipation can be brought about. SSM lacks any theory about the wider features of the social structure because of its interpretive foundations. They condemn it to regulation.

This conclusion, it might be noted, would be shared by proponents of the postmodern paradigm who would see SSM as helpless in the face of the power of the 'system'. Its role is to readjust the ideological status quo by engineering human hopes and aspirations in a manner that responds to the system's needs and so ensures its smoother functioning.

Checkland believes that the results achieved during 30 years of action research, using SSM, fully justify the interpretive perspective he brings to the social world. If, during his experiences using SSM, he had found other theoretical perspectives and their associated systems methodologies useful, he would have employed them. He finds it disappointing (Checkland, pers. commun. 2003) that '... most of the critique of SSM gives the impression of deriving from nothing more than a casual reading of some of the literature, rather than from real-world experience – which could provide a legitimate grounding for criticism.' The trouble with this, as Churchman would put it, is that no data ever destroyed a *Weltanschauung*. Unless you are willing and able to view the world through alternative theoretical lenses you are likely to go on finding confirmation for the one you favour, however much real-world experience you gain.

10.5   THE VALUE OF SOFT SYSTEMS METHODOLOGY (SSM) TO MANAGERS

SSM asks managers to replace the goal-seeking approach with which they have been inculcated with a model based on relationship maintaining. Using human activity system models they can then learn their way to what changes to the problem situation are desirable and feasible, given the accommodations between concerned actors that are possible. This is a process they can conduct aided by SSM (a methodology they can internalize and employ without losing touch with the dynamics of the problem situation). With this orientation, it is not surprising that it brings much of value to managers. Here are five major things:

- SSM does not require the establishment of clear goals before problem resolving can begin; rather, it maps onto the normal managerial tasks of considering the 'mess', suggesting ways forward and seeking agreements for action – thus it is easily absorbed into organizational processes.
- SSM offers an excellent way of exploring purposes, using human activity system models to find out what is possible given the history, culture and politics of the problem situation.
- SSM articulates a learning system that challenges existing ways of seeing and doing things, and can lead to some surprising shifts in *Weltanschauungen*, opening up novel and elegant proposals for change.
- SSM has shown that the effective design of support systems, such as information systems, depends on a clear understanding of the purposeful activity that is to be supported in the higher order human activity system.
- Some powerful methods, such as rich pictures, root definitions and conceptual models, have been developed and refined to assist with using SSM.

10.6   CONCLUSION

Checkland's break with the predominant goal-seeking tradition in management science and his recognition of the significance of relationship maintaining as an alternative have led to a revolution in systems thinking. The development of SSM, based on an action research programme that linked ideas and experience directly, operationalized this and enabled the continual refinement of soft systems thinking. Checkland's clear understanding that he was engaged in making an 'epistemological break', reframing systems thinking on new philosophical foundations, helped to steer the revolution through. SSM, with its associated principles and methods, is an achievement that revitalized the systems approach and has hugely increased its relevance to business and management.

REFERENCES

Checkland, P.B. (1976). Towards a systems-based methodology for real-world problem-solving. In: J. Beishon and G. Peters (eds), *Systems Behaviour* (pp. 51–77). Harper & Row, London.

Checkland, P.B. (1981). *Systems Thinking, Systems Practice*. John Wiley & Sons, Chichester, UK.

Checkland, P.B. (1982). Soft systems methodology as process: A reply to M.C. Jackson. *Journal of Applied Systems Analysis*, **9**, 37–39.

Checkland, P.B. (1983). OR and the systems movement: Mappings and conflicts. *Journal of the Operational Research Society*, **34**, 661–675.

Checkland, P.B. (1987). The application of systems thinking in real-world problem-situations: The emergence of soft systems methodology. In: M.C. Jackson and P. Keys (eds), *New Directions in Management Science* (pp. 87–96). Gower, Aldershot, UK.

Checkland, P.B. (1999). *Systems Thinking, Systems Practice* (new edn, including a 30-year retrospective). John Wiley & Sons, Chichester, UK.

Checkland, P.B. and Holwell, S. (1998). *Information, Systems and Information Systems*. John Wiley & Sons, Chichester, UK.

Checkland, P.B. and Scholes, P. (1990). *Soft Systems Methodology in Action*. John Wiley & Sons, Chichester, UK.

Flood, R.L. and Carson, E. (1988). *Dealing with Complexity: An Introduction to the Theory and Application of Systems Science*. Plenum Press, New York.

Gaisford, P.J. (1989). A systemic analysis of female street prostitution within the environs of central London. M.Phil. thesis, City University, London.

Jackson, M.C. (1982). The nature of soft systems thinking: The work of Churchman, Ackoff and Checkland. *Journal of Applied Systems Analysis*, **9**, 17–28.

Jackson, M.C. (1983). The nature of soft systems thinking: Comments on the three replies. *Journal of Applied Systems Analysis*, **10**, 109–113.

Jackson, M.C. (2000). *Systems Approaches to Management*. Kluwer/Plenum, New York.

Mingers, J.C. (1984). Subjectivism and soft systems methodology – A critique. *Journal of Applied Systems Analysis*, **11**, 85–103.

Mingers, J.C. (2000). An idea ahead of its time: The history and development of soft systems methodology. *Systemic Practice and Action Research*, **13**, 733–755.
Vickers, G. (1965). *The Art of Judgement*. Chapman & Hall, London.
Vickers, G. (1970). *Freedom in a Rocking Boat*. Allen Lane, London.

Type C

Ensuring Fairness

Here we detail two systems approaches that aim to assist managers improve their enterprises by ensuring fairness. These approaches are critical systems heuristics and team syntegrity. They were developed because of the failure of functionalist and interpretive systems approaches to give appropriate attention to ensuring the proper participation of all stakeholders in taking decisions and to addressing the disadvantages faced by some groups in and affected by organizations. The two approaches emphasize the empowerment of those discriminated against in terms of the way they are treated and their emancipation so that they can take full advantage of their rights. In sociological terms they are emancipatory in character, oriented toward eliminating sources of power and domination that illegitimately oppress particular individuals and groups in society. They have explored the horizontal axis of the System Of Systems Methodologies (SOSM) to the point where they see conflict and coercion as endemic in organizations and as deserving of primary attention. The psychic prison and instruments of domination metaphors guide their recommendations for systems intervention.

Critical Systems Heuristics

11

> *Likewise, the meaning of critique threatens to be lost if we do not link it properly to the **emancipatory interest**, that is, if we do not give the latter an adequate methodological status and place in CST [critical systems thinking].*
>
> Ulrich (2003)

11.1 INTRODUCTION

The publication of Werner Ulrich's *Critical Heuristics of Social Planning*, in 1983, stands as a landmark in the development of systems thinking. This is because the book describes, for the first time, a systems approach that takes as a major concern the need to counter possible unfairness in society by ensuring that all those affected by decisions have a role in making them. In doing so it established emancipatory systems thinking and provided it with a methodology that can be used by planners and concerned citizens alike to reveal and challenge the normative content of actual and proposed systems designs. By normative content Ulrich means both the underlying value assumptions that inevitably enter into planning, and the social consequences and side effects for those at the receiving end. Critical Systems Heuristics (CSH) is a practically orientated, emancipatory systems approach that can ensure planning and decision-making include a critical dimension, and can enable the designs emanating from other systems approaches, whether hard or soft, to be suitably interrogated to reveal whose interests they serve.

11.2   DESCRIPTION OF CRITICAL SYSTEMS HEURISTICS (CSH)

11.2.1   Historical development

In setting out his approach, Ulrich (1983) distances himself from the currently dominant (in 1983) use of the systems idea in what he calls 'systems science': Operational Research (OR), systems analysis, systems engineering, cybernetics. In systems science, which he sees as premised on the limited mechanistic and organismic analogies, the systems idea is used only in the context of instrumental reason to help us to decide *how to do things*. It refers to a set of variables to be controlled. Ulrich's purpose is to develop the systems idea as part of practical reason, to help us decide *what we ought to do*.

As a PhD student of Churchman's, Ulrich was in an excellent position to get the inspiration he needed to achieve his purpose. In particular he took two of Churchman's central ideas and drove each of them in a slightly more radical direction (see Ulrich 1988, 2003).

One of Churchman's greatest contributions to systems thinking was establishing the fundamental idea that the drawing of boundaries is crucial to determining how improvement is to be defined and what action should be taken. He was also the first to argue that justifying systems interventions requires continually redrawing the boundaries to 'sweep in' stakeholders previously excluded from consideration. With Churchman it is the responsibility of the systems designer to ensure that boundaries are redrawn so that the system comes to serve all its customers. In one of his examples he notes that women have not been taken into consideration in some proposed systems designs. Ulrich readily accepts the significance of boundary judgements, but does not want to leave responsibility for getting them right to the individual systems designer. He is influenced here by Habermas who argued that rationality emerges from dialogue. On this basis Ulrich suggests that appropriate boundaries can only be established through dialogue, especially between those involved and those likely to be affected by a systems design.

Another theme of Churchman's, developed by Ulrich, focuses on the apparent need for social systems design to take on the whole system. To critics this makes Churchman's work appear hopelessly idealistic and impractical. All that Churchman is doing, however, is pointing out the fate of all the applied sciences, which have no option but to live with the prospect that localized action based on partial understanding can lead to unexpected consequences in terms of whole system improvement. Ulrich (1983) argues, therefore, that the critics are blaming the messenger for the bad news. Reading Churchman positively we see that he is using the theoretical indispensability of comprehensive systems design as an ideal standard to force us to recognize the inevitable lack of comprehensiveness of our actual designs. Ulrich is intent on finding a way of proceeding given Churchman's insight that what is necessary if we are to justify our designs (understanding the whole system) is in practice impossible. His approach is about making the lack of comprehensiveness of our designs transparent so that we can reflect critically on their limitations.

11.2.2 Philosophy and theory

Ulrich calls his approach 'critical systems heuristics', interpreting each of these words as did the philosopher Kant. To be *critical* means reflecting on the presuppositions that enter into both the search for knowledge and the pursuit of rational action. Systems designers must make transparent to themselves and others the normative content of their designs so that they can be subject to inspection and debate. The *systems* idea in Kant refers to the totality of elements – ethical, political, ideological and metaphysical – on which theoretical or practical judgements depend. In trying to grasp the whole system we inevitably fall short and produce limited accounts and suboptimal decisions based on particular presuppositions. What we should try to do, therefore, is unearth the partial presuppositions that underpin the 'whole system' judgements we make. *Heuristics* refers to the process of continually revealing these presuppositions and keeping them under review. Systems designers should never be allowed to get away with the claim that their designs are objective.

These concepts are further developed in a debate with the ideas on social systems design present in or inferred from the writings of Popper, Habermas and Kant (again).

Popper's position is that critical reason can only assist social systems design with technical issues, such as the most efficient means to achieve predetermined ends. Rational answers to questions about ends, and even about the value content of means, are apparently not possible. This is the attitude Ulrich sees as assumed in systems science. The goals served go unexamined and all the effort is put into finding the most efficient means of achieving taken-for-granted ends. Ulrich wants to bring the central question of practical reason – 'what ought we to do?' – back within the scope of critical reflection and rational guidance.

Habermas' work is of great help to Ulrich because he has sought to show that both practical reason and emancipatory reason (aiming at freedom from oppression) are capable of being brought within the domain of critical reflection and reasoned argument. In order that such questions as 'what ought to be done' may be properly decided, according to Habermas, a process of rational argumentation must be established. All citizens, or at least all those affected by a social systems design, must be allowed to participate in the debates and decisions concerning the design. This echoes the soft systems thinkers' call for participation, but Habermas goes much further. The debates surrounding the design must be so arranged that all ideological and institutional constraints on discussion are eliminated, and the force of the better argument wins the day. Through an analysis of the structure of actual speech situations, Habermas is able to determine what an 'ideal speech situation', free from all distortion, must be like. This is his theory of 'communicative competence'.

Ulrich is willing to follow Habermas in grounding rationality on dialogue (a break from Kant), but he worries about the applicability of Habermas' musings. In essence he sees Habermas' work as providing a theoretical basis for critical reflection, but as having little practical usefulness. In order to enter Habermas' debate it appears that speakers must already be willing and able to exhibit communicative competence. This presupposes the very rationality the debate is designed to ensure. Habermas, in attempting to ground critical reflection theoretically, cuts himself off from the real world in which personal and group interests inevitably contaminate any such debate. Far better, Ulrich argues, to ground critical reflection on social systems designs *heuristically*, to provide a methodology that enables practical judgements to be constantly reviewed and their partiality revealed by ordinary, everyday accounts of the nature of social experience.

Ulrich returns to Kant's philosophy for clues on how the judgements we make can be unearthed and reflected on. Kant wanted to find a way of justifying the kind of knowledge we have about the world. He was particularly concerned about what he called *synthetic* a priori concepts. These concepts were deeply implicated in the production of knowledge, but were little understood and difficult to justify. Kant attempted to show the theoretical necessity for thought and knowledge about the world of three sets of *synthetic* a priori concepts. First are two 'pure forms of intuition' – space and time – present in the very possibility of things as appearances. Second are 12 'categories', pure concepts of understanding necessary to connect perceptions together. Finally, there are three 'transcendental ideas' – the

World, Man and God. These reveal to us the necessary conditional character of our understanding of the totality.

11.2.3 Methodology

Ulrich now has to transform the philosophy and theory he finds attractive into a methodology applicable to planning and systems design. The result is CSH.

He begins (Ulrich, 1983) by outlining the 'purposeful systems paradigm' that underpins his methodology. Kant had argued that space and time are necessary mapping dimensions for the objects studied by Newtonian natural science. Social systems designers inevitably come up against human intentionality (self-consciousness, self-reflectiveness and self-determination) as well as space and time. Ulrich reasons, therefore, that if we wish to understand and improve social reality, we must add an additional dimension of 'purposefulness' and design social systems to become purposeful systems. In a purposeful system the ability to determine purposes must be spread throughout the system; the system should produce knowledge relevant to purposes and encourage debate about purposes; and all plans or design proposals should be critically assessed in terms of their normative content.

The next step is to construct some principles for the methodology around Kant's three transcendental ideas. In Kant these notions are employed to reveal the necessarily limited character of our understanding of the whole. They are adjusted by Ulrich to yield the 'systems', 'moral' and 'guarantor' concepts (quasitranscendental ideas more suited to social reality and capable of acting as critical standards against which the partiality of particular social system designs can be compared). The systems idea (as we saw) requires us to reflect on the inevitable lack of comprehensiveness of attempts to map social reality and produce system designs. The moral idea instructs the systems designer to use his or her designs to improve the human condition for all, but at the same time to question constantly the values built into designs and consider their moral imperfection. Moral limitations are best revealed by listening to the views of those affected, but not involved in planning. The guarantor idea insists that there can be no absolute guarantee that planning will lead to improvement; but, the systems designer should seek to incorporate as many sources of imperfect guarantee as possible. This means taking into account any scientific data available, evaluation feedback, etc., as well as the views of experts and other stakeholders.

The next stage of the methodology is intended to assist systems designers to make transparent to themselves and others the 'whole system' judgements (limited by knowledge, ethics and guarantee) that inevitably enter into social systems designs. Ulrich suggests using the concept of 'boundary judgements'. When planners design systems they inevitably make assumptions about what is inside the system of concern and what belongs to its environment. These boundary judgements reflect the designers' whole system judgements about what is relevant to the design task. If they are not made transparent, they also represent 'justification break-offs', revealing the scope of responsibility accepted by the designers in justifying their designs. Thus boundary judgements provide an access point to the normative presuppositions entering into systems designs. The task is to find a means of interrogating systems designs to reveal the boundary judgements currently being made and a means of asking what other boundary judgements might be possible.

Ulrich proceeds to look at the nature of the boundary judgements that must inevitably enter into any social systems design. These are said to have *heuristic* necessity and so the status of *synthetic*, relatively a priori concepts. They are heuristically necessary because only by making them explicit does it become possible to reflect critically on the presuppositions conditioning a social systems design. The boundary judgements meeting this criterion are 12 in number (like Kant's 12 'categories') and are arranged around a distinction between those 'involved' in any planning decision (client, decision-taker, designer) and those 'affected but not involved' (witnesses).

To reveal the boundary judgements involved, boundary questions must be asked for each of the four groups – client, decision-taker, designer and witnesses. The questions relating to the client concern the 'sources of motivation' flowing into the design. They are about its purposes. The questions relating to the decision-taker examine 'sources of control'. They are about the design's 'basis of power'. The questions relating to the designer concern 'sources of expertise'. They ask for the basis of guarantee. And the questions relating to the witnesses reflect on the 'sources of legitimation' considered in the design. So they ask about the values it incorporates.

There are three questions asked of each of the four groups – giving the complete set of 12 boundary questions. The first question is about the 'social roles' of the involved or affected; the second refers to 'role-specific concerns'; and the third to 'key problems' surrounding the determination of boundary judgements with respect to that group.

The power of the 12 questions to reveal the normative content of systems designs is best seen if they are asked in an 'is' mode and an 'ought' mode, and the answers contrasted. For example, we could compare the answer to the question 'who is the actual *client* (beneficiary) of the system S to be

Table 11.1 Ulrich's 12 boundary questions in the 'ought' mode.

1. Who ought to be the *client* (beneficiary) of the system S to be designed or improved?
2. What ought to be the *purpose* of S (i.e., what goal states ought S be able to achieve so as to serve the client)?
3. What ought to be S's *measure of success* (or improvement)?
4. Who ought to be the *decision-taker* (i.e., have the power to change S's measure of improvement)?
5. What *components* (resources and constraints) of S ought to be controlled by the decision-taker)?
6. What resources and conditions ought to be part of S's *environment* (i.e., not be controlled by S's decision-taker)?
7. Who ought to be involved as *designer* of S?
8. What kind of *expertise* ought to flow into the design of S (i.e., who ought to be considered an expert and what should be his role)?
9. Who ought to be the *guarantor* of S (i.e., where ought the designer seek the guarantee that his design will be implemented and will prove successful, judged by S's measure of success (or improvement))?
10. Who ought to belong to the *witnesses* representing the concerns of the citizens that will or might be affected by the design of S (i.e., who among the affected ought to get involved)?
11. To what degree and in what way ought the affected be given the chance of *emancipation* from the premises and promises of the involved?
12. On what *worldview* of either the involved or the affected ought S's design be based?

designed or improved?' with answers to the question 'who ought to be the *client* (beneficiary) of the system S to be designed or improved?' The 12 questions are set out, in the 'ought' mode, in Table 11.1.

Using the 12 boundary questions makes explicit the normative premises that inevitably flow into systems designs. For Ulrich, no systems design can be regarded as rational unless it does reveal its own normative content. This, however, is not the only criterion of rationality. The final justification for practical action, Ulrich insists (following Habermas), must come from some sort of participative debate involving all relevant stakeholders. Habermas' forum of speakers exhibiting communicative competence has, however, already been dismissed as impracticable. Ulrich suggests instead, as the final element of his methodology, a 'dialectical solution' to the problem.

It is not enough that the involved, making use of the heuristically necessary concepts, be self-reflective about the partiality of their designs.

They must also be subject to a dialogue with the witnesses – in practice, representatives of those affected, but not involved. The witnesses need only state their concerns in everyday language since the 'polemical employment of reason' (Kant) in itself will be enough to reveal that the social systems designs of the involved are based on challengeable assumptions. It will become clear that only agreement among all involved and affected citizens can finally lead to conclusions about what ought to be done. Ulrich's dialectical solution, therefore, is to bring the systems rationality of the planners directly into contact with the 'social rationality' of those who have to live in and experience the social systems designs.

11.2.4   Methods

Methods are provided for assisting with the exposure of the normative assumptions entering into social systems designs and to ensure proper dialogue between those involved in planning and those affected, but not involved.

In the first case we have Ulrich's list of 12 boundary questions, which we detailed in the previous subsection because they are so intrinsically embedded in his methodology. These can be used to interrogate existing or proposed systems designs and, as we mentioned, in an 'is' or 'ought' mode. Midgley (2000) has suggested that they include some jargon and that it can be useful to employ other versions of the questions in plain English. There will be other alternative methods that can be used for getting at normative assumptions. It is also clear that the 12 questions can be extracted from Ulrich's overall approach and used as a tool to support other methodologies. They are very much a method in these senses.

To ensure proper dialogue Ulrich suggests a tool called the 'polemical employment of boundary judgements'. This is a practical method that ordinary citizens can employ to cause the involved to reflect on their design's normative content even if they should appear less than willing to do so.

The main obstacle that might seem to lie in the way of the affected is their lack of expertise and, therefore, their apparent lack of 'objectivity'. However, as Ulrich shows, this is not really such a difficulty. All designs are based on boundary judgements incorporating justification break-offs and these are, of course, beyond the reach of expertise to justify. Anyone who understands the concept of boundary judgements knows that planners who justify their proposals on the basis of expertise or 'objective facts' are in fact employing boundary judgements whether cynically or unreflectively. If they can be made to debate their boundary judgements they are put in a position where they are no better off than ordinary affected citizens. It becomes a matter of trading value judgements about what assumptions should influence plans and what consequences are desirable or otherwise.

In order to put recalcitrant planners into a position where they have to admit their boundary judgements, Ulrich advocates the 'polemical employment of boundary judgements'. Affected citizens use different boundary judgements, reflecting an alternative value position, purely with critical intent against the planners. This is quite good enough to shift the burden of proof onto the planners because it demonstrates:

- that the planners' proposals are governed by their boundary judgements;
- that the knowledge and expertise of experts is insufficient to justify their boundary judgements or to falsify those of others;
- that planners or experts who seek to justify designs on the basis of knowledge or expertise are, in fact, employing boundary judgements dogmatically or cynically, and so disqualify themselves.

The technique should secure a position in the dialogue for any ordinary citizens who care to employ it.

11.2.5 Recent developments

In his more recent writings Ulrich (1998) has been propounding a research programme called 'Critical Systems Thinking for Citizens'. The aim is to contribute to the revival of civil society by further developing and simplifying his 'emancipatory systems approach', particularly the idea of boundary critique, so that it can be used by ordinary citizens to help them participate fully in decisions over matters of public concern.

In a similar vein, Gerald Midgley and coworkers at the Centre for Systems Studies at the University of Hull are seeking to extend and pragmatize the work of Churchman and Ulrich on boundary critique. This has involved theoretical innovation as well as the use of CSH alongside other systems methodologies. Midgley (2000) argues that conflict between groups often arises when they possess different ethical positions and thus repeatedly make different boundary judgements. These boundary judgements can become stabilized by social attitudes and rituals. The tendency to unreflectively accept stabilized boundary judgements, and so buttress the status quo, needs addressing at the beginning of a systems intervention. It is necessary, Midgley believes, to challenge whatever consensus exists on boundaries by seeking to involve all those who might have a relevant

perspective on the issue of concern. Having addressed issues of marginalization through boundary critique and ensured the 'sweeping in' of a wide
variety of viewpoints, Midgley recommends proceeding by the 'creative
design of methods'. In negotiation with the various stakeholders, research
questions are identified, each of which may require resolution using a
different method or part of a method. Inevitably, the research questions
will be systemically interrelated, and thus it is necessary to achieve a synthesis
among the methods used to address them, at the same time as ensuring the
continued involvement, if possible, of marginalized groups. If their continued involvement is prevented by the exercise of power, then the researcher
needs to consider whether there might be other ways to represent their
views or contemplate withdrawing his or her services.

11.3   CRITICAL SYSTEMS HEURISTICS (CSH) IN ACTION

The intervention described was conducted by Gerald Midgley, Isaac Munlo
and Mandy Brown of the Centre for Systems Studies, University of Hull,
and was funded by the Joseph Rowntree Foundation (see Midgley et al.,
1997, 1998). Its initial aim was to review how policy for the development
and provision of housing services for older people was informed by data
aggregated from assessments made of individual applicants. Overall, it was
hoped that improvements to the process of information collection, handling
and use would lead to more general improvements in housing services for
older people. The research was to cover possible adaptations to properties
or other assistance needed to enable older people to stay in their homes, as
well as housing itself, and to involve all forms of provision, whether
public, private or by voluntary means.

The researchers suggested a two-stage approach. In a first phase a wide
perspective would be taken on the problems associated with the identification of need, the handling of information and its use for planning. In a
second phase, various stakeholders would be engaged in designing actual
improvements to the information provision aspects of the problem situation.
The researchers were clear that, since this purposeful system was about
designing housing services for older people, it was essential that the affected,
the older people who were clients, should participate in the design.

The first phase – problem identification – consisted of interviews with
relevant stakeholders in two geographical areas. Rather than trying to
determine at the beginning exactly which stakeholders to interview, the

researchers used the approach of 'rolling' out the boundaries of the people they should talk to. This required starting off with an obvious set of interviewees and inviting them, as part of the interview, to suggest who else might reasonably be questioned. Interviewees were asked which other stakeholders were relevant, perhaps because they held a different opinion on the problem situation, and in particular who else was involved in or affected by the interviewee's activities. This process continued until no new names came forward and produced some surprising additions to the original list. In the end 131 interviews were conducted with clients, potential clients, carers, councillors, senior and middle managers, wardens and assessment officers. Local government departments, health purchasers and providers, housing associations, voluntary organizations, private providers, building companies, users and other stakeholders were all represented.

After about 20 of these interviews it was clear that an important choice had to be made, which would impact on the whole of the rest of the study. The interviews revealed that the second phase of the intervention would miss many of the most significant problems that concerned stakeholders if it remained limited to looking only at issues of information provision. This was especially the case because the procedures for collecting information ensured that needs that could not be met within current spending priorities were not even recorded. Older people were asking why there was such a mismatch between what they asked for in terms of housing services and what they got. Further, a number of the agencies involved were highlighting, as their primary concern, the difficulties they encountered in co-operating with other interested parties (i.e., in multiagency working). Neither of these issues could be addressed given the existing narrow specification of the second stage of the project.

The researchers saw this as an ethical problem about where the boundaries were drawn in this problem situation. If they followed the narrow specification they would only be able to increase efficiency and efficacy in the context of current resource distribution. This might lead to improvements in the provision of housing services for older people from the point of view of those who believed current levels of spending appropriate. It could hardly bring about improvements from the perspectives of older people or many of the managers or planners. In terms of the 'systems', 'moral' and 'guarantor' ideas propounded in CSH, accepting the narrow boundaries of the study as originally prescribed could detract from rather than enhance 'whole system improvement'.

The researchers called a meeting of the Advisory Group for the project at which the ethical consequences of different boundary judgements were considered. It was decided that the boundaries of the research should be widened to ensure that the larger problems now identified by some of the stakeholders could be embraced in the next stage of the study. The first phase ended, therefore, with the production of two 'problem maps' showing the interrelationships between key issues, including issues of multi-agency co-operation and of capturing the stated needs of older people.

A workshop was now suggested so that discussions could be held on how the second phase would be conducted. During the preparations for this, however, it became clear that, because of certain sensitivities and the internal politics of the situation, the Housing and Social Services Departments wanted the workshop to be restricted to their own managers. The researchers were concerned that this would lead to the marginalization of the values and interests of users and other involved stakeholders and that they would be implicated in reinforcing this marginalization if they went ahead. Weighing the ethical pros and cons they decided to let the workshop proceed, but to put in place certain safeguards to ensure that the boundaries remained wide. One of the researchers was given the role at the workshop of being advocate for the stakeholders who were not directly represented. And all of the researchers insisted throughout the workshop that the managers who were present try to put themselves in the position of other stakeholders and speak on their behalf. The decision to go ahead was justified and the tactics vindicated when it was clearly specified that the improvements sought in the second phase would be based on the desires of all stakeholders including older people and their carers.

The discussions at the workshop now turned to the methods that would be used to design improvements in the second phase. This again required care on the part of the researchers, lest their knowledge of the intricacies of systems methodologies and use of systems jargon marginalized the managers who would be responsible for the outcomes. The 'systems discussion' was initially conducted by the researchers alone, with the permission and in the presence of the managers. The results were then explained to the managers, and further general debate took place before actual decisions on methods were taken.

The second phase of the intervention – designing improvements – had two parts. In the first part Ackoff's 'idealized design' technique was used alongside Ulrich's 'boundary questions' to discover what the stakeholders felt an ideal housing system for older people needed to be like. This was in response to the outcome of the first phase of the project, which had shown all the various issues to be so interrelated that only a 'problem dissolving' approach was going to be useful. The second part used Beer's viable system model to assist managers from the various involved agencies to design a form of multiagency structure that could support the 'idealized design'.

The first part of the second phase consisted of workshops held separately with three stakeholder groups: older people in receipt of housing services, carers and representatives of relevant community groups and voluntary organizations, and managers and front line professionals working for statutory agencies concerned with housing. The choice of these three groups of affected and involved stakeholders ensured the boundaries continued to be wide. Holding the workshops separately, so that each group had its own space, ensured that 'professional discourses' did not dominate over the ordinary language of users. It avoided the risk of drawing the boundaries back in again.

Employing Ackoff's idealized design technique (see Chapter 9), each group was asked to design an 'ideal' housing system on the basis that the existing service system had disappeared the night before and they could construct its replacement as they wished, so long as it was technologically feasible, viable and adaptable. The natural 'boundary-busting' features of Ackoff's approach were enhanced by using Ulrich's boundary questions to lead the discussions. For example, it was asked 'who should benefit from the provision of housing services to older people?', 'who should be considered an expert?', etc. Ulrich's questions ensured that important boundary matters, which might otherwise have been taken for granted, were raised and debated. To ensure the maximum benefit was obtained from the questions they were translated into plain English and phrased specifically to relate to housing for older people. The workshops produced three long lists of the desired properties of the housing service from the perspectives of the three stakeholder groups.

The three lists defining ideal housing systems were so similar that it was possible for the researchers themselves to produce a first draft synthesis reflecting a single vision. This, together with the disagreements that did exist, was discussed and debated at a further workshop of managers from relevant agencies. At this workshop the researchers again acted as advocates for those groups not directly represented and asked the managers to be careful that the finalized list of desired properties reflected the concerns of users and carers.

In the second part of the second phase the same managers and the researchers used Beer's Viable System Model (VSM) (see Chapter 6) to construct an organizational structure capable of delivering the ideal service while overcoming the existing problems of multiagency working. Beer's model was originally chosen because it was non-hierarchical in the sense of demanding that the primary focus should be on facilitating the work of those directly providing the service (the System 1 elements). During the workshop the model was discussed in simple English to ensure that the expertise of the researchers did not dominate and some changes were made to it as a result. The managers were then asked to use it to provide an organizational design in which each of the five key functions described in the VSM was performed in accordance with the list of desired properties. At the end of the process the final design was validated by systematically checking it against the lists of desired properties of the housing service system produced by the various stakeholders.

This case study offers an excellent example of the design of a purposeful system, the provision of housing services for older people, in which a wide range of involved and affected stakeholders participated to ensure whole system improvement in the way required by the systems, moral and guarantor concepts. Ulrich's boundary questions were employed to ensure critical reflection during the design of an ideal service system. The researchers were able to use the 'polemical employment of boundary judgements' method while acting as advocates for the users. Midgley and his coresearchers added to CSH, in this intervention, an acute awareness that the choice of methods and techniques is itself an important element in ensuring that vulnerable stakeholder groups are not marginalized.

11.4   CRITIQUE OF CRITICAL SYSTEMS HEURISTICS (CSH)

Ulrich's work provides a solid philosophical foundation for the purposeful systems approach and, in CSH, a methodology and techniques to realize the benefits of that approach in practice. If they are to be justifiable, plans for purposeful systems should reflect the values of the widest possible constituency of stakeholders. Particular attention needs to be paid to ensuring representation of those affected by proposed or actual systems designs, but not involved in their formulation. In order that all the stakeholders can evaluate the plans it is essential that they are transparent with regard to the 'boundary judgements' they express — what they focus on and what they exclude from their remit. Groups that do feel excluded can call systems designers to account using the 'polemical employment of boundary judgements' and so secure for themselves a position in the argument. Ulrich believes that this approach can be used by all concerned citizens and thus contribute to an increase in rational decision-making in society.

It will be clear from this brief summary, and the longer account that precedes it, that Ulrich's work expands on soft systems thinking in the way it devotes attention to the interests of those who might otherwise be excluded from debate about social systems design. The values of the 'affected, but not involved', who have to live the consequences of the designs, are emphasized. The debate has to be made accessible to them, and they must be enabled to participate without being cowed by the expertise or power of others. CSH seeks to emancipate all 'citizens' by empowering them to take part in dialogue about the shape and direction of the purposeful systems their actions and interactions produce and which they inhabit.

How successful is it?

Critics argue (see Jackson, 1985, 2000; Midgley, 1997) that CSH is limited by the type of critical thinking, emanating from Kant and Churchman, that it embraces. Kant and Churchman are seen as 'idealists' and as providing Ulrich with a form of critique that is only able to reflect on the values and ideas that enter into social systems designs. Philosophers and sociologists of a 'materialist' persuasion (e.g., Marx and the theorists associated with the Frankfurt School) want to extend critique to the material conditions that give rise to particular values and beliefs. They argue that the social positions of stakeholders, in organizations and the wider society, go a long way to explaining the ideas that they hold. A historical materialist analysis would reveal how values and beliefs arise; how they are related to the political and economic aspects of the totality; and how power, deriving from the very structures of society, determines that certain ideologies dominate at particular times.

This neglect of the structural aspects of social systems leads directly to another criticism: Ulrich's recommendations are ultimately just as Utopian as those of Habermas. Critics are led to ask 'why should the involved bother to take account of the views and interests of those who are affected but not involved?', 'which class, group or agency has the power, will and interest to bring about a rational society in which the better argument wins through?' It is because Ulrich neglects this type of question that Midgley (1997) believes the successful use of CSH depends on there already existing a situation in which some kind of forum for debate is in operation where planners have to consider their accountability. It is hardly, therefore, an adequate response to power and coercion since these are likely to lead to closure of debate. If Ulrich wanted to be genuinely 'emancipatory' he would have to develop an appropriate social theory and then confront the forces in organizations and society that prevent rational argumentation and participative decision-making.

A third line of criticism is intimately related to these first two. If CSH does not possess a social theory it cannot provide much assistance, let alone an answer, to the question of where the boundaries should be drawn in undertaking a social system design. In Mejia's (2001) terms it is a 'content-less' form of critique. The answers to the 12 critically heuristic categories need 'filling in', perhaps by the stakeholders in the design situation, perhaps by those who bring CSH to that situation. In the former case this may simply be on the basis of the knowledge held tacitly and unquestioningly by those stakeholders, who may not, for example, recognize that they are discriminating against women. In the latter case it can lead to the imposition of the analyst's predetermined views in the name of critique. These dangers are reinforced if certain stakeholders are inarticulate, lack confidence, suffer from learning disabilities or, for whatever other reason, are unable to engage effectively in rational argumentation. They are highlighted by studies that suggest CSH and the 12 questions are not so 'commonsensical' and easy to use as Ulrich believes.

Finally, Flood and Jackson (1991) accuse CSH of methodological immaturity. It lacks the well-tried methods, tools and techniques to support it that, for example, soft systems methodology has developed. Moreover, Ulrich has not thought through the relationship of his approach to others and is overly dismissive of those systems methodologies that serve 'instrumental reason'. This is unfortunate because rational social action depends on what it is possible to do and on the choice of efficient means (matters of instrumental reason) as well as on what we ought to do (a matter of practical reason and, as we know, Ulrich's overriding concern). Recently, case studies have begun to emerge, from Midgley and others, that employ CSH and seek to develop it to make it more usable. It is noticeable, however, that in all these instances CSH is used alongside other, more established systems approaches.

At a more theoretical level, in terms of the System Of Systems Methodologies (SOSM) outlined in Chapter 2, Ulrich has moved systems thinking along the horizontal 'participants dimension', noting the possible existence of coercion and seeking ways to counter it in order that all stakeholders can take part in debate about change. In doing so, he follows soft systems thinking in continuing to honour the culture and political system metaphors and expands on it by responding, to a degree, to the psychic prison and instruments of domination metaphors. CSH does not see its role as managing complexity along the 'systems dimension' of the SOSM, and it is not surprising, therefore, that Ulrich rails against the machine, organism and brain metaphors that dominate what he calls 'systems science'. It is arguable, however, that this lack of attention to complexity in the real world defeats his intention of supplying an 'emancipatory' systems approach. CSH can respond to transparent causes of coercion, but is useless in the face of complex–coercive situations where, for example, power might find its expression through a mobilization of bias expressed in the very structures of society, or in the existence of 'false consciousness'.

In paradigm language, CSH rejects functionalism and takes seriously the need to extend interpretive thinking in an emancipatory direction. It wants to enlighten all stakeholders, especially disadvantaged ones, about the nature of the social systems designs they encounter and empower them to participate in debate about the validity of such designs. It is, however, an emancipatory approach of a very limited kind. CSH fails to provide any account of the social structures that may lie behind and determine the character of the debate and its outcomes.

11.5 THE VALUE OF CRITICAL SYSTEMS HEURISTICS (CSH) TO MANAGERS

CSH's value to managers can be summarized in the following five points:

- It offers an 'inclusive' systems approach that emphasizes the benefits of incorporating the values of all stakeholders in planning and decision-making.
- CSH puts the concept of 'boundary' at the centre of systems thinking and makes it easy to see that drawing the boundary around a problem situation in different ways impacts massively on how it is seen and what is done.
- It allows managers and others to question whose values are being respected and whose interests served by particular systems designs.
- CSH demands that attention be given to disadvantaged stakeholders, especially those affected by a design, but not involved in it.
- CSH empowers managers and other stakeholders by undermining the notion that expertise rules in planning and design, and allows them to fully participate in discussions and decisions about purposes.

11.6 CONCLUSION

The systems tradition has long been strong in methodologies for the efficient design of systems to achieve known goals. More recently, soft systems thinking has provided approaches capable, in pluralistic situations, of achieving sufficient accommodation among stakeholders for some agreed course of action to follow. Until the publication of Ulrich's *Critical Heuristics of Social Planning*, however, there was no systems approach that provided a means for critically reflecting either on the goals sought and the means used in hard systems thinking or on the nature of the accommodations achieved and the changes brought about through soft systems thinking. CSH has, therefore, helped to fill a significant gap.

CSH is now most frequently used in multiagency situations where it is important to gain the commitment of all parties and to take account of the wishes of clients who may have limited opportunity, otherwise, to have their perspectives taken into account. It will be interesting to see if its range can be extended to more hierarchical settings. Managers of all types are increasingly being asked to account for the performance of their organizations on such matters as provision for disabled people, sexual discrimination, racial equality, equal opportunities for people from different social classes and environmental protection. Perhaps if they incorporated CSH in their repertoires they would already know they were acting responsibly and their organizations would benefit as a result.

REFERENCES

Flood, R.L. and Jackson, M.C. (1991). *Creative Problem Solving: Total Systems Intervention*. John Wiley & Sons, Chichester, UK.

Jackson, M.C. (1985). The itinerary of a critical approach: Review of Ulrich's 'Critical Heuristics of Social Planning'. *Journal of the Operational Research Society*, **36**, 878–881.

Jackson, M.C. (2000). *Systems Approaches to Management*. Kluwer/Plenum, New York.

Mejia, A. (2001). *The Problem of Knowledge Imposition: Paulo Freire and Critical Systems Thinking* (Research Memorandum No. 29). University of Hull Business School, Hull, UK.

Midgley, G. (1997). Dealing with coercion: Critical systems heuristics and beyond. *Systems Practice*, **10**, 37–57.

Midgley, G. (2000). *Systemic Intervention: Philosophy, Methodology and Practice*. Kluwer/Plenum, New York.

Midgley, G., Munlo, I. and Brown, M. (1997). *Sharing Power*. Policy Press, Bristol.

Midgley, G., Munlo, I. and Brown, M. (1998). The theory and practice of boundary critique: Developing housing services for older people. *Journal of the Operational Society*, **49**, 467–478.

Ulrich, W. (1983). *Critical Heuristics of Social Planning*. Haupt, Bern.

Ulrich, W. (1988). Systems thinking, systems practice and practical philosophy: A program of research. *Systems Practice*, **1**, 137–153.

Ulrich, W. (1998). *Systems Thinking as if People Mattered: Critical Systems Thinking for Citizens and Managers* (Working Paper No. 23). University of Lincoln, Lincoln, UK.

Ulrich, W. (2003). Beyond methodology choice: Critical systems thinking as critically systemic discourse. *Journal of the Operational Research Society*, **54**, 325–342.

Team Syntegrity   12

*When I started to construct physical polyhedra with my own hands, it was truly a revelation to follow Bucky's route. An unwholesome mess of wooden doweling, panel pins, rubber bands, string, and glue, strengthened with gratuitous contributions from skin and beard, quite suddenly transformed itself into a polyhedron so strong that I could actually **stand** on it.*

Beer (1990)

12.1 INTRODUCTION

Stafford Beer, the founder of organizational cybernetics and inventor of the Viable System Model (VSM) (see Chapter 6), devoted his last years to the development and refinement of an approach to democratic decision-making called Team Syntegrity.

Team syntegrity provides a theory and a set of procedures (a 'protocol') that support non-hierarchical, participative and effective decision-making around a topic that is interesting for a group of people who share some knowledge and experience relating to it. It is of obvious value in organizations that are already democratic and in multiorganizational settings where, of necessity, the commitment of a variety of stakeholders to action has to be obtained. White (1994, 1998) illustrates the latter scenario, describing team syntegrity sessions that debated the questions 'how can we, sovereign world citizens, govern our world?' and 'how should we run London?' But its use is by no means confined to such situations. Indeed in the postindustrial age, where democracy and decentralization are coming to be valued more highly than hierarchy and centralization, there is likely to be an increasing need for Team Syntegrity to promote inclusiveness, flatter structures and self-management even in otherwise conventional organizations.

Beer's book *Beyond Dispute: The Invention of Team Syntegrity*, published in 1994, presents all the theoretical and practical aspects of the approach. Since that time the protocol has been used extensively and has shown its worth in supporting teamwork, particularly (according to Schwaninger, 1997) in relation to problems of planning, innovation and knowledge acquisition.

This chapter draws heavily on previous work by Angela Espinosa (2003) who was also the organizer and a facilitator of the 'Gorgona Syntegration' described in Section 12.3. I am grateful to her for her help.

12.2   DESCRIPTION OF TEAM SYNTEGRITY

12.2.1   Historical development

The origins of team syntegrity lie, on the one hand, in what Beer sees as a misunderstanding of his VSM and, on the other, in a necessary requirement of that model (see Beer, 1990).

The misunderstanding is that the VSM is hierarchical. Beer believes that this arises from people taking at face value the diagram that usually depicts System 5, 'the boss', at the top. A more sophisticated grasp of the model reveals that the sole purpose of Systems 2 through 5 is to facilitate the functioning of the embedded System 1. After all, Beer protests, 'are not the lowest autonomic functions in the human body represented in the cortex?' and 'is not the leadership of a democracy supposed to embody the will of the people?' In this sense the emphasis Beer has given to developing a protocol for democratic dialogue is his rebuke to all those he feels have got the VSM wrong. But, what essential requirement of the model does it meet?

In his work on the VSM, Beer highlighted the need for organizations to develop conversational tools that can handle the divergent and often conflicting viewpoints of their members and facilitate the emergence of a shared social consciousness. In order to define and specify a resolution to most policy, control, co-ordination and monitoring issues it is important to have proper communications mechanisms that can deal with the variety the participants necessarily bring to their discussions. For example, as we saw in Chapter 6, it is essential to promote rich and productive debate at the point in an enterprise where information about its internal state (generated by System 3) is brought together with information about the external environment (generated by System 4); a point known as the 'operations room' in VSM parlance. Beer knew, based on Ashby's work on variety, that most organizational structures are variety inhibitors and constrain interaction and debate because they impose barriers reflecting organizational rules and practices. If the required conversations and debates are to take place at the high variety levels necessary and achieve the kinds of balances demanded throughout the architecture of the VSM, it is important to pay attention to the design of the negotiation spaces in which they occur and to create the democratic conditions in which all relevant viewpoints and world views can be fully expressed and taken into account.

Beer set out in search of a mechanism that could integrate, through democratic dialogue, the ideas and experiences of participants, promote effective synergy and translate the outcome into social knowledge. As a cybernetician, he looked for useful analogies that could be drawn between other scientific fields and the social domain in which he was interested. He explored holography (the study of wholes that are manifest in their parts), experimented with lasers and toyed with various abstruse areas of mathematics. One day, in a completely different context, Beer remembered Buckminster Fuller's dictum: 'All systems are polyhedra.' At once he recognized that no structure could be less hierarchical than a regular polyhedron – an example being the geodesic dome that Fuller had designed. Furthermore, in a geodesic dome the whole gains its cohesive strength from the tension existing between the faces. This was the example of 'structural synergy' that he wanted, and he began to construct physical polyhedra himself in order to understand better their nature and properties. Beer (1990) found to his amazement that using wooden dowelling, panel pins, rubber bands, string, and glue, together with, as he put it, 'gratuitous contributions from skin and beard', he was able to build a polyhedron so strong that he, a man of large stature, could stand on it.

To a holistic thinker, like Beer, the geodesic dome was likely to be just one expression of a 'natural invariance' that would be repeated throughout the natural and social worlds. Fuller, indeed, was already producing designs for cars, ships and houses based on the same structural characteristics. He determined, therefore, to investigate the phenomenon as a possible guide for democratic and effective dialogue. The analogy he developed was of a group of participants (an 'Infoset') that is consciously trying to express its integrity by compressing a shared idea into a cohesive statement, but is also experiencing the tension that discussions and arguments produce in the process. A Fullerian tensegrity (tensile integrity) balance would help as a model for designing this conversational space.

12.2.2   Philosophy and theory

Beer (1990, 1994) follows Fuller in regarding the icosahedron as the most interesting of the regular polyhedra and as the type exhibiting the most perfect tensegrity in nature. He sees it, therefore, as a possible model for an ideal democracy. Using the analogy, democracy and the robustness and effectiveness of the process are guaranteed by organizing discussion according to this particular geometric structure. To understand the theory underlying Team Syntegrity, therefore, we have to know about the peculiar properties of the icosahedron.

The icosahedron has 20 triangular sides described by 30 edges. It has 12 vertices each connecting five edges. Figure 12.1 shows the shape of the icosahedron. We now have to think through how these properties can be transferred to the social domain to provide for democratic and synergistic conversations.

Taking the icosahedron to represent an organization, or the 'Infoset', Beer asks us to regard each of the edges as a person. There are therefore 30

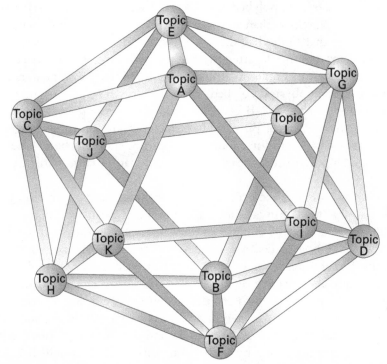

Figure 12.1   An icosahedron showing how 30 'people' (edges) are connected to 12 'topics' (vertices).

people. Each of the 12 vertices gathers five edges together. If a vertex is regarded as a discussion group, there are, therefore, 12 groups and 60 group members. As each edge (or person) has two ends, each of the 30 people belongs to two groups and no two people belong to the same two teams. Again:

- There are 30 people, divided into 12 discussion groups.
- Each person belongs to two groups, which might be called his or her left-hand and right-hand group. Thus there are 60 team members. No person belongs to the same two teams as anyone else.

Beer regards this as a good start for a model of a perfect democracy because it exhibits no global hierarchy – each of the 12 teams have identical structures, connectivities and relative position. Moreover, this arrangement demonstrates total closure; it is in logical terms self-referential. If the discussions are appropriately ordered, this should produce the phenomenon of 'reverberation'. Views emanating from one discussion group will reverberate around the structure, gaining and losing adherents, consolidating and subtly changing, and this should ensure maximum creativity among the groups and generate synergy.

The other benefit of the icosahedron, for Beer, lies in its structural strength. Fuller had discovered that polyhedral structures, like the icosahedron, are held together by what he called 'tensile integrity', or 'tensegrity' for short. Tensegrity is defined by Fuller as the unity of the structure of any physical object as determined by its distributed tensile stresses. In structures like the geodesic dome the forces of compression and tension achieve a natural, reinforced balance. The integrity of the structure then derives not from the local compressor stresses where elements conjoin, but from the overall tensile stresses governing the entire system.

Fuller achieved cohesive strength in the geodesic dome by running struts between the centres of adjacent triangular faces, thus providing for a thick two-dimensional skin. Beer recognized that in his theoretical construct, of an organization exhibiting tensegrity, even greater strength could be obtained by driving the 'struts' straight through the central spaces that, in the architectural design, had to be kept open. He now had to work out what the correlate of a strut is in organizational terms.

Beer came up with the idea of 'critics', appointed to each of the teams formed at the vertices, from positions across the phase space. Critics were to offer constructive advice to the team on the basis that they were relatively disinterested members of the whole organization and individuals having detailed specialized knowledge of one other, but unadjacent team. The tension created by each critic was to be balanced by appointing a member of the receiving team as a critic to another distant team – in fact, the second team of which the original critic is also a member. Again:

- Each person is appointed a critic of a team of which he or she is not a member. The team to which he or she is appointed as a critic will appoint a critic to his or her right-hand team.
- Similarly, each person becomes a critic in that team of which he or she is not a member, but of which a right-hand teammate is a member. And that team will appoint a critic to his or her left-hand team.
- Since each person has two critical appointments, there are 60 critics spread with tensegrity over 12 teams. So, each five-member team has five more quasimembers who are critics as defined.

We now have a model of an organization generating synergy out of perfect democracy and, at the same time, demonstrating great strength and cohesion because of its tensegrity. The model exhibits synergistic tensegrity or 'syntegrity'. It remains necessary to specify how this theory can be translated into practice through the 'protocol' of team syntegrity.

12.2.3 Methodology

Essentially, team syntegrity is a process that guides non-hierarchical group decision-making for an 'Infoset' of 30 people who share an interest in addressing an issue of particular concern to them and about which they will inevitably have different opinions. The 30 individuals must agree to a communications protocol – a set of procedures designed to extract maximum advantage from the qualities of the icosahedron. The protocol establishes how these individuals share information about the issue, develop their conversations and reach conclusions. It places the participants in roles of equal status so that every voice is heard and no individual is allowed to dominate. People are divided into groups, meetings are sequenced and information is distributed in such a way as to ensure a highly interactive and democratic event, which offers the best opportunities for balancing tension and synergy as the groups negotiate different viewpoints. It should be clear that the protocol simply specifies the form of the interactions and conversations in the Infoset. It puts no restrictions and makes no comment on the content of what is said. That is left up to the judgement of individuals and the teams.

A team syntegrity exercise, in its classic form, will last for around five days and have five stages:

- opening;
- generation of the agenda;
- topic auction;
- outcome resolve;
- closing session.

Once the decision to use the methodology has been made, the first step is to agree on an 'opening' question that captures the issue on which all participants hope to reach agreement. Participants are then selected and should include a rich variety of perspectives on the opening question; in a multi-agency situation, for example, representatives from different geographical regions, ethnic, age, gender and status groups, and from communities and institutions affected by the issue. The participants are invited to the opening of the event.

During the first actual session the participants concentrate on 'generating an agenda' that will help them to address the opening question. Since they are going to be divided into 12 groups, this requires clustering the concerns of all the 30 individual participants around 12 main issues, or 'topics', that will be the focus of discussion.

The 'topic auction' sees the 30 participants allocated in different groups according to their preferences among the topics and the logic of the icosahedron. Individuals are asked to rank their preferred topics and an algorithm is employed to ensure that the highest level of satisfaction is obtained while respecting the constraints imposed by the structure of the icosahedron. Each of the 12 vertices is taken to represent 1 of the 12 topics for discussion (topics A–L in Figure 12.1) and, as we know, each edge represents one participant. Thus every discussion group is allocated five people, corresponding to the vertex that is formed by five edges joining together. And each participant ends up assigned to two groups defined by the ends of their edge. The structure then determines which two other topics the person will be a critic of. There are, therefore, 12 teams each developing 1 of the topics and consisting of 5 members and 5 critics. Each of the 30 people involved plays 2 roles: a participant in the 2 groups defined by their edge and a critic in the 2 groups defined by the edge on the opposite side of the icosahedron. Once the groups are fixed in the topic auction they remain the same for the remainder of the exercise.

The topic auction ensures that maximum lateral communication is obtained and, in Beer's view, enables 'reverberation' to happen in the closed system represented by the icosahedron. Participants feel ideas rebounding back to them in a different and enhanced form.

The fourth stage, the 'outcome resolve', takes up the majority of the 5 days and consists of a series of meetings of the 12 groups. The meetings typically last between 45 and 75 minutes and each group will meet 3 or 4 times depending on the time available. The sequence of meetings is determined by the protocol, which stems from the geometry of the icosahedron. As each participant is involved in developing 2 issues and as a critic of 2 others, it turns out that only 2 groups can meet at any one time. The 5 discussants in each group seek to work up their thinking on the topic into an insightful Final Statement of Importance (FSI). The 5 critics on the team must remain silent while this process is going on, but may then join in with 10 minutes of relevant questioning. The critics should act as devil's advocates by challenging the group to review any agreements reached and questioning the assumptions behind apparent agreements. Observers may also be present from other groups that are not meeting and, while they may not intervene, they can scrawl on any written outcomes ('graffiti') and make use of the information they garner from being present in the sessions when they are discussants or critics.

Given that each participant belongs to four teams (two as participant, two as a critic), they act as information diffusion channels, rapidly spreading information around the different teams. This produces the desired reverberation or 'echo effect', so that all the team members share information about all the others thanks to the icosahedron structure. It has been demonstrated that after the third iteration around 90% of the information initially generated about the opening question has been distributed among all the participants.

After each iteration of meetings there is a plenary session at which the 12 teams present the current results of their conversations and raise questions and proposals concerning the content of the discussions or the methodology itself.

At the end of the whole event there is a 'closing' plenary session where the teams present their FSIs. There are 12 of these, one for each team, which by now should meet with general assent in the Infoset. Teams are also invited to assess the event and methodology, and their own learning and experience as participants. Plans for further meetings or actions can be made at this closing session.

12.2.4 Methods

Team Syntegrity Inc., the company that brought the methodology to market, has developed special tools for supporting the planning and delivery of team syntegrity sessions. We have already mentioned the optimization software for deciding team membership. There are also various brainstorming, visual applause, and other creative and democratic techniques for sharing information and promoting enhanced group learning. Here we describe one approach to generation of the agenda (to give an idea of what can be done) and comment on the important role that facilitators play in Team Syntegrity as well.

A much used technique for helping to generate the agenda is called the 'problem jostle'. The 30 participants and the facilitators assemble in a large room with extensive wall space, to which documents can be affixed, and containing 12 tables with a few chairs around each. The problem jostle begins with each player submitting to the facilitators at least one Statement of Importance (SI) that he or she feels is particularly relevant to the opening question. An SI should be a concise, one- or two-sentence assertion. The facilitators scrutinize the SIs, eliding any that say similar things, type them up and make them available to the players. Any player who then regards a particular SI of extreme importance can move to one of the 12 tables (called 'hours' because they are arranged in the pattern of a clock), name the SI and start a discussion group around that topic. Other players are free to champion alternative SIs in this way, join existing discussion groups or simply wander around the room. When, at a given table, enthusiasm develops around a particular topic, its advocates can write the topic down and seek further adherents to their cause. Any topic that gains five signatories is classed as an Aggregated Statement of Importance (ASI). While this self-organizing process is taking place, the facilitators assist by pointing out similarities between certain ASIs and by seeking to position 'polar opposite' statements at polar extreme 'hours' (e.g., 6 and 12). The first session of the problem jostle should end with all 12 hours having ASIs beside them. The next three sessions are designed to promote further reflection on existing ASIs, the emergence of new ASIs, and the reduction and refinement of these to just 12 Composite Statements of Importance (CSIs) arranged according to the prescribed pattern. This is known as 'hexadic reduction'. If necessary, a rating system can be employed to decide on the best CSIs.

If the facilitators have an important role in helping generation of the agenda, they are crucial in the outcome resolve. During each team meeting a facilitator is responsible for handling the variety of the conversations and integrating the contributions from all the participants and critics. He or she moderates the amount of time taken by each discussant in the conversation, making sure all have the opportunity to have an equal say. The critics too must be allocated time to make their contribution. The facilitator aims to give the participants the space and time they need to have an impact. It is not his or her role to influence the content of what is said. The facilitator needs skills in hearing, understanding and feeding back the participants' conversations. He or she is also responsible for making a visible record of the important issues addressed. In this he or she may have the support of a technical assistant, with a computer, who records an electronic version of the development of team conversations so that they can be reproduced for the plenary sessions.

12.2.5 Recent developments

In *Beyond Dispute* Beer describes the traditional form of team syntegrity involving 30 people over around 5 days. However, he was, from the beginning, aware of the difficulties created by the strict demands of this form. More recently, Joe Truss, of Team Syntegrity Inc., has developed protocols called *ShortForms* and *SmallForms*. The most widely used *Short-Form* involves 24 to 30 people over 3.5 days. A *SmallForm* event requires 12 people over 2 to 3 days.

One of the main questions asked of team syntegrity is what it does to assist with implementation after the event. To answer this Joe Truss has continued to refine 'FACE planning' (see Beer, 1994) to co-ordinate further meetings of willing and available Infoset members. This has been tested and found to work following a number of syntegrations in recent years.

12.3 TEAM SYNTEGRITY IN ACTION

Readers of Chapter 6 will recall that the Colombian Constitution of 1991 established a Ministry of the Environment together with a set of organizations – the national environmental system (SINA) – and charged them, at the national, regional and local levels, to deal with environmental issues in a more holistic and participatory way in order to promote sustainable development. The organizational design and policies of SINA sought to respect these goals. Nevertheless, by 1996 it was clear that many organizational problems remained at SINA, and its practices and results were actually far removed from its objectives. For this reason, the Ministry of the Environment and the National Auditing Office decided to sponsor a syntegration to get agreement on the main strategic issues still plaguing SINA's development and operation. The event took place on the Colombian island of Gorgona, a beautiful and valuable ecological reserve in the Pacific Ocean. The principal organizer was Angela Espinosa and the following account (2003) is hers. She was assisted with facilitation by Chris Cullen and Joe Truss of Team Syntegrity Inc., the Canadian company holding the copyright for the methodology.

Senior managers from the national institutions sponsoring the event and the consultants organizing it agreed that the opening question should be:

How should public, private and voluntary sector organisations and institutions be co-ordinated in order to preserve the natural environment in Colombia?

They then drew up criteria for inviting participants in order to achieve a varied and balanced representation of individuals from different bodies involved with strategic environmental matters around the country. Issues of ethnicity, gender, age, geographical spread, political and professional background, etc. were taken into account. The final list of participants involved (a) senior managers from the following public sector institutions:

- Ministry of Environment;
- National Auditing Office;
- Risaralda – the county auditing office;
- Ministry of Agriculture;
- national parks;
- La Macarena – a regional environmental corporation (CAR);
- Environmental Development Institute (IDEAM);
- a Colombian petroleum enterprise (Ecopetrol);
- National Planning Department;
- Van Humboldt Research Institute;
- Cartagena's environmental agency (DAMA);
- the city of Cordoba (an ex-governor);
- the National University;

and (b) individuals representing different communities, organizations and institutions:

- representative of black communities;
- senior manager from a private sector company – Antioquia;
- women's leader;
- researcher – environmental issues;
- postgraduate student (studying environmental issues);
- countryside and peasants' representative;
- editor of *Environmental and Socio-Economic Review*;
- Ecology Teachers' Association – Cundinamarca;
- Colombian Environmental Funding Agency (Ecofondo);
- environmental non-governmental organization – Popayan;
- Los Andes University;
- Colombian Association of Small and Medium Sized Enterprises (ACOPI).

The organizers made the necessary travel and accommodation arrangements and the participants gathered on the first afternoon for the opening. At this session the methodology and protocol were explained, as well as the roles of participants, facilitators and assistants, and the various facilities available were described.

The rest of that afternoon and evening focused on generation of the agenda using the problem jostle technique. More than a hundred SIs were produced. With the help of the facilitators these were then collapsed and prioritized, during hexadic reduction, into ASIs and, finally, 12 CSIs – the 12 issues relevant to the opening question, which would guide later conversations. This whole process was stressful for the participants, already tired from travelling, and it was 9 p.m. before agreement was reached on the following 12 issues:

- participatory mechanisms;
- search for peace – war, corruption and environment;
- culture and education;
- equity and agrarian reform;
- institutionalization;
- territorial and environmental ordering;
- management and development;
- gender and environment;
- ethical values;

- environmental conservation;
- rationalization of environmental control;
- sustainable development and the international dimension.

Once the CSIs were agreed, the topic auction stage began with the participants each expressing their preferences for discussing particular issues. The computer program did the best it could to satisfy these preferences within the constraints imposed by the icosahedron structure, and the results were announced first thing on the second day. Not everyone was satisfied: three participants in particular were unhappy with being allocated to the gender group. Nevertheless, everyone eventually accepted membership of the groups to which they had been assigned.

The outcome resolve could now commence. It lasted for 3 days and the participants worked well in the 12 teams, as discussants, critics and observers, to address the 12 CSIs. They were supported throughout by the facilitators and technical assistants who recorded the conversations and their outcomes, and fed them back to the whole Infoset during the plenary sessions. There were certain problems arising from faulty installation of computers and software, but these were overcome by good teamwork and everything ran to schedule.

The closing session saw the groups sharing their conclusions on the 12 issues, and the Infoset discussing the experience and the learning they had derived. A few individuals had been upset by conflict in their teams and were disappointed with the outcomes. The great majority, however, as shown by evaluation questionnaires, had a positive and pleasant learning experience and declared themselves satisfied both with their contributions and with the quality of the final results.

FACE planning, which would have brought together participants after the event to ensure implementation of the outcomes, was not implemented following Gorgona. However, some of the organizers and participants did meet again to work out a final version of the 12 FSIs, and some months after the event the organizers published the *Gorgona Manifesto* setting out their conclusions. A very brief summary follows:

- Participatory mechanisms. The State should encourage communities to take advantage of the opportunities for participation open to them – unless they learned to participate sustainability could not be achieved.
- Search for peace – war, corruption and environment. War and corruption are social phenomena that destroy the environmental and social milieus.

- Culture and education. Environmental education should be introduced at all educational levels and there is the need to value, conserve and transmit traditional wisdom.
- Equity and agrarian reform. It is necessary to agree on a new development model promoting agrarian reform on the basis of equity. Without this there cannot be democracy, peace, political stability or sustainable development.
- Institutionalization –
  - SINA must grant autonomy to institutions involved in environmental management at the local level, but they must still act cohesively as a whole;
  - its components should cohere by region and theme so they can act jointly to tackle complex, transdisciplinary and inter-regional issues;
  - there should be strategies promoting environmental investments aimed at key programmes and institutions, and encouraging participation and responsibility;
  - it is essential to involve universities and research institutes in developing environmental educational programmes;
  - monitoring and control systems should be put in place to assess the impact of the development programmes and industrial projects on sustainability;
  - SINA should review current environmental laws and design effective control and punishment mechanisms.
- Territorial and environmental ordering. An integrated regional strategy was needed to manage the water basins of the main rivers, and an integrated national strategy to ensure all possible benefits are obtained from environmental reserves.
- Management and development. Knowledge, science, technology and local wisdom form the basis for sustainable development and these need to be co-ordinated to support decision-making contributing to sustainable development at the local level in the context of a shared national ethos.
- Gender and environment. The participation of women in environmental issues is fundamental because of their traditional roles in the family, education, agriculture and the community, and relevant female values should be more highly valued and shared by males.
- Ethical values. An environment of ethical responsibility should be collectively built, based on trust, throughout society – thus enabling co-operative behaviour between individuals and between communities.
- Environmental conservation. We need to monitor environmental

damage, understand its causes and be prepared organizationally and economically to prevent or respond to it.

- Rationalization of environmental control. Communities must be involved participatively in defending their local environments.
- Sustainable development and the international dimension. Colombia needs to improve its negotiating skills on environmental issues at international fora in order to protect its national interests.

Following the publication of the *Gorgona Manifesto* there were no more meetings of the organizers or participants. Nevertheless, many of those who took part in the syntegration continued to be involved with SINA, and it does seem that the event and the *Manifesto* made an important contribution to the debate about organizational development going on within SINA at that time and is likely to do so into the future. For example, in the 'environmental strategic plan' for the period of the last Colombian government, 1998–2002, the section on the 'institutional development strategy' of SINA shows a precise alignment with the conclusions on 'institutionalization' set out in the *Manifesto*. Three of the main action lines – 'organizing actions by region and theme', 'strategies for promoting participation and responsibility' and 'developing monitoring and control systems' – echo the sentiments and even employ many of the same words used in the *Manifesto*. At a broader level, an evaluation report on SINA's performance during the same period of government, produced by the National Council of Socio-economic Development (COMPES), highlights results that relate closely to the guidelines for action established at the Gorgona syntegration.

12.4 CRITIQUE OF TEAM SYNTEGRITY

Those who have experienced a syntegration attest to the fact that the process feels non-hierarchical, open and self-organizing. Based on the structure of the icosahedron it supports participative decision-making by ensuring that no individual or group dominates the conversations. Furthermore, it guarantees that the views of each participant are taken seriously and are 'heard', through reverberation, even in groups that they do not belong to. The approach is, therefore, an effective vehicle for achieving truly democratic dialogue. It can promote fairness in decision-making by neutralizing the baneful influence power and hierarchy can have on discussion.

Team syntegrity additionally offers a communications design that maximizes the constructive engagement of participants and achieves the greatest

possible learning from the resources brought to the event. Using the geometry of the icosahedron, as a guide to organizing the conversations, produces
robust and effective dialogue because it allows a balance to be struck
between integrating the knowledge and experience of the participants
about an area of concern to them and creating a healthy tension from multiple
viewpoints. The protocol ensures that information circulates freely, that
people are exposed to the views of others and so can experience learning,
and that new synergistic knowledge emerges because of the reverberation
of ideas set in train. The end result of a syntegration should be the agreement
and commitment of the Infoset to a final document, structured around 12
issues, which represents the best of the participants' understanding and
experience brought to bear to answer the opening question.

Critics (see Jackson, 2000) inevitably argue that, whatever the apparent
success of a syntegration, it cannot guarantee that anything will actually get
implemented in practice. Good intentions arrived at in the context of a democratically organised Infoset can soon dissolve when they encounter power
relationships and hierarchy in the real world. This is likely to be the case
whatever attention is given to follow-up meetings using FACE planning.

This criticism suggests some limitations to the usefulness of team
syntegrity, but should not be seen as detracting from what it was designed
for and what it does well. A syntegration opens up a conversational space
and helps to achieve a coherent understanding at a certain stage in the development of thinking about a matter of public concern or an organizational
issue. This kind of outcome might be of particular benefit in arriving at
agreement on strategic issues or the design of an organizational change
programme. As we saw with the Gorgona syntegration, the event can
produce a climate in favour of change that resonates through future action
and, of course, that creates a coterie of critical, active learners. Nevertheless,
to properly implement and institutionalize the results of a syntegration is
likely to require that the methodology be used in combination with other
systems approaches.

Other critics (including Jackson, 2000) baulk at the cybernetic logic that
connects icosahedra, geodesic domes and participative decision processes.
To them the constraints imposed by team syntegrity, which require 30
people to take 5 days out of their lives to discuss 12 topics, seem artificial.
Efforts have been made, as we know, to increase flexibility by offering alternative protocols – although these too reflect other geometric designs. And
the effectiveness of these alternatives still needs to be fully researched.

Another line of criticism (Mejia, 2001; Espinosa and Mejia, 2003) points
out that while Team Syntegrity can ensure democratic interaction, it cannot

impact on the actual content of the conversations that take place. It has to rely on the content brought to the sessions by the participants or developed as part of the learning process that occurs during the conversations. The content-less type of critical approach offered by team syntegrity (and criticized in relation to critical systems heuristics – see Chapter 11) cannot guarantee that emancipatory concerns are recognized since it depends on the existing level of understanding and awareness of the participants. As Mejia and Espinosa note, if distorted forms of knowledge have been imposed on participants in the past, then under the guise of democratic dialogue those forms can easily be passed over or even legitimized again during a syntegration.

Furthermore, it has been argued that team syntegrity assumes that participants will have the same fundamental capacity to enter into dialogue and to grasp meaning. White (1994, 1998) notes the lack of specific mechanisms to involve the silent or inarticulate. He also suggests that there is a danger that discussions can degenerate into 'networking sessions' rather than being topic-focused. This hints at a more general concern. Beer seems to assume that people are willing to enter into dialogue because they want to reach a consensus. Others, however, see dialogue as an arena for struggle and dissension in which speakers seek to defeat their opponents, often for the simple pleasure of the game. From this perspective dialogue is simply a different form of power struggle and whatever issues forth from 'democratic debate' represents just another claim to power. Beer is relying on the participants wanting to play the same language game that he prefers.

At the theoretical level team syntegrity uses the properties of the icosahedron, as transferred to the social domain, to maximize the interplay between the culture and political system metaphors in order that the benefits of both integration and tension are gained. And it does so with a full awareness of the problems highlighted by the psychic prison and instruments of domination metaphors. To ensure the benefits are won, people must be empowered so that they can take part in dialogue on an equal and fair basis. In this way team syntegrity pays attention to issues of coercion that arise as we move along the horizontal dimension of the System Of Systems Methodologies (SOSM) (see Chapter 2) and that are ignored in soft systems thinking.

Team syntegrity, therefore, responds to the emancipatory paradigm by establishing ground rules that enable democratic participation in decision-making. It does not seek out procedures for predicting and controlling the behaviour of complex adaptive systems – and so offers little to functionalism. It differs from interpretive approaches in paying more attention to the form than to the content of conversations. Interpretive thinkers have little time for the elaborate protocol developed as part of team syntegrity to ensure democratic dialogue. It finds its severest critics among postmodernists who question the role Beer assigns to language as offering the possibility of achieving a genuine consensus among participants. As we shall see in the next chapter, postmodernists believe that we live in a world of multiple truths that give rise to incommensurable interpretations of reality and think that we should promote difference rather than seek to subsume it in the quest for agreement and consensus.

12.5 THE VALUE OF TEAM SYNTEGRITY TO MANAGERS

Team syntegrity's value to managers can be summarized in the following five points:

- It offers a 'democratic' systems approach that emphasizes the benefits of the equal and participative involvement of stakeholders in defining and clarifying social and organizational concerns, and seeking their resolution. Team syntegrity promotes fairness.
- Team syntegrity produces robust and effective dialogue though a protocol that takes advantage of the tensions induced by multiple viewpoints, integrating these to strengthen the agreements reached among participants about an area of concern to them.
- The end result of a syntegration, a record of the agreed responses to 12 topics, will reflect the very best of the participant's shared understanding and experience of the opening question, enhanced by their involvement in highly interactive and participative group processes.
- Participants in a syntegration emerge with a shared understanding of a matter of concern and interest to them, and with a commitment to some ways of addressing it. These will serve later to help with implementation of particular actions in the real world.
- Participants in a syntegration gain an understanding and respect for participative processes and have their learning capacities enhanced.

12.6 CONCLUSION

Since 1994 there have been well over a hundred team syntegrity events in different countries. According to the evaluations these have yielded very good results. Beer's development of team syntegrity, and the associated methods and concepts (many new to the systems field), has added considerably to the armoury of applied systems thinkers. It is essential, however, to recognize what a syntegration can and cannot achieve. The main purpose of a syntegration is to provide a proper context for developing democratic and insightful agreements about complex policy or strategic topics. It cannot guarantee that after the event the agreements reached will be respected or effectively implemented by relevant organizations. A syntegration event in isolation will not ensure that long-term organizational or societal changes are realized. Beer originally designed it as a complementary approach to be employed along with the viable system model, and it is this combination that perhaps offers the best possibilities for profound organizational development.

REFERENCES

Beer, S. (1990). On suicidal rabbits: A relativity of systems. *Systems Practice*, **3**, 115–124.

Beer, S. (1994). *Beyond Dispute: The Invention of Team Syntegrity*. John Wiley & Sons, Chichester, UK.

Espinosa, A. (2003). Team Syntegrity as a tool to promote democratic agreements: An example from the national environmental sector in Colombia. *Proceedings of the 2003 Annual Conference of the ISSS [International Society for the Systems Sciences]*, *Crete, Greece*.

Espinosa, A. and Mejia, D. (2003). Team Syntegrity as a learning process: Some considerations about its capacity to develop critical active learners. *Proceedings of the 2003 Annual Conference of the ISSS [International Society for the Systems Sciences]*, *Crete, Greece*.

Jackson, M.C. (2000). *Systems Approaches to Management*. Kluwer/Plenum, New York.

Mejia, A. (2001). *The Problem of Knowledge Imposition: Paulo Freire and Critical Systems Thinking* (Research Memorandum No. 29). University of Hull Business School, Hull, UK.

Schwaninger, M. (1997). Self organisation and self reference in the cognition of organisations. In: V. Braitenberg, et al. (eds) *Interdisciplinary Approaches to a New Understanding of Cognition and Consciousness* (pp. 70–80). Unipress, Augsburg, Germany.

White, L.A. (1994). Let's syntegrate. *Operational Research Insight*, **7**, 13–18.

White, L.A. (1998). Tinker, tailor, soldier, sailor: A syntegrity to explore London's diverse interests. *Operational Research Insight*, **3**, 12–16.

Type D

Promoting Diversity

Here we detail the postmodern systems approach. This aims to assist managers improve their enterprises by promoting diversity. The approach was developed because the dominating and 'totalizing' discourses of modernism – represented by functionalist, interpretive and emancipatory systems thinking – are seen as suppressing difference and creativity. The postmodern systems approach by contrast emphasizes the exceptional, seeks to make a space for suppressed voices to be heard and hopes to unleash creativity and a sense of fun by engaging people's emotions. In sociological terms postmodernism stands opposed to the other modernist paradigms, subverting and ridiculing their attempts to impose order on a world that is inevitably too complex, coercive and diverse. Postmodern thinkers believe only local and temporary resolutions of difficulties can be achieved because they see problem contexts as lying toward the extreme ends of both axes making up the System Of Systems Methodologies (SOSM). The carnival metaphor has been suggested as a lens through which to capture the diversity and creativity called for by postmodern systems thinking.

Postmodern Systems Thinking   13

The answer is: Let us wage a war on totality; let us be witnesses to the unpresentable; let us activate the differences and save the honor of the name.

Lyotard (1984 – replying to the question 'what, then, is the postmodern?')

13.1   INTRODUCTION

Postmodernists would classify all of the various systems approaches considered so far, whether their aim is to improve goal seeking and viability, to explore purposes or to ensure fairness, as being 'modernist' in character. They are expressions of a European intellectual movement, with its origins in the 18th century, known as the Enlightenment. This movement sought to use rational modes of thought to sweep away superstition, ignorance and prejudice, and to build a better world.

Lyotard, in his book *The Postmodern Condition* (1984), recognizes two major manifestations of modernism that can be labelled, following Cooper and Burrell (1988), 'systemic modernism' and 'critical modernism'. Systemic modernism is concerned with increasing the 'performativity' of systems, in terms of input – output measures, and with handling environmental uncertainty. It relies on science to discover what is logical and orderly about the world, and on technology to assist with prediction and control. This form of modernism is expressed in classical accounts of hard systems thinking, system dynamics, organizational cybernetics and complexity theory.

Critical modernism sees its task as the progressive realization of universal human emancipation. It depends on language being 'transparent' so that it can act as a means whereby humans arrive at agreement about the purposes they wish to pursue. This form of modernism can be recognized in soft systems thinking and in the work of emancipatory systems thinkers. In the latter case it is felt necessary to take careful precautions to ensure that any consensus or accommodation reached emerges from rational discourse and not from 'distortions' that reflect the current system and simply lead to its reproduction.

Postmodernists attack the whole Enlightenment rationale and, therefore, the pretensions of both systemic and critical modernism. They reject particularly the belief in rationality, truth and progress. They deny that science can provide access to objective knowledge and so assist with steering organizations and societies in the face of complexity. They deny that language is transparent and can function as a regulative principle of consensus. Postmodernists emphasize, instead, that we have to learn to live with the incommensurable, accepting multiple interpretations of the world and being tolerant of difference. Indeed, they want to ensure diversity and encourage creativity by reclaiming conflict and bringing marginalized voices forward to be heard. Postmodernism offers little security. Rather it thrives on instability, disruption, disorder, contingency, paradox and indeterminacy.

Even this brief introduction suggests that there are difficulties in managing a fit between the systems approach and postmodern thinking.

13.2   DESCRIPTION OF POSTMODERN SYSTEMS THINKING

13.2.1   Historical development

The roots of postmodernism are traced, by Brocklesby and Cummings (1996), to a break with the Enlightenment tradition established by Nietzsche and followed up by Heidegger. Nietzsche questioned the emphasis placed by Enlightenment philosophers, such as Kant, on the human essence and individual rationality and ridiculed the notion that history revealed that humanity was making 'progress'. The self, for Nietzsche, is a contingent product of various physical, social and cultural forces. To be free, an individual has to restyle himself by critically questioning all received opinion and accepted ways of doing things. People need power in order to do this and, therefore, people's 'will to power' is something to be celebrated. Taking his lead from Nietzsche, Heidegger sought to undermine the Western philosophical tradition and to reorientate philosophy around the study of *Being*, concentrating particularly on the uniqueness of each person's 'being in the world'. To be 'authentic', he argued, it is necessary to face up to the contingency of our own existence and make of it what we will.

Emancipation is a personal matter, not something provided by history in the form of a shared Utopia.

The work of Nietzsche and Heidegger promoting self-emancipation provides an alternative, therefore, to the Enlightenment tradition, mapped out by Kant, Hegel and Habermas, which is engaged on the quest for universal or collective human emancipation. This alternative proved particularly attractive to various French philosophers, among them Foucault, Derrida, Lyotard and Baudrillard, who were reacting against the 'structuralism' that dominated much of French intellectual life in the 1960s and 1970s. Structuralism, the reader may recall from our study of system dynamics and organizational cybernetics, seeks to uncover the causal relationships that are seen to exist 'beneath the surface' and that give rise to system behaviour. The new breed of French philosophers, labelled poststructuralists or postmodernists (and we do not seek to make a distinction here), rejected the idea that such determining structures existed and, therefore, could be 'objectively' revealed by social scientists.

They were drawn instead to the 'surface' meanings, appearances and representations that structuralists ignored, to how these are inextricably linked to power relationships and to the impact they have on how individuals understand themselves and are able to express themselves in the world. As a result the somewhat marginal opposition that existed to Enlightenment thinking, as found in the writings of Nietzsche and Heidegger, became transformed into a fully fledged alternative position across a whole swathe of social science disciplines. This alternative way of thinking and doing came, most commonly, to be called postmodernism.

13.2.2   Philosophy and theory

In order to show the relevance of postmodernist writers to organizational research, Alvesson and Deetz (1996) highlight seven common themes that they pursue. These are explained below, each by reference to the work of one postmodernist thinker. This will do for our purposes; although it certainly cannot be inferred that all postmodernists share exactly the same views on each theme. For more on the individual theorists see Jackson (2000).

(a) The loss of power of the 'grand narratives'

In the introduction to this chapter we followed Lyotard in identifying two forms of modernism – 'systemic modernism' and 'critical modernism'.

Lyotard is opposed to both, believing that the quest for precise, objective knowledge about systems and the hope that language can operate as a regulatory principle of consensus are both misguided. Moreover, both types of modernism are dangerous because they give rise to 'grand narratives' about, for example, continuous economic growth or the emancipation of humankind.

Lyotard wants to construct a postmodern alternative opposed to all 'totalizations'. This should emphasize dissension, instability and unpredictability, and activate 'difference'. The blind spots of modernism, those things rendered unpresentable and unspeakable in its narratives, must be brought to the fore. Science needs to be seen as only one kind of language game with limited relevance to social affairs. Language should be regarded not as orientated to achieving consensus, but as necessarily characterized by struggle and dissent. It is a vehicle for promoting innovation, change and renewal, for energizing and motivating human action, and so refusal of conformity should be encouraged. Consensus is possible only in very localized circumstances and is only desirable if subject to rapid cancellation.

(b) The centrality of discourse

Foucault's early work sought to provide an 'archaeology' of discursive formations in different human sciences, such as medicine, psychiatry and criminology. In his view every field of knowledge is constituted by sets of discursive rules that determine whether statements are adjudged true or false in that field. The discursive formations and classificatory rules that operate in a discipline will alter over time, but there is no reason to believe the current arrangements give rise to more 'objective' classifications than earlier ones – in the sense that they resemble reality more closely. The idea of accumulation of knowledge is, therefore, rejected by Foucault. So is the notion of a constant human subject who can autonomously engage in promoting emancipation. Individuals have their subjectivities formed by the discourses that pertain at the time of their birth and socialization. These not only structure the world but shape individuals in terms of their identity and way of seeing as well.

(c) The power/knowledge connections

If Foucault's earlier work was 'archaeology', looking at the origins and nature of discourses, his later writings emphasize the need to study the power relations with which they are inextricably connected. Particular discourses come to the fore because of power relations. They also embody knowledge and, Foucault argues, knowledge offers power over others: the power to define others. Discourses therefore play a role in establishing patterns of domination, benefiting the meanings favoured by some while marginalizing the voices of others.

This explanation of the power/knowledge relationship is usually seen as Foucault's most valuable contribution to social theory. Discourses depend on power relationships. On the other hand, they carry power in the way they make distinctions and so open or close possibilities for social action. A claim to power can, therefore, be seen as present in any claim to knowledge. Because of the nature of power, understood in this way, it is omnipresent in social relations.

(d) Research aimed at revealing indeterminacy and encouraging resistance rather than at maintaining rationality, predictability and order

Foucault gives the name 'genealogy' to the accounts he offers of the power struggles associated with the rise to dominance of particular forms of discourse. Genealogy is aimed at unmasking the pretensions of 'totalizing discourses'. It dismisses their claims to provide objective knowledge. In particular, it offers criticisms directed at the power/knowledge systems of the modern age and support for 'subjugated' knowledge. In this way a space is opened up that makes resistance possible, albeit on a local basis in response to specific issues. By paying attention to difference at the local level, to points of continuing dissension, it becomes feasible to give a voice back to those silenced or marginalized by the dominant discourses.

(e) The discursive production of natural objects rather than language as a mirror of reality

Derrida accepts one aspect of structuralism – the notion that linguistic meaning derives from the structure of language. According to this argument, the meaning of a 'sign' in a language is determined not by its correspondence to some objective thing in the world, or to the intentions of the speaker, but results from its relationships with other signs. He goes much further than the structuralists, however, in embracing what might be described as a relativistic position. Once the relationship between signs and what is signified in the world is broken, it appears to Derrida that it must be possible to create an infinite number of relational systems of signs from which different meanings can be derived. Rather than simply mirroring objects, language creates objects. To take the distinctions made in any particular discourse as representative of reality is an illegitimate privileging of that discourse, which involves hiding other possible distinctions. Derrida's 'deconstructive' method seeks to reveal the deceptiveness of language and the work that has to go on in any 'text' to hide contradictions (which might reveal alternative readings) so that a certain unity and order can be privileged and 'rationality' maintained.

(f) The discursive production of the individual

The shift to the study of the structure of language and away from the intentions of the speaker, as the route to discovering the meaning of 'texts', puts Derrida at the forefront of the postmodernist assault on humanism. In his view it is discourse that speaks the person and not the person who uses language. In the contemporary world, where there are many possible discourses, the idea of an integrated, self-determining individual becomes untenable. From this follows a rejection of the notion of historical progress, especially with humans at the centre of it.

(g) Hyper-reality – simulations replace the real world in the current world order

Baudrillard takes the idea that signs gain their meaning from their relation-ships to other signs, and not from reflecting some reality, and uses it to interpret the contemporary world. In this world signs and images are every-thing, and 'reality' counts for nothing. We inhabit 'simulations', imaginary worlds which consist of signs that refer only to themselves. Disneyland is an exemplar, but Los Angeles too offers a make-believe world with no connection to any other reality. Writing at the time of the war against Iraq, it is impossible not to add that campaign as another example. Television is a significant culprit in much of this.

If the postmodernists are right there are considerable implications for tradi-tional systems thinking. If there is no rationality or optimum solution to problems, then its problem-solving techniques will lack legitimation. Deep analysis of systems in search of laws and regularities is not going to yield dividends. It would be more productive to pay attention to the local, to con-centrate on image, to take note of accidents, and to respect arbitrariness and discontinuity. In a world of multiple truths competing for prominence, even soft and emancipatory systems thinkers are left impotent unless they recognize the importance of power and engage with (rather than seek to avoid) the social and political contexts of their work. Overall, if there are no acceptable grand narratives to guide progress, then systems thinking has to abandon the idea of universal, verifiable improvement to which it often seems to aspire, and recognize that it can bring about only temporary and contested improvements.

The fit between postmodernism and the systems thinking we have been studying to date may not look good. Certainly we must recognize that postmodernism does not offer us a systemic theoretical framework or even a systemic manner of proceeding in intervention. Nevertheless, we shall discover in the next couple of subsections two ways in which systems thinking and postmodernism can collaborate. The first is using various systems methods, models and techniques, but in the spirit of postmodernism. The second is by postmodernism providing some new methods and tools that can assist the systems practitioner.

13.2.3 Methodology

It would be inconsistent with the philosophy of postmodernism to offer a structured methodology for turning theory into practice. Accordingly, Foucault (see Brocklesby and Cummings, 1996) refers to his work as providing a 'toolkit', which anybody can make use of, as they see fit, in order to short-circuit or disqualify systems of power. Taket and White (2000), adopting a postmodernist stance in management science, see themselves as offering a 'cookbook' that sets out some favourite recipes, but then encourages variation and innovation in the actual cooking. Nevertheless, Taket and White do set out quite clearly what they see as the main features of intervention in the spirit of postmodernism, and it is their guidelines that are set out here.

Taket and White give the name PANDA – Participatory Appraisal of Needs and the Development of Action – to the approach to intervention that they endorse. PANDA is said to embrace 'pragmatic pluralism' and to have grown from postmodern roots. It is an attempt to work holistically and pragmatically to address the diversity and uncertainty found in multi-agency settings and, increasingly, in modern organizations. PANDA rejects prescription based on totalizing theories and instead encourages mixing different perspectives, accepting contradiction, recognizing and affirming difference and diversity, taking an open and flexible stance, and responding to the characteristics of the moment.

Table 13.1 The four Ds and nine tasks of PANDA (Participatory Appraisal of Needs and the Development of Action).

Deliberation I	Selecting participants
	Defining purpose/objectives
	Exploring the situation
Debate	Identifying options
	Researching options (which could include consulting on options)
	Comparing options
Decision	Deciding action
	Recording decisions
Deliberation II	Monitoring/Evaluating

PANDA has four phases and nine tasks or foci to be addressed during the phases, as set out in Table 13.1. 'Deliberation I' involves opening a space for discussion, selecting participants, respecting and multiplying diversity, and enabling and facilitating participation. Taket and White produce a list of their favourite, tried-and-tested methods, which can be mixed and matched to make a success of this phase. 'Debate' may require more forceful facilitation than Deliberation I because the aim is to deepen understanding of the options under consideration, structure them, lose some and combine others. This demands more systematic appraisal of the options, explicit negotiation over preferences and continued striving toward full and equitable participation. Another list of methods is supplied, which have been found useful in Debate. 'Decision' involves not only discussion about the options to take forward but also about the methods to be used in deciding between these options. 'Deliberation II' oversees the monitoring and evaluating of the effects of the agreed actions. Taket and White again provide lists of favourite methods for Decision and Deliberation II.

This may look very much like a classical methodology, but Taket and White insist that its application is more an art or craft than a science. In particular, in order to remain true to the spirit of postmodernism, it is essential to recognize and respond to pluralism in each of four areas:

- in the nature of the client;
- in the use of specific methods;
- in the modes of representation employed;
- in the facilitation process.

Pluralism in the nature of the client refers to the diverse viewpoints held by various stakeholders, all of which must be acknowledged and respected. This demands attention to the three Cs:

- Critical – ensuring the widest possible range of viewpoints and values are heard and any that are being suppressed are brought to the fore;
- Consent – acknowledging that consensus may be impossible and that we might have to be satisfied with a 'system of consent';
- Contingent – accepting that the only 'truths' are those relevant to the local circumstances at the moment.

Pluralism in the use of specific methods requires that we 'mix and match' methods, adopting a flexible stance according to 'what feels good' in the situation we are confronting. To do this well we should bear in mind the four Ms:

- Mixing – using whole methods, or parts of different methodologies, together and at different times during an intervention;
- Modify – being aware of the need to change and adapt methods to particular circumstances;
- Multiply – trying out different methods for the same task;
- Match – choosing an appropriate mix of methods according to the preferences of the stakeholders and facilitators, and the nature of the situation addressed.

Pluralism in the modes of representation employed acknowledges the shift, signalled in postmodernism, from the idea of 'representation' as picturing objects 'out there' to representation as capturing only other impressions of the world. This implies that we need to develop modes of representation that allow participants the freedom to express themselves naturally. Remembering the three Vs will help:

- Verbal – making use of traditional verbal forms of representation;
- Visual – employing also visual modes of representation, such as rich pictures (see Chapter 10);
- Vital – encouraging participation and learning through techniques such as sociodrama.

Pluralism in the facilitation process requires facilitators to mix and match different roles and guises at different times during an intervention and in

relation to the different individuals/groups involved. This is encapsulated in
the four Fs:

- Flexibility – responding and adapting to the dynamics of the situation;
- Forthrightness – challenging and intervening when appropriate;
- Focus – keeping a sense of purpose, progress and place;
- Fairness – engaging in critical reflection about whether equitable partici-
  pation is being achieved and about the facilitator's own role and ethical
  position.

Following their postmodern logic, Taket and White are unable to provide
any formal justification for embracing pragmatic pluralism and employing
PANDA. They have to accept that all knowledge is partial, provisional and
contingent and that improvement can only be defined according to the
local context. This does not, however, mean that 'anything goes'. Rather, it
replaces futile questions about 'the truth' (according to Taket and White)
by responses to issues such as:

- How does this feel?
- Is this fun?
- Does this do what we want?
- Does viewpoint or action a seem better than b, at least for the moment?
- Are we achieving a novel and exceptional outcome, at least locally?
- Am I being self-critical about my own involvement?

It seems that an engagement can be deemed successful if it appeals to our
emotions, brings about the exceptional and is conducted according to a
personal code of ethics.

13.2.4   Methods

We now turn to another way in which systems thinking and postmodernism
can work together. This involves the appropriation of certain postmodern
ideas and their conversion into postmodern methods that can be used in
the course of a systems intervention. This systems intervention might itself
be in the spirit of postmodernism (e.g., follow the PANDA guidelines) or
it might be guided by a methodology serving another paradigm (e.g.,
functionalist, interpretive or emancipatory). Here we briefly describe four
postmodern methods drawn from the work of Foucault, Derrida and
Lyotard.

Knowledge systems diagnostics is a method, developed by Topp (1999), based on Foucault's early work on the 'archaeology of knowledge'. It seeks to uncover and inquire into the 'formative system' operating in an organization. The formative system is a system of 'second-order' knowledge production that enables and regulates what it is possible for organizational actors to think and express at any point in time. This system is not usually understood by people in the organization. Organizational change, therefore, becomes a matter not of shifting individual perspectives, but of altering the knowledge matrix governing the organization that is determining what it is possible for individuals to say. Understanding the formative system is achieved by asking a series of critical questions derived from the work of Foucault. These questions inquire into matters such as the following:

- How is new knowledge created or adopted by the organization?
- What are the sources of the generation or regulation of knowledge?
- What rules underlie such generative or regulative processes?
- Why are some concepts and systems ideas adopted and circulated within conversation while others are discounted and never established as guides for action?

Once a map of the formative system has been completed, it becomes possible to examine it and aim organizational interventions at the points of leverage likely to have the greatest impact in transforming the first-order knowledge of organizational actors. If this works, individuals will be able to think and discuss new things relevant to their business context.

Foucault's later work on 'genealogy', the reader will recall, focused on unmasking the characteristics of totalizing discourses. Brocklesby and Cummings (1996) concentrate on the practical aspects of this and argue that it enables individuals to understand the extent to which they are determined by existing structures of power and knowledge. It also allows them to grasp some of the mechanisms by which the current order is sustained and offers them tools and techniques to use, as they see fit, in local strategizing and subversion to undermine the status quo. They cannot hope to proceed on the basis of consensus to achieve universal emancipation – they must accept that difference will prevail. But, in Taket and White's (2000) terms, they may be able to achieve 'consent to act'.

Taket and White have found Derrida's 'deconstruction' a powerful device in a number of interventions using their pragmatic pluralism. Deconstruction is aimed at exploring the values or deep structure of a 'text' (and for Derrida everything can be seen as a text) in order to expose the biases inherent

Table 13.2 Examples of deconstructive strategies.

a. Focusing on marginalized elements
b. Exploring a false distinction
c. Exploring a false identification
d. Looking at claims or assertions that depend on something other than what is clearly stated – especially those that make explicit or implicit recourse to claims of 'naturalness'
e. Examining what is not said, what is omitted (deliberately or not)
f. Paying attention to disruptions and contradictions
g. Examining use of metaphor
h. Examining use of *double entendres*

in it. Various strategies are used to probe texts for contradictions and ambivalences. They can then be taken apart to reveal what they privilege or ignore, and alternative meanings can be derived. Building on Beath and Orlikowski, Taket (2002) provides examples of deconstructive strategies, as set out in Table 13.2.

Drawing on Lyotard's key work *The Differend*, Topp (1999) proposes 'generative conversation' as a postmodern method that can lead to the emergence of new concepts, systems ideas and themes that may guide future action in organizations. The strategy in generative conversation is to replace one 'language game' with another in order to create new knowledge. The only rule is that any new phrase brought forth in the conversation must always link to the previous phrase. This prevents the recurrence of phrases that take the conversation back to some 'higher regulatory business stake'. Beyond that, certain 'guides' can be provided:

- generative conversation is a game in which we play with ideas, not against each other;
- appoint a facilitator at the start to monitor the application of the linking rule;
- there is no rush – 'regulative conversations' (those that do not escape from existing concerns) are characterized by speed;
- allow at least three seconds of silence between each phrase;
- watch the pull of habit and pattern and be aware of the tension to link in a certain way;
- keep a notebook to jot down ideas so that they are not forgotten;
- questions can form part of the conversation, but must obey the linking rule;

- make use of creative misunderstanding;
- listen, take a few breaths, think, link;
- remember, silence is a phrase;
- try to link multiple previous phrases.

Later analysis of the conversation transcripts should allow the facilitator and participants to identify new themes and concepts that have emerged during the conversation.

13.2.5 Recent developments

The acceptance of postmodern approaches in systems thinking is a relatively new phenomenon. Those persuaded by postmodernism continue to experiment and so learn about how the idea can best be used to facilitate interventions. They also seek to refine the postmodern methods they employ (e.g., Taket, 2002). More traditional management scientists have started to look at some of the postmodern methods to see if they can be incorporated as tools in more orthodox interventions (e.g., Ormerod, 2003).

13.3 POSTMODERN SYSTEMS THINKING IN ACTION

A variety of case studies are described by Taket and White (2000) that show PANDA in action, including five fuller accounts chosen to illustrate its use in a diversity of settings. A brief description of an engagement to assist a development agency in Belize shows attention to pluralism in the nature of the client and pluralism in relation to the use of methods (at different stages, Participatory Rapid Appraisal (PRA), elements of Team Syntegrity and aspects of 'Strategic Choice' are all employed). There is a longer account of another intervention in Belize, for the Association of National Development Agencies, which was designed to help them reach strategic decisions in the face of reduced funding. Emphasis on pluralism in the nature of the client and mixing and matching methods – in this case cognitive mapping, nominal group technique, a composite causal map, role playing, etc. – is still strong. In this example, however, attention is also paid to pluralism in the modes of representation and in the facilitation process. The existence of more powerful groups in the network represented by the Association and the lack of facility of some other groups with verbal approaches meant that the facilitators had to work hard and employ non-verbal forms of representation, to develop fuller and more equitable participation.

We do not have space to show all the various postmodern methods in use so will restrict ourselves to an account of an application of 'deconstruction' provided by Taket (2002).

Deconstruction, the reader will recall, involves analysing a text to see what is being suppressed in order that the discourse can be made to appear a unity. Tensions and conflicts in the text are pinpointed so that its partiality becomes obvious and a space is opened for suppressed sides of the discourse to be heard. The example given by Taket is of deconstruction employed as part of the evaluation of a 'linkworker' project in an inner city district. The 'linkworkers' were bilingual individuals employed to assist communities whose mother tongue was not English to gain access to primary health care services. As part of the evaluation a number of meetings were held with stakeholder groups and these meetings were taped and transcribed. Taket provides a transcript of one part of one meeting and shows how the participants themselves were able, with the help of facilitators, to employ deconstructive techniques to open out and move on their dialogue and understanding.

The facilitator begins by commenting on certain problematic aspects of the linkworker scheme, to do with communications, record keeping and safety, and inviting further discussion of these. Taket sees this as the use of deconstructive strategies d. and f. in Table 13.2. Three participants then come in to emphasize that, despite these problems, the linkworkers are doing a great job, are well respected, are seen as 'brilliant'. This amplifies a tension that seems to exist between the positive way the linkworkers are perceived and the problems that, nevertheless, surround the scheme.

The facilitator then asks 'so where do these problems come from?' This continues the application of strategy d., but reinforced by e. – examining what is omitted. A further brief discussion yields general agreement that the problems arise not from the actual work of the linkworkers (which is positively evaluated), but come up in the course of meetings of other staff held to discuss the scheme. At these meetings the problems of communications, records and safety dominate.

The facilitator probes further: 'what do you think makes the staff say the scheme caused all these problems?' (strategies c., d., e. and f.). The participants themselves are then able to push the deconstruction forward. One suggests that some people simply want to do the scheme down, however well it is working. Another argues that although the scheme is seen as the cause of the problems this is not really the case (strategy c.). What is being suggested here is that the scheme is revealing issues that need addressing in the wider social services directorate. The scheme makes these apparent, but is not the cause of them.

This analysis is generally accepted and two participants begin to provide examples that support it. One points to the issue of what have been represented as the 'overprotective' safety guidelines issued to the linkworkers. Perhaps the problem is the safety guidelines issued to staff in the directorate more generally. The other focuses on the issue of the accountability of the linkworkers and points out that a similar problem has, for many years, plagued school nurses and their auxiliaries. Taket sees this as the employment of deconstructive strategies b. and a. – it reveals a false distinction made between the linkworkers and others, and demonstrates that discussion of the circumstances of other staff groups in the directorate has been marginalized in the discourse. The earlier discussant returns with another example concerned with record keeping. Linkworkers have been criticized because they keep separate records. This participant points out that this is also true of district nurses, school nurses and health visitors (strategy b.). It seems that the usual practice of these groups has been marginalized in the discussion (strategy a.). What is really required is to look at record keeping across the directorate as a whole – not concentrate just on the linkworkers.

The problem can now be restated as one of not having 'teams working in partnership'. The issues surrounding the linkworker scheme are seen as effects rather than the cause of this, and new ways forward can be explored.

Taket regards this as a good example of deconstruction carried out as a group activity. She is well aware that others might see it just as 'probing interviewing', but suggests that the deconstructive strategies add great value because of their ability to bring to the fore the implicit assumptions that are not obvious, but which often shape discussion.

13.4 CRITIQUE OF POSTMODERN SYSTEMS THINKING

According to Taket and White (2000), we are entering 'new times' in which new organizational forms are coming into being based on fragmentation, decentralization and networks. In these postmodern times, individuals have more choices available to them, there is a greater diversity of stakeholders involved in decision-making and the turbulence of the organizational environment demands greater levels of co-operation between different enterprises. We seem to be entering an age in which participation and partnership, and decision-making in 'multiagency settings' (broadly defined) will be crucial. Other systems approaches draw upon modernist theories of rational action that, with their reliance on rationality, abstraction and verbal competence, can suffocate diversity, spontaneity and creativity. An alternative postmodernist approach is required, Taket and White argue, that encourages diversity by strengthening the opportunity for different stakeholders to participate and enabling them to explore the possibilities available and the constraints limiting them. It then becomes possible to build, out of various 'fragmented rationalities', a local and provisional plan for action. The great strength of postmodernism/poststructuralism, therefore, is that it seems appropriate to the new times in which we live.

Topp's (1999) experience in trying to change business organizations supports this argument. In the postmodern world, he suggests, traditional systems approaches still have a role in helping businesses to achieve goals efficiently and efficaciously, and in assisting managers to regulate debate. What have become crucial to the success of postindustrial businesses, however, are creating new knowledge and using existing knowledge more productively. Modernist systems methodologies tend to be frustrated in this endeavour by 'subtle systemic resistance'. All they can achieve are new moves in the same game. There is a need, therefore, for new systems methods appropriate to the creation of new knowledge in postindustrial business. Topp provides a number of private business examples (e.g., Southern Life in South Africa) in support of his contention. These complement the multiagency examples, in Taket and White, and suggest that postmodern systems thinking has a wide field of application.

There is much that is attractive in Taket and White's PANDA, whether or not you share their allegiance to postmodernism. The complete abandonment of unitary assumptions, and the willingness to see problem situations as arenas for dialogue in the context of diversity, are exhilarating. Their extension of the normal meaning of pluralism in management science to embrace modes of representation and facilitator roles and guises is of great utility. The flexibility provided for the employment of methods, the redirection of attention to 'local improvement' and the emphasis on the ethical responsibilities of facilitators are all to be welcomed.

Critics are likely to remain sceptical, however, about the value of a postmodern orientation in the great majority of organizational settings. In traditional organizations concerns about efficiently and effectively pursuing goals still seem to be paramount. No doubt many managers value diversity and having fun, but these will be secondary compared with other aims, such as improving the functioning of the system or achieving a consensus around goals. Taket and White argue that other aims and objectives are misleading because they require us to deal with 'unanswerable' questions posed by the complexity of the situation or the need to achieve genuine consensus. It is a matter of engaging people's emotions, having fun and leaving the rest for ethical decision. But are we not then left heavily dependent on the ethical practice of the facilitators? And isn't their ability to recognize disadvantaged groups and marginalized issues simply another form of unargued expertise?

Theoretically, and making use of the System Of Systems Methodologies (SOSM) (see Chapter 2), postmodernism seems determined to explore the far reaches of both the 'complexity' and 'participants' dimensions. Problem situations are deemed to be so extremely complex that they are impossible to understand and participants are regarded as subject to power/knowledge relationships they cannot control. The response is to do what feels right, seeking only local improvement of the situation. The usual metaphors that inform systems thinking, such as the organism, brain, flux and transformation, culture, even psychic prison and instruments of domination, are regarded as simplistic and misleading. A more appropriate metaphor, suggested by Alvesson and Deetz (1996), is the carnival. Carnivals are subversive of order, they allow diversity and creativity to be expressed, they encourage the exceptional to be seen, they are playful and engage people's emotions.

We have, of course, no difficulty in recognizing the 'paradigm' to which pragmatic pluralism and PANDA respond. Whereas other systems approaches relied on particular paradigms implicitly or, having established themselves through practice, sought the explicit assistance of a paradigm to help them develop further, postmodern systems thinking has been consciously constructed on the basis of the postmodern paradigm since its inception. Whether the result is seen as good or bad depends on the paradigm you yourself favour.

If the 'grand narratives' of economic growth, emancipation, religion, etc. have inspired human endeavour in the past, it is also true to say that they have, on occasion, given birth to extremely destructive ideologies. The scepticism of postmodernism to all grand narratives has, therefore, much to recommend it. So has, in many ways, its prioritizing of the local and its emphasis on how we achieve our own identities by engaging in local 'struggles'. The debunking of pomposity and the constant challenge to cultural elitism and the notion of expertise are also positive aspects of postmodernism. The original contributions of the approach to our understanding of discourse and power will not need further emphasis.

Adherents of other paradigms are, however, horrified by postmodernism. Functionalists see it as a retreat into irrationalism. They regard the achievements of science and technology as contributing to the progressive improvement of the human condition and will not have them denigrated. Interpretive thinkers wish to promote mutual understanding and learning through the widest possible participation in decision-making. The postmodern injunction to value diversity and conflict above all else seems, to them, more of a call for anarchy than improvement based on accommodation. Emancipatory thinkers are not convinced that postmodernism can contribute in any way to human fulfilment and emancipation. Diversity is not necessarily a good in itself. Within the variety of human experience lie viewpoints and actions propelled by some pretty nasty forces (e.g., racism). It is surely legitimate to keep an 'emancipatory check' on the emergence of such forces. Furthermore, from the emancipatory position, collective emancipation is an absolute prerequisite for the self-emancipation the postmodernists seek. How can we restyle ourselves without also remaking the power/knowledge relations that create us? Many of the ills we face, such as gender, race and class inequality, seem to be system-wide. Others are literally global in nature (e.g., pollution and world poverty). It seems clear that individual and local resistance are going to be futile in the face of the forces that sustain such problems. A wider, more universal coalition for change needs to be constructed if they are to be addressed.

Finally, it can be disputed whether postmodernism really provides an alternative paradigm. Some use its ideas as part of consulting practice, others in support of soft systems thinking, still others as part and parcel of an emancipatory rationale. This very promiscuity should give us pause. Certainly the lack of clear methodological guidance binding postmodern insights, methods and techniques to the overall theoretical framework (and forbidden by that framework) makes it difficult to do research on postmodernism. What are the methods and techniques seeking to achieve if they can serve any paradigm? How then can we judge the value of methods like deconstruction, genealogy and generative conversation?

13.5 THE VALUE OF POSTMODERN SYSTEMS THINKING TO MANAGERS

The value of postmodern system thinking to managers can be summarized in the following five points:

- It emphasizes a number of things, such as having fun at work, engaging emotions, etc., which may appear 'superficial', but are very significant (and are ignored in many more traditional systems approaches).
- It recognizes the importance of encouraging diversity and creativity if we want to maximize learning and so be successful in modern organizations as well as in the increasingly common multiagency situations we confront.
- Postmodernism challenges the notion that there are universal solutions to management problems, deriving from expertise, or universal ways of arriving at them, perhaps thorough appropriately designed participative processes.
- It encourages managers to experiment with and learn from a whole variety of forms of pluralism (i.e., of client, methods, modes of representation and facilitative processes).
- Postmodernism has given rise to some highly original postmodern systems methods (e.g., deconstruction) that can be employed in the spirit of postmodernism or in the service of some other systems approach.

13.6 CONCLUSION

It is worth concluding by referring to a series of 12 lectures by Habermas (1987) in which he seeks to respond to the postmodern attack on his own modernist position. In the process he develops a critique of postmodernists, such as Nietzsche, Heidegger, Derrida and Foucault. In each case he shows that the theorist he is critiquing has something valid to say, but exaggerates it out of all proportion. Foucault, for example, focuses on certain dysfunctions associated with rationalization processes in society. He ignores the undeniable achievements of those same forces. Derrida concentrates on certain defects that arise in argumentation. Habermas acknowledges they exist, but details all the positive aspects of language as a means of dealing with problems in the world. We should continue to value it and develop communicative approaches that increase mutual understanding and learning. Language remains a vehicle through which reason can reach out to the ideals of truth and justice.

In short, Habermas recognizes that the postmodernists have something to say, but believes that rather than abandoning the Enlightenment vision we need to renew and revitalize it. To do this requires more reason – to overcome the difficulties on which the postmodernists focus – rather than less. This is the argument followed by critical systems thinking in the final part of the book.

REFERENCES

Alvesson, M. and Deetz, S. (1996). Critical theory and postmodernist approaches to organizational studies. In: S.R. Clegg, C. Hardy and W.R. Nord (eds), *Handbook of Organization Studies* (pp. 191–217). Sage Publications, London.

Brocklesby, J. and Cummings, S. (1996). Foucault plays Habermas: An alternative philosophical underpinning for critical systems thinking. *Journal of the Operational Research Society*, **47**, 741–754.

Cooper, R. and Burrell, G. (1988). Modernism, postmodernism and organizational analysis: An introduction. *Organizational Studies*, **9**, 91–112.

Habermas, J. (1987). *Lectures on the Philosophical Discourse of Modernity*. MIT Press, Cambridge, MA.

Jackson, M.C. (2000). *Systems Approaches to Management*. Kluwer/Plenum, New York.

Lyotard, J.-F. (1984). *The Postmodern Condition: A Report on Knowledge*. Manchester University Press, Manchester.

Ormerod, R.J. (2003). Taket's suggestions for the OR toolkit. *Journal of the Operational Research Society*, **54**, 322–323.

Taket, A. (2002). Facilitation: Some contributions to theorising the practice of operational research. *Journal of the Operational Research Society*, **53**, 126–136.

Taket, A.R. and White, L.A. (2000). *Partnership and Participation: Decision-making in the Multiagency Setting*. John Wiley & Sons, Chichester, UK.

Topp, W.K. (1999). Towards heuristic systems methods for generating new knowledge in post-industrial business. PhD thesis, University of Cape Town, South Africa.

Part III

Creative Holism

Part III, which provides the book with its subtitle, 'creative holism', is concerned with how to maximize the benefit of the different holistic approaches studied in Part II by using them creatively in combination. I would argue that managers can become more successful if they possess the capacity to view their organizations through the lenses offered by the four sociological paradigms and the various metaphors of organization referred to in Chapter 3. They also need the ability to choose and to use the different systems approaches discussed in Part II, which reflect the variety of metaphors and paradigms, in an informed manner in order to improve organizational performance. To cope with the complexity, turbulence and diversity of the problem situations they are confronted by in the 21st century, managers must give attention to: improving goal seeking and viability, exploring purposes, ensuring fairness and promoting diversity. They need to measure against standards of efficiency, efficacy, effectiveness, elegance, emancipation, empowerment, exception and emotion. It is the essence of managerial creativity to pursue improvement, systemically, in all these areas, although of course managers will have to prioritize and to place a different emphasis on what their actions are intended to achieve at any particular conjuncture.

The commitment to using a plurality of systems approaches, their related methodologies and some appropriate systems methods, together, is sometimes called Critical Systems Thinking (CST), sometimes multimethodology practice. I am employing the phrase 'creative holism' in this book to refer to the same thing because it is, perhaps, more resonant of what I am actually trying to encourage: the creative use in combination of different ways of being holistic. Chapter 14 describes 'Total Systems Intervention', the best known critical systems or multimethodological approach. Chapter 15 brings the reader up to date in terms of the latest research in 'Critical Systems Practice'.

Part III

Creative Holla

Total Systems Intervention 14

The future prospects of management science will be much enhanced if (a) the diversity of issues confronting managers is accepted, (b) work on developing a rich variety of problem-solving methodologies is undertaken, and (c) we continually ask the question: 'What kind of issue can be "managed" with which sort of methodology?'.

Flood and Jackson (1991a)

14.1 INTRODUCTION

Early approaches to applied systems thinking, labelled hard systems approaches, were suitable for tackling certain well-defined problems, but were found to have limitations when faced with complex problem situations involving people with a variety of viewpoints and frequently at odds with one another.

Systems thinkers, as we saw in Part II, responded by developing: system dynamics, organizational cybernetics and complexity theory to tackle complexity and change; strategic assumption surfacing and testing, interactive planning and Soft Systems Methodology (SSM) to handle pluralism; Critical Systems Heuristics (CSH) and team syntegrity to empower the disadvantaged in situations involving conflict; and pragmatic pluralism to manage diversity. There has been a corresponding enlargement in the range of problem contexts in which systems practitioners feel competent to intervene.

It was becoming apparent, however, in the 1980s and 1990s, that something more was needed if systems thinking was ever to realize its potential as a guide for managers. It was Critical Systems Thinking (CST) that provided this 'something more'. CST has supplied the bigger picture, has allowed systems thinking to mature as a transdiscipline and has set out how the variety of approaches, methodologies, methods and models, now available, can be used in a coherent manner to promote successful intervention in complex organizational and societal problem situations.

Once CST had been formulated as a philosophy and theory, it needed guidelines that would enable it to be applied in practice. These were provided in 1991 with the publication of Flood and Jackson's (1991a) book *Creative Problem Solving: Total Systems Intervention*. Total Systems Intervention (TSI) was heralded as a new approach to planning, designing, problem-solving and evaluation based on CST. This chapter outlines the development of CST and highlights the first critical systems methodology: TSI.

14.2   DESCRIPTION OF TOTAL SYSTEMS INTERVENTION (TSI)

14.2.1   Historical development

The development of CST and TSI can be traced to three sources: a growing critical awareness of the strengths and weaknesses of individual systems approaches; an appreciation of the need for pluralism in systems thinking; and the rise of emancipatory systems thinking.

The major steps in the development of critical awareness in systems thinking were the assaults launched, in the 1970s, by soft systems thinkers on hard systems thinking and the critique of soft systems thinking, elaborated in the 1980s, by those of an 'emancipatory' persuasion. In the first case, soft systems thinkers sought to demonstrate that hard systems thinking is ineffective in the great majority of problem situations. Checkland, as we saw in Chapter 10, argues that hard systems thinking is a special case of soft systems thinking, applicable only in those rare cases when problem situations present themselves in terms of systems with clearly defined goals and objectives. In the second case, the critics argued that soft systems thinking, too, had a limited domain of application. The kind of open participative debate that is essential for the success of the soft systems approach, and that is used to validate the recommendations that emerge, is impossible to obtain in problem situations involving significant conflict between interest groups that have access to unequal power resources.

As the 1980s progressed the level of informed critique of individual systems approaches grew, culminating in Jackson's (1991) review of five strands of systems thinking – 'organizations as systems', 'hard', 'cybernetic', 'soft' and 'emancipatory' – from the point of view of some appropriate social theory. It had become obvious that all systems methodologies had certain weaknesses as well as certain strengths.

Our second source of CST is 'pluralism'. There has always been a tendency to pluralism in systems thinking applied to management – presumably on the basis that it assists with being holistic. Sociotechnical systems theory (concerning itself with the social, technical and economic subsystems of organizations) and contingency theory (interested in the goal, human, technical and managerial subsystems) are cases in point. However, while these early systems approaches identified different aspects of the organization to look at, they always looked at them from the same point of view – taking an essentially functionalist perspective (see Jackson, 2000). The sort of pluralism that inspired CST did not emerge until 1984. In that year Linstone released his book *Multiple Perspectives for Decision Making* and Jackson and Keys first published their System Of Systems Methodologies (SOSM). These two events signalled the birth of a more advanced form of pluralism that required systems practitioners both to look at problem situations from a variety of different perspectives and to use different systems methodologies in combination.

Linstone's form of multiperspective research seeks to use three different viewpoints to gain a rich appreciation of the nature of problem situations. The Traditional or technical (T) perspective, dependent on data and model-based analysis, is augmented by an Organizational (O) or societal perspective, and a Personal (P) or individual perspective. The T, O and P perspectives act as filters through which systems are viewed, and each yields insights that are not attainable with the others. Linstone argues that the different perspectives are most powerfully employed when they are clearly differentiated from one another, in terms of the emphasis they bring to the analysis, yet are used together to interrogate the same complex problem. Nor, he believes, can one expect consistency in findings: two perspectives may reinforce one another, but may equally cancel each other out.

Jackson and Keys were motivated to explore the relationships between the different systems methodologies that had arisen as guides to intervening in problem situations and to understand their capacities and limitations. To this end, during 1983/1984, a research programme was established at the University of Hull (UK) that used as its primary research tool the SOSM described in Chapter 2. This research programme was successful enough to open up a new perspective on the development of systems thinking. Previously, it had seemed as if the discipline was undergoing a Kuhnian 'paradigm crisis' (Kuhn, 1970) as hard systems thinking encountered increasing anomalies and was challenged by other approaches. The SOSM, by contrast, demonstrated that alternative systems approaches could be seen as complementary rather than in competition. Each systems approach is useful for certain purposes and in particular types of problem situation. The diversity of approaches, therefore, heralds not a crisis but increased competence in a variety of problem contexts.

The SOSM offered a way forward from the prevailing systems thinking 'in crisis' debates. In doing so it established pluralism as a central tenet of CST and encouraged mutual respect between proponents of different approaches who had previously seen themselves as being at war with one another. Furthermore, going beyond Linstone, the SOSM recognized that pluralism could be achieved based on methodologies (hard, cybernetic, soft, etc.) that were developed from more than one paradigm.

The centrality of pluralism was reinforced by Jackson, in 1987, in an article that compared it with 'isolationism', 'imperialism' and 'pragmatism' as a development strategy for systems thinking. Isolationists, who believed in just one systems methodology, divided the discipline and discredited the profession. Imperialists, who sought to incorporate different methodologies within their favoured systems–theoretical orientation, ignored the benefits of other paradigms and 'denatured' many of the approaches they used. Pragmatists, who eschewed theoretical distinctions and concentrated on building up a 'toolkit' of methods and techniques on the basis of what 'worked' in practice, limited the possibilities for learning (e.g., why the method worked) and passing on knowledge to future generations.

Pluralism, however, offered excellent opportunities for future progress. It respected the different strengths of the various strands of systems thinking, encouraged their theoretical development and suggested ways in which they could be appropriately fitted to the diversity of management problems that arise. It was argued that a *metamethodology* (TSI was still to come) would develop that could guide theoretical endeavour and advise practitioners, confronted with problem situations, which approach or combination of approaches is most suitable.

The third element that was important in the development of CST was the emergence of the 'emancipatory systems approach'. Indeed, in the early days of both approaches they could hardly be separated. There was a good reason for this, which can be understood using the SOSM. Once the strengths and weaknesses of existing systems methodologies were better understood, it became possible to ask whether there were any 'ideal-type' problem contexts for which no currently existing systems approach seemed appropriate. The most obvious candidates were the 'coercive' contexts, defined as situations where there is fundamental conflict between stakeholders and the only consensus that can be achieved arises from the exercise of power. Recognition that such contexts were important for systems thinking led to the first explicit call (Jackson, 1982a, 1985) for a 'critical approach' that could take account of them.

This call for (essentially) an emancipatory systems approach, inspired by the SOSM, was met by the arrival of Ulrich's CSH (see Chapter 11). Although Ulrich's (1983) approach represented an independently developed strand of CST, deriving from Kantian idealism and Churchman's reflections on systems design, when the approach became known at Hull it was like the discovery of an element that filled a gap in the periodic table (the SOSM). CSH was capable, where soft systems thinking was not, of providing guidelines for action in certain kinds of coercive situation.

This early involvement of CST with emancipatory systems approaches, led to a concern with 'emancipation' becoming one of its defining characteristics.

14.2.2 Philosophy and theory

By the time of the creation of TSI, in 1991, CST could be summarized (Jackson, 1991) as having five main commitments to:

- critical awareness;
- social awareness;
- pluralism at the methodological level;
- pluralism at the theoretical level; and
- 'emancipation'.

We have dealt with 'critical awareness', 'pluralism at the methodological level' and 'emancipation' in the previous subsection, but we did not detail their philosophical and theoretical underpinnings. We do that now and combine this with a discussion of 'social awareness' and 'pluralism at the theoretical level', these two commitments having emerged more directly from theoretical considerations.

The philosophy of the social sciences provided the major theoretical prop in developing critical awareness. Of particular importance has been work that allows an overview to be taken of different ways of analysing social systems and intervening in organizations. For example, Burrell and Morgan's (1979) book on sociological paradigms and organizational analysis was used by Checkland (1981) to demonstrate that hard systems thinking is functionalist in nature and that its shortcomings (in Checkland's eyes) can be understood in those terms. The same source allowed Jackson (1982b) and Mingers (1980, 1984) to argue that soft systems thinking is interpretive in nature; embracing both subjectivism and regulation. Jackson's 1991 book, *Systems Methodology for the Management Sciences*, made use of Burrell and Morgan's classification, Morgan's (1986) work on 'images' of organization, Habermas' (1970) theory of three human interests (technical, practical, emancipatory) and the modernism versus postmodernism debate, to critique the assumptions different systems approaches make about social science, social reality and organizations. This kind of critique allows a much richer appreciation of the theoretical assumptions lying behind their strengths and weaknesses.

As well as facilitating critical awareness, the social sciences drew the attention of critics to the importance of the social context in which systems approaches are used – and so to the need for 'social awareness'. Social awareness considers two things. First, it looks at the organizational and societal circumstances that lead to certain systems theories and methodologies being popular for guiding interventions at particular times. For example, hard systems thinking and management cybernetics were widely used in the old Soviet Union, and the communist states of Eastern Europe, because of their fit with hierarchy and bureaucracy. Second, social awareness makes users of systems methodologies contemplate the consequences of use of the approaches they employ. For example, using soft systems approaches in circumstances where open and free debate are not possible may simply reinforce the status quo.

The desirability of pluralism at the methodological level was established, as we saw, by the work of Linstone (1984), Jackson and Keys (1984) and Jackson (1987). Following Jackson's (1987) paper, debate about pluralism in systems thinking began to focus at the theoretical level. This was because of philosophical difficulties posed for the pluralist position by arguments in favour of 'paradigm incommensurability' derived from Kuhn (1970) and Burrell and Morgan (1979). It seemed inconceivable to proponents of paradigm incommensurability that different systems methodologies, based on what were (to them) irreconcilable theoretical assumptions, could ever be employed together in any kind of complementarist way. This would require standing 'above' the paradigms. How could such a privileged position be attained?

To find an answer to this problem, and therefore to give coherence to pluralism at the methodological level, critical systems thinkers turned to Habermas' theory of human interests.

Habermas (1970, 1975, 1984) has argued that there are two fundamental conditions underpinning the sociocultural life of the human species. These he calls 'work' and 'interaction'. *Work* enables us to achieve goals and to bring about material well-being through social labour. Its success depends on achieving technical mastery over natural and social processes. Human beings, therefore, have a 'technical interest' in the prediction and control of natural and social systems. The other anthropologically based cognitive interest is linked to *interaction* and is labelled the 'practical interest'. Its concern is with securing and expanding the possibilities for mutual understanding among all those involved in social systems. Disagreements between individuals and groups are just as much a threat to the sociocultural form of life as a failure to predict and control.

While work and interaction have pre-eminent anthropological status, the analysis of 'power' and the way it is exercised is equally important, Habermas argues, if we are to understand past and present social arrangements. The exercise of power can prevent the open and free discussion necessary for the success of work and interaction. Human beings have, therefore, an 'emancipatory interest' in freeing themselves from constraints imposed by power relations and in learning, through a process of genuine participatory democracy conducted in 'ideal speech situations', to control their own destiny.

Now, if we all have a technical, a practical and an emancipatory interest in the functioning of organizations and society, then an enhanced systems thinking that can support all of these various interests must have an extremely important role to play in securing human well-being. But this is exactly what CST, with its commitment to pluralism, offers. It seems clear that hard, system dynamic, organizational cybernetic and complexity theory approaches can support the technical interest, soft systems thinking the practical interest, and CSH and team syntegrity can assist the emancipatory interest.

By 1991, based on Habermas' thinking, it was possible for Flood and Jackson (1991a) to suggest that the concern about paradigm incommensurability could be resolved at the level of human interests. As a result the SOSM could be rescued as a vehicle for promoting methodological pluralism. Complementarism at the theoretical level provided the basis and justification for complementarism at the methodological level. The SOSM could point to the strengths and weaknesses of different strands of systems thinking and put them to work in a way that respects and takes advantage of their own particular theoretical predispositions in the service of appropriate human interests.

As we saw in the previous subsection, the SOSM benefited CST by providing a warm embrace to emancipatory approaches. By 1991, however, it was possible to see that it was necessary to keep emancipatory systems thinking at arm's length as far as becoming a permanent partner was concerned. The appropriate relationship became clear once CST had attached itself to Habermas' theory of three human interests: the technical, practical and emancipatory. It then became possible to define CST's 'emancipatory commitment' in terms of a much broader dedication to 'human improvement'. Flood and Jackson (1991a) saw this as meaning bringing about those circumstances in which all individuals could achieve the maximum development of their potential. This, in turn, means raising the quality of work and life in the organizations and societies in which they participate. Habermas had shown that human improvement required that each of his three interests needed serving by systems methodologies. Critical systems thinkers made the point that this was exactly what their approach wanted to achieve.

Emancipatory systems thinking is, therefore, narrower than CST. Its role is to provide methodologies that, through critique, enable the open and free discussion necessary for the success of work and interaction. The domain of effective application of emancipatory approaches is 'coercive' problem contexts, or organizations as psychic prisons and/or instruments of domination. But not all problem situations are usefully regarded as coercive; some are better seen as unitary or pluralist. Emancipatory systems thinking, therefore, just like hard and soft approaches, possesses a limited domain of application. CST, by contrast, is about putting *all* the different system approaches to work, according to their strengths and weaknesses, and the social conditions prevailing, in the service of a more general project of improvement.

14.2.3   Metamethodology

TSI aims to put into practice the commitments adhered to by CST. Briefly, it regards problem situations as messes that cannot be understood and analysed on the basis of only one perspective. For this reason, it advocates viewing them from a variety of perspectives, perhaps as encapsulated in different metaphors. Once agreement is reached among the facilitators and participants about the major issues and problems they are confronting, an appropriate choice needs to be made of systems methodology, or set of systems methodologies, for managing the mess and tackling the issues and problems. This choice should be made in the full knowledge of the strengths and weaknesses of available systems approaches as revealed, for example, by the SOSM. When selecting methodologies it is important that the idea of pluralism is kept in mind. Different methodologies can be used to address different aspects of problem situations and to ensure that the technical, practical and emancipatory interests are all given proper consideration. Furthermore, the initial choice of methodology or methodologies must be kept constantly under review and may need to change as the nature of the mess itself changes. In this way TSI guides intervention in such a way that it continually addresses the major issues and problems faced in an organization or multiagency situation.

From this brief account it will be clear that, because it organizes and employs other systems methodologies, TSI should strictly be described as a *metamethodology*. Flood and Jackson (1991a) see seven principles as underpinning this metamethodology:

- problem situations are too complicated to understand from one perspective and the issues they throw up too complex to tackle with quick fixes;
- problem situations, and the concerns, issues and problems they embody, should therefore be investigated from a variety of perspectives;
- once the major issues and problems have been highlighted it is necessary to make a suitable choice of systems methodology or methodologies to guide intervention;
- it is necessary to appreciate the relative strengths and weaknesses of different systems methodologies and to use this knowledge, together with an understanding of the main issues and concerns, to guide choice of appropriate methodologies;
- different perspectives and systems methodologies should be used in a complementary way to highlight and address different aspects of organizations, their issues and problems;
- TSI sets out a systemic cycle of inquiry with interaction back and forth between its three phases;
- facilitators and participants are engaged at all stages of the TSI process.

The sixth principle refers to the three phases of the TSI metamethodology, which are labelled *creativity*, *choice*, and *implementation*.

The task during the *creativity* phase is to highlight the major concerns, issues and problems that exist in the problem context that is being addressed. Various creativity-enhancing devices can be employed to help managers and other stakeholders during this phase. It is mandatory, however, that a wide range of different perspectives is brought to bear so that the picture built up of the problem situation is derived from viewing it from different paradigms. TSI uses 'systems metaphors' as its favoured method for ensuring this happens.

The key aspects of the problem situation revealed, by whatever creativity-enhancing devices are employed, are subject to discussion and debate among the facilitators, managers and other stakeholders. The outcome (what is expected to emerge) from the creativity phase is a set of significant issues and concerns. There may be other important but less immediately crucial problems that it is also sensible to record and pursue into the next phase. These 'dominant' and 'dependent' concerns, issues and problems then become the basis for designing an appropriate systems intervention approach.

The second phase is known as the *choice* phase. The task during this phase is to construct a suitable intervention strategy around a choice of systems methodology or combination of systems methodologies. Choice will be guided by the characteristics of the problem situation, as discovered during the examination conducted in the creativity phase, and knowledge of the particular strengths and weaknesses of different systems methodologies. A method is therefore needed that is capable of interrogating these method-ologies to show what they do well and what they are less good at. Tradition-ally, TSI has used the SOSM, but any of the devices employed by Jackson (1991) could be adopted for this purpose (i.e., metaphors, sociological para-digms, Habermas' three 'interests', positioning in the modernism versus modernism debate). The most probable outcome of the choice phase is that there will be a dominant methodology chosen, to be supported if necessary by dependent methodologies to help with secondary problem areas.

The third phase of TSI is the *implementation* phase. The task is to employ the selected systems methodology or methodologies with a view to bringing about positive change. If, as is usual, one methodology has been deemed dominant, it will be the primary tool used to address the problem situation. TSI stipulates, however, the need always to be open to the possibilities offered by other systems methodologies. For example, the key problems in an organization suffering from an inability to learn and adapt may be structural, as revealed by the organism and brain metaphors. But the cultural metaphor might also appear illuminating albeit in a subordinate way given the immediate crisis. In these circumstances, organizational cybernetics could be chosen to guide the intervention, but with a soft systems method-ology taking on other issues in the background. Of course, as the problem situation changes, it may be necessary to reassess the state of the organization, by re-entering the creativity phase, and then select an alternative method-ology as dominant. The outcome of the implementation phase should be

Table 14.1 The TSI metamethodology.

Creativity	
Task	To highlight significant concerns, issues and problems
Tools	Creativity-enhancing devices including systems metaphors
Outcome	Dominant and dependent concerns, issues and problems identified
Choice	
Task	To choose an appropriate systems intervention methodology or methodologies
Tools	Methods for revealing the strengths and weaknesses of different systems methodologies (e.g., the SOSM)
Outcome	Dominant and dependent methodologies chosen for use
Implementation	
Task	To arrive at and implement specific positive change proposals
Tools	Systems methodologies employed according to the logic of TSI
Outcome	Highly relevant and co-ordinated change that secures significant improvement in the problem situation

co-ordinated change brought about in those aspects of the problem situation currently most in need of improvement.

The three-phase TSI approach is summarized in Table 14.1.

It is important to stress, as a final point, that TSI is a systemic and interactive process. Attention needs to be given during each phase to the likely outcomes of other phases. As the problem situation changes in the eyes of the participants, a new intervention strategy will have to be devised. The only way to attend to these matters is to continually cycle around creativity, choice and implementation, ready to change those methodologies that are dominant and dependent. TSI is a dynamic metamethodology.

14.2.4 Methods

In the previous subsection we hinted at some of the methods that can be used by TSI in support of its three phases. Here we add a little more detail about some of them.

To encourage managers and other participants to think creatively about the problem situation they face, TSI will often ask them to view it through the lenses of various systems metaphors. Different metaphors focus attention on different aspects of the problem context. Some concentrate on structure, while others highlight human and political aspects. By using a varied set of Morgan's (1986) 'images' of organization, TSI ensures that it is gaining a holistic appreciation of the problem situation and taking on board perspectives that draw their meaning from different paradigms. Some of the common metaphors used by TSI are:

- machine;
- organism;
- brain;
- culture;
- coalition;
- coercive system.

The sorts of question it is useful to ask during metaphor analysis are:

- What metaphors throw light onto this problem situation?
- What are the main concerns, issues and problems revealed by each metaphor?
- In the light of the metaphor analysis, what concerns, issues and problems are currently crucial for improving the problem situation?

If all the metaphors reveal serious problems, then obviously the organization is in a crisis state!

Flood (1995) has suggested supplementing metaphor analysis: by allowing participants to create their own metaphors ('divergent' metaphorical analysis); by using techniques such as brainstorming and 'idea writing' to enhance creativity; and by paying attention to the 'ergonomics' of reflection – providing participants with the time and space to be creative. These are useful additions as long as they are not seen as a replacement for the discipline of metaphor analysis, which as has been emphasized is necessary to achieve a genuinely pluralistic appreciation of the problem situation.

The SOSM is the traditional tool employed by TSI in the choice phase. As we know from Chapter 2, it unearths the assumptions underlying different systems approaches by asking what each assumes about the system(s) in which it hopes to intervene and about the relationship between the participants associated with that system. Combining the information gained about the problem context during the creativity phase and the knowledge provided by the SOSM about the strengths and weaknesses of different systems approaches, it is possible to move toward an informed choice of systems intervention strategy. For example, if the problem context can reasonably be characterized as exhibiting clear and agreed objectives (unitary) and as being transparent enough so that it can be captured in a mathematical model (simple), then a methodology based on simple–unitary assumptions can be used with every hope of success.

One of the main methods associated with the implementation phase is the use of dominant and dependent methodologies together and in a potentially changing relationship. More details will be given about this technique in Chapter 15.

14.2.5   Recent developments

Since its formulation TSI has been taken in rather different directions by its two originators, Flood and Jackson. In a 1995 book, Flood suggests additions to the methods that can be used in each of the three phases of the metamethodology and specifies three 'modes' in which TSI can be used. The three modes are the traditional 'problem-solving' mode, the 'critical review' mode and the 'critical reflection' mode. The critical review mode applies TSI to the assessment of candidate methodologies that might be incorporated in the metamethodology. It is an elaboration of critical awareness. The critical reflection mode sees TSI used to evaluate its own interventions after the event in order to improve TSI itself. This seems to me to be essential, if properly specified, for ensuring that TSI fulfils its obligation to pursue research as well as practice. In further books (1996, with Romm, and 1999), Flood has explained the relationships between TSI and postmodernism, and TSI, chaos and complexity theory, respectively.

Jackson's more recent work has focused on developing 'critical systems practice', which is the topic covered in the final chapter of this book.

14.3   TOTAL SYSTEMS INTERVENTION (TSI) IN ACTION

The intervention described here was one of a series that took place, using TSI, within North Yorkshire Police (NYP) in the mid-1990s. NYP is the largest police force in England in terms of geographical area, covering some 3,200 square miles. It serves a population of over 750,000, some living in towns and cities, such as York, and others in low population areas such as the North Yorkshire Moors. NYP, in 1993, had a budget of over £70 million per annum and employed over 2,750 police officers and civilian support staff.

NYP was commanded, from the Force Headquarters, by a chief constable and two assistant chief constables. A civilian finance director oversaw all

the finance and administrative activities. This group of senior staff constituted the Chief Officer Team of NYP. There were seven divisions, each
headed by an officer of superintendent rank, which were responsible for
operational policing.

The intervention was conducted by Keith Ellis, an academic and
consultant with experience of TSI, and Andrew Humphreys, a divisional
commander in NYP who was on secondment, learning about systems thinking. I am grateful to Keith Ellis for allowing me to draw heavily on, and
take extracts from, his account of the project (Ellis, 2002).

The Chief Constable had determined that NYP should develop a long-
term organizational strategy that would enable it to realize its mission.
First, however, it was necessary to create a strategic planning process that
could produce such a strategy. That was the aim of this particular intervention, which according to the brief should develop 'a top level corporate
strategic planning process . . . together with the approach to be used.'

The consultants (Ellis and Humphreys) were under no illusions about the
scale of the task given the complexity of the organization and its environment, and the current propensity in NYP toward reactive planning. They
also recognized the major importance of the project for the Chief Officer
Team, who were the clients and who were expecting major changes to the
management of the organization to result from it. It was agreed that the
intervention would last about a year with regular reports back to the Chief
Officer Team. The consultants also secured a free hand to utilize any methodology they considered appropriate. They chose TSI and used it in a pure
form so that they could learn as much as possible about the metamethodology itself as well as improve the situation in NYP. This allows the three
phases to be described very precisely.

The creativity phase had two interrelated aspects: an interview programme and a metaphor analysis.

In order to gain a holistic understanding of the problem situation
surrounding the strategic planning process in NYP, it was essential to
gather opinion from the widest possible range of stakeholder groups. The
following stakeholder groups were identified:

- NYP chief officers;
- divisional commanders and police officer departmental heads;
- police staff associations;
- special constabulary;
- police authority chairpersons;
- North Yorkshire County Council senior officials;

- community consultation representatives;
- Her Majesty's Inspector of Constabulary;
- Police Staff College, Bramshill;
- Humberside Police Force;
- Northumbria Police Force.

Forty-two representatives of these groups were interviewed. The interviews were semistructured, based around a set of 'trigger questions', and were tape-recorded, but with contributions to remain anonymous to all but the consultants.

A metaphor analysis was conducted immediately after each interview and the results combined to build up a 'metaphoric picture' of the organization. The metaphors used for this were of the organization as a:

- machine;
- organism;
- brain;
- culture;
- coercive (political) system.

The majority of stakeholder representatives saw NYP as a goal-seeking machine dominated by hierarchy, engaged in repetitive functions and controlled through financial constraints. It was hindered as a 'machine' by a lack of clear direction from the top. Moreover, because NYP operated like a machine, current top-level planning ignored environmental influences.

Despite its machine-like character, NYP simply had to recognize environmental disturbances and react accordingly in some areas of its activity. Use of the organism metaphor revealed that this had gone furthest at the divisional and local service levels, where stakeholders were becoming involved in planning. This was not, however, mirrored at the top level of the organization.

The Viable System Model (VSM) (see Chapter 6) was used to help interpret the interview results from a brain perspective. It revealed that NYP was weak in terms of its capacity to learn and adapt. It possessed only a limited development function, connecting it to the outside world, and lacked an audit function that would enable senior managers to get feedback about the performance of the operational elements. As a result the Chief Officer Team tended to forget about their environment and to spend their time trying to find out what was going on lower down. This was inevitably perceived as interference by the divisional commanders who retaliated by actively withholding information. NYP, it seemed, was very far from the ideal of a learning organization.

The culture metaphor, applied to the results of the interviews, showed that NYP was a complex mix of cultures, with different camps distinguished by phrases such as 'shapers' and 'doers', 'dreamers' and 'implementers', 'innovators' and 'applicators'. Many interviewees identified separate 'language zones' and pleaded for a 'common language', 'management speak-free documents', 'clarified value statements' and 'targeted documents'. In general there seemed to be a divide between those whose thinking was dominated by the 'single issue of policing with ever-diminishing resources' and those most concerned about 'socially demanded 24-hour policing in a multifaceted community'. NYP seemed to be in the process of shifting from unitary to pluralist internal relations, but with no means of managing pluralism.

Externally, NYP was entwined in a complex web of political engagements involving itself, central government and local government. Internally, there were also a number of political agendas. Nevertheless, the 'coercive' exercise of power did not seem to be a problem. It existed in terms of top-down planning and decision-making, but this was seen as normal for a goal-driven organization.

On the basis of the interviews and the metaphor analysis, the consultants concluded that the dominant concerns and issues for NYP revolved around the need for viable organizational structures that would enable the shift from a 'closed mechanistic entity', through an 'open organismic body' into a 'learning brain organization'. Also important was the need for a strategic planning process, owned by the Chief Officer Team, that would assist this shift at the same time as introducing a more pluralistic approach to planning. Rapid change meant that pluralism and politics were inevitable facts of life that had to be embraced.

Using the SOSM as the main vehicle for the 'choice' phase, it seemed clear to the consultants that the NYP strategic planning problem situation could be described as systemic–pluralist.

NYP was a complex system containing many sub-subsystems, which themselves contained components that were made up of elements. There was no doubt that the wider system, of which NYP was a part, was becoming more turbulent.

One aspect of that environmental turbulence was a growing diversity of opinion about the role of police in a modern society. The debates taking place were reflected internally in NYP itself. There was increasing divergence of values and beliefs, not least between the chief officers and lower ranks.

The SOSM analysis pointed at Ackoff's interactive planning (see Chapter 9) as a suitable systems methodology to help develop the strategic planning process. Its strengths were its ability to marshal pluralism to productive ends together with its willingness to entertain models that could help design complex systems. At the same time, it had to be borne in mind that the metaphor analysis had pointed strongly to the need to develop viable organizational structures capable of supporting an effective strategic planning process. And the brain perspective, based on the VSM, had seemed particularly insightful in revealing what problems existed in this respect.

In the event the consultants decided to proceed with the VSM as the dominant approach, to tackle structural weaknesses in the organization, closely coupled with Interactive Planning (IP), in a dependent role, to move forward with actually developing the strategic planning process.

Implementation therefore proceeded using the VSM and IP in combination. The VSM diagnosis brought to the fore a variety of structural issues that needed addressing:

- System 5 –
  - o identity weak and fragmented;
  - o chief officers did not act as a team;
  - o lack of strategy-making process left NYP without corporate direction;
  - o chief officer-thinking dominated by lower level tactical and operational issues;
  - o chief officer interference in operational activities.
- System 4 – almost non-existent development function.
- System 3 – poor operational control by the managerial team.
- System 3* – limited and ineffective audit of operational unit activities.
- System 2 – lack of co-ordination of operational units.

The initial, mess formulation, stage of IP could draw from the outcomes of the creativity phase of TSI. A reference scenario was constructed that revealed the absence of a strategic planning process in NYP and lack of clarity about how to get one. It also highlighted the need for: improvements in clarifying organizational values; involving stakeholders in planning; agreeing a planning terminology; and communicating, disseminating and co-ordinating plans.

Working with a number of the stakeholders, the consultants then produced an idealized design for a strategic planning process. This had as key attributes:

- involving all those who might affect, or be affected by, strategies relating to policing in North Yorkshire;
- informing and communicating through involvement, thus avoiding the pitfalls associated with 'retelling the strategy';
- enhancing the relevance of strategic planning to operational policing by concentrating on core service areas;
- ensuring continuity in the planning process;
- providing a clarity of purpose within community consultative bodies;
- providing a basis for innovation within a dynamic and unstable environment.

Having decided on the ends, it was now necessary to agree means (as informed by the VSM diagnosis), secure resources and begin implementation. To this end, the draft, idealized design, strategic planning process was presented at a two-day workshop attended by the chief officers, as clients, and representatives of the wider set of stakeholder groups.

Initially, there were severe problems. The chief officers had become aware of findings critical of them that had emerged during the interview programme. The Chief Constable, particularly unwilling to see his authority challenged in the presence of influential outsiders, reacted against this information in an autocratic and coercive manner. In turn this led to other stakeholders modifying their 'messages'. Some persuasion had to be used to overcome the Chief Constable's defensive mindset of 'I'm in charge' and replace it with one that recognized that involving others assists with creativity and 'spreads the risk'. Eventually, this worked, the situation was recovered and the workshop achieved its aims. In particular, a NYP five-year strategic planning process was agreed and fully operationalized in 1995.

Ellis argues that TSI provided a powerful guiding metamethodology for this intervention, which produced useful output for NYP. The following list of successful outcomes reflects both the VSM and IP inputs:

- a strategic planning process that replaced *ad hoc* tactical planning;
- an acceptance by the Chief Constable that wider stakeholder input to strategic planning is useful;
- Police Authority input to strategic planning;
- a generalized, systemic understanding of the nature of NYP as a complex organization undergoing radical change;

- a recognition by the Chief Officer Team of the strategic nature of their roles in terms of boundary scanning and the relationship between NYP and the wider system at local and national levels;
- an understanding that NYP needed to become a learning organization and of the need to overcome organizational defensive routines.

As a result of the intervention Ellis was able to: suggest improvements to TSI, particularly with regard to its ability to recognize and respond to coercion; learn much about using TSI to bring about change, which he was able to incorporate into his own 'systemic theory of organisational change' (Ellis, 2002); and use the considerable knowledge he gained of NYP to secure further consultancy contracts.

14.4 CRITIQUE OF TOTAL SYSTEMS INTERVENTION (TSI)

It can reasonably be argued that CST rescued systems theory from a crisis produced by warring paradigms and offered it a coherent developmental strategy, as a transdiscipline, based on firmer foundations. A similar claim can be made for TSI in relation to systems practice. By setting out a meta-methodology for using methodologies adhering to different paradigms in the same intervention and on the same problem situation, TSI suggested that the approaches and skills developed by different systems practitioners could be brought together and co-ordinated to achieve a more successful form of systems intervention.

TSI rejects isolationism and moves beyond imperialism. Imperialism, it will be recalled, is prepared to use different tools and techniques, but only in the service of its favoured theoretical assumptions and methodology. TSI suggests a way of managing, in a coherent way, very different methodologies built on the foundations of alternative paradigms. This puts it a step ahead of other systems approaches in dealing with the complexity, heterogeneity and turbulence of the problem situations we face today. At the same time TSI rejects pragmatism, insisting that the use of a variety of methodologies and methods must remain theoretically informed to ensure that learning can take place and be passed on to others.

TSI does not try to disguise the difficulties inherent in using different methodologies alongside one another in highly complex situations. Indeed, it argues that, although this is desirable, if it proves practically impossible, then the best way to handle methodological pluralism is to clearly state that one methodology is being taken as dominant (and others as dependent) for some period of time. One methodology, encapsulating the presuppositions of a particular paradigm, is granted imperialistic status – but only temporarily; its dominance is kept under continuous review.

Another strength of TSI has been to bring together pluralism in the creativity phase (looking at the problem situation from different perspectives) with pluralism in terms of the management of different methodologies in combination (in the choice and implementation phases).

If TSI's great strength is operating at the metamethodological level, this also leads to some weaknesses. As Mingers and Brocklesby (1996) point out, TSI requires the use of 'whole' methodologies. This has two consequences. First, TSI is dependent on the set of systems methodologies it has inherited, such as system dynamics, organizational cybernetics, interactive planning, CSH, etc. These were not always carefully formulated with explicit reference to their theoretical foundations. It can be argued that TSI would be better developing its own 'pure' methodologies that are clearly related to the theoretical paradigms it recognizes. Second, it seems that, once you have chosen a particular methodology as dominant, you must employ only the methods and techniques closely associated with it and in exactly the manner prescribed by that methodology. For example, having chosen Checkland's SSM you get rich pictures, root definitions and conceptual models, but are prevented from using causal loop diagrams or idealized design. There is an unnecessary lack of flexibility here that needs addressing. There is nothing philosophically wrong with using a selection of methods and techniques, as long as they are employed according to an explicit logic. Indeed, it allows a much greater responsiveness to the peculiarities of each problem situation as it evolves during an intervention.

Another criticism centres on the lack of attention given to the process of using TSI. For example, Taket and White (2000) find little guidance on the roles and styles that facilitators might adopt. Most detail is provided on the implementation phase, whereas they suspect users of TSI have greatest difficulty with the creativity and choice phases.

A further gap in the TSI armoury is highlighted by those management scientists who give attention to the users of methodologies. TSI, which demands multimethodological competence and adherence to a variety of 'commitments', clearly asks a great deal from would-be users. Brocklesby (1997), for example, identifies severe cognitive difficulties for individuals trying to work across paradigms. TSI does not detail whether or how the relevant competences can be obtained.

Again, there are those who accuse TSI of partiality in seeking improvement. TSI suggests it is in favour of human emancipation, but tends to ignore environmental concerns. For Midgley (1996), the two are inextricably linked.

TSI receives support from CST, which has spent a considerable amount of time and effort establishing, developing and promoting its theoretical tenets. Inevitably, this openness has drawn the attention of critics. The two main lines of criticism come from those who take a strong paradigm incommensurability stance and from postmodernists.

TSI grounds its pluralism, or complementarism, on Habermas' early theory of human interests – a theory that he has himself subsequently abandoned. This theory suggests that TSI can, on the basis of the three human interests, stand 'above the paradigms' and pick out appropriate methodologies according to the particular human interest to be served. Tsoukas (1993), however, notes that different paradigms constitute different realities and, therefore, seek to provide answers to all three human interests. If TSI claims to stand above the paradigms, adjudicating between them, how can this claim be grounded? If it has to abandon this claim, does it mean that CST constitutes a paradigm in its own right? If this is the case what has happened to pluralism?

From their postmodern perspective, Taket and White (2000) see TSI as an approach that seeks to tame pluralism and diversity rather than embracing them. The emphasis on rigour and formalized thinking in TSI sets up a tension, they believe, with the espoused purpose of employing a plurality of methodologies and methods. A deconstruction of the language of TSI reveals a contradiction between statements that imply closure and those encouraging an openness to other approaches and ways of proceeding. Taket and White also worry that the emphasis on rationality and abstraction in TSI leads to the privileging of methods that are verbally based and that this can hinder the participation of some groups. Another problem with giving primacy to rationality is that the feelings and emotions of participants in decision processes get ignored.

14.5 THE VALUE OF TOTAL SYSTEMS INTERVENTION (TSI) TO MANAGERS

Proponents of TSI have always warned managers not to be fooled by those who peddle fads and quick fixes. The problems they face are too complicated and diverse to be handled by anything other than considered, and often prolonged, holistic endeavour. TSI seeks to guide and structure this holistic endeavour, in particular by:

- Advocating and enabling the maximum creativity when the problem situation is being analysed.
- Helping managers to evaluate the usefulness to them, in their situation, of different management solutions and, particularly, different systems approaches.
- Opposing a 'one best way in all circumstances' mentality and ensuring that managers have available to them a variety of systemic problem-resolving strategies that can be used in combination if necessary.
- Asking managers to take into account a number of considerations – technical (prediction and control), practical (mutual understanding) and emancipatory (fairness) – when planning and evaluating interventions.
- Providing a learning system that, through critical self-reflection, managers can tap into to improve their own practice.

14.6   CONCLUSION

The early years of CST were ones of huge intellectual excitement, providing for very rapid theoretical and practical development of the approach. These years culminated in the publication, in 1991, of three books that took their inspiration from CST and tried to present the main findings as they stood at that date. Flood and Jackson's (1991b) *Critical Systems Thinking: Directed Readings* was a collection of papers, accompanied by a commentary, that traced the origins and development of CST. Jackson's *Systems Methodology for the Management Sciences* sought to provide a comprehensive critique of the different systems approaches, drawing on the social sciences as the basis for that critique. Flood and Jackson's (1991a) *Creative Problem Solving: Total Systems Intervention* introduced the TSI metamethodology as a means of operationalizing CST in practice. This latter volume, in particular, spawned a myriad of applications of CST using TSI. By 1991, therefore, a position had been established from which creative holism could be further developed.

REFERENCES

Brocklesby, J. (1997). Becoming multimethodology literate: An assessment of the cognitive difficulties of working across paradigms. In: J. Mingers and A.

Gill (eds), *Multimethodology: The Theory and Practice of Combining Management Science Methodologies* (pp. 189–216). John Wiley & Sons, Chichester, UK.

Burrell, G. and Morgan, G. (1979). *Sociological Paradigms and Organizational Analysis*. Heinemann, London.

Checkland, P.B. (1981). *Systems Thinking, Systems Practice*. John Wiley & Sons, Chichester, UK.

Ellis, R.K. (2002). Toward a systemic theory of organisational change. PhD thesis, City University, London.

Flood, R.L. (1995). *Solving Problem Solving*. John Wiley & Sons, Chichester, UK.

Flood, R.L. (1999). *Rethinking 'The Fifth Discipline': Learning within the Unknowable*. Routledge, London.

Flood, R.L. and Jackson, M.C. (1991a). *Creative Problem Solving: Total Systems Intervention*. John Wiley & Sons, Chichester, UK.

Flood, R.L. and Jackson, M.C. (eds) (1991b). *Critical Systems Thinking: Directed Readings*. John Wiley & Sons, Chichester, UK.

Flood, R.L. and Romm, N.R.A. (1996). *Diversity Management: Triple Loop Learning*. John Wiley & Sons, Chichester, UK.

Habermas, J. (1970). Knowledge and interest. In: D. Emmet and A. MacIntyre (eds), *Sociological Theory and Philosophical Analysis* (pp. 36–54). Macmillan, London.

Habermas, J. (1975). *Legitimation Crisis*. Beacon Press, Boston.

Habermas, J. (1984). *Reason and the Rationalization of Society*. Beacon Press, Boston.

Jackson, M.C. (1982a). Verifying social systems theory in practice: A critique. In: L. Troncale (ed.), *A General Survey of Systems Methodology* (pp. 668–673). Society for General Systems Research, Louisville, KY.

Jackson, M.C. (1982b). The nature of soft systems thinking: The work of Churchman, Ackoff and Checkland. *Journal of Applied Systems Analysis*, **9**, 17–28.

Jackson, M.C. (1985). Social systems theory in practice: The need for a critical approach. *International Journal of General Systems*, **10**, 135–151.

Jackson, M.C. (1987). Present positions and future prospects in management science. *Omega*, **15**, 455–466.

Jackson, M.C. (1991). *Systems Methodology for the Management Sciences*. Plenum, New York.

Jackson, M.C. (2000). *Systems Approaches to Management*. Kluwer/Plenum, New York.

Jackson, M.C. and Keys, P. (1984). Towards a system of systems methodologies. *Journal of the Operational Research Society*, **35**, 473–486.

Kuhn, T. (1970). *The Structure of Scientific Revolutions* (2nd edn). University of Chicago Press, Chicago.

Linstone, H.A. (1984). *Multiple Perspectives for Decision Making*. North-Holland, New York.

Midgley, G. (1996). Evaluating services for people with disabilities: A critical systems perspective. *Evaluation*, **2**, 67–84.

Mingers, J.C. (1980). Towards an appropriate social theory for applied systems thinking: Critical theory and soft systems methodology. *Journal of Applied Systems Analysis*, **7**, 41–49.

Mingers, J.C. (1984). Subjectivism and soft systems methodology – A critique. *Journal of Applied Systems Analysis*, **11**, 85–103.

Mingers, J.C. and Brocklesby, J. (1996). Multimethodology: Towards a framework for mixing methodologies. *Omega*, **25**, 489–509.

Morgan, G. (1986). *Images of Organization*. Sage Publications, Beverley Hills, CA.

Taket, A.R. and White, L.A. (2000). *Partnership and Participation: Decision-making in the Multiagency Setting*. John Wiley & Sons, Chichester, UK.

Tsoukas, H. (1993). The road to emancipation is through organizational development: A critical evaluation of Total Systems Intervention. *Systems Practice*, **6**, 53–70.

Ulrich, W. (1983). *Critical Heuristics of Social Planning*. Haupt, Bern.

Critical Systems Practice   15

This is the source of the trouble. Persons tend to think and feel exclusively in one mode or the other and in so doing tend to misunderstand and underestimate what the other mode is all about ... To reject that part of the Buddha that attends to the analysis of motorcycles is to miss the Buddha entirely.

Pirsig (1974)

15.1 INTRODUCTION

The subtitle of this book is 'Creative Holism for Managers'. Being 'holistic', in the managerial domain, means using systems ideas and concepts to understand and intervene in problem situations. However, there are different ways of being holistic, as we have seen. This is an advantage because it allows us to be 'creative' in the manner in which we employ systems thinking. Creative holism is about the creative use in combination of different ways of being holistic. Once understood, it allows managers to be holistic in a more profound sense.

Creative holism evolves as its philosophy and theory – Critical Systems Thinking (CST) – and its metamethodology – called Critical Systems Practice (CSP) – change. In the previous chapter we looked at the early development of CST and considered Total Systems Intervention (TSI) as the best known version of CSP. In this chapter we bring the story up to date, by reviewing the further development of both CST and CSP in the 1990s and early years of this century.

15.2 DESCRIPTION OF CRITICAL SYSTEMS PRACTICE (CSP)

15.2.1 Historical development

As we saw in the last chapter, CST and CSP had a significant impact on the systems thinking scene within a relatively short period of time. By 1991 it was firmly established, and further development took on a dynamic of its own. This was propelled by an internal logic (e.g., learning from applications of TSI) and by the responses made to challenges from the outside, such as from postmodernism. We started to consider both of these in the last chapter and will continue to do so in this. To them, however, was added a third motor of change, which we will refer to specifically at this point.

This third motor was fuelled by pluralism in method use becoming popular among practitioners. To put it simply there was a clamour for pluralism in the applied disciplines. This was true of organization theory, information systems, operational research, evaluation research and management consultancy. Munro and Mingers (2002) report on a survey of operational research, management science and systems practitioners, which demonstrates just how widespread multimethod use had become in those fields by 2002. For those working on real-world problems, pluralism seemed to be necessary and, judging from the response of Munro and Mingers' sample, combining methods brought success.

The fact that multimethod use was becoming common in practice, and was apparently successful, spurred on its advocates. The year 1997 saw the publication of Mingers and Gill's (eds) *Multimethodology – The Theory and Practice of Combining Management Science Methodologies*. This was a definitive collection of papers on multimethodological thinking addressed to an operational research/management science/systems audience. It drew on highly theoretical work in CST as well as on multimethod applications by consultants. The result was the emergence of something of a community of those interested in CST or multimethodology, call it what you will, which led to a further round of rapid progress in the development of creative holism.

15.2.2 Philosophy and theory

The five 'commitments' of CST (Section 14.2.2) in 1991 had, by 2000 (see Jackson, 2000), been transformed into three: with 'critical awareness' swallowing 'social awareness', and 'methodological pluralism' and 'theoretical pluralism' now usually treated together. We can consider the philosophy and theory of CSP, therefore, by looking at the three, revised commitments: to 'critical awareness', 'improvement' and 'pluralism'.

Critical awareness retains as its main purpose critiquing the theoretical underpinnings, strengths and weaknesses of different systems methodologies and methods. Work of this kind continued throughout the 1990s, and the results have been reported in Jackson (2000) and summarized in Part II of this book. The other aspect of critical awareness (which was previously dealt with as social awareness) considers the societal and organizational 'climate' within which systems approaches are used. This impacts on their 'popularity' and the results they can generate. As Flood and Romm (Flood, 1990; Flood and Romm, 1996) have insisted it must include consideration of the effects that power at the microlevel can have on the development and use of knowledge. This idea derives, of course, from postmodernism and, in particular, from the work of Foucault (see Chapter 13). A related point has been urged on critical systems thinkers by Brocklesby (1994, 1997). He asks that more attention be given to the various 'constraints' (cultural, political, personal) that hinder acceptance of CST.

Turning to the second commitment, CST has since its inception made somewhat grand statements about being dedicated to human 'emancipation'. Putting fairness and empowerment on the agenda, by promoting emancipatory system thinking, has certainly been one of its main achievements. As we saw in the previous chapter, however, this led to some initial confusion between critical and emancipatory systems thinking. Eventually, it became clear that emancipation was only one of the three human interests that, following Habermas, CST sought to support. CST in 1991, therefore, still embraced emancipation, but as part of a much broader commitment to realizing those circumstances in which all individuals could realize their potential (Flood and Jackson, 1991).

These days, following the attack on the 'grand narratives' of universal liberation conducted by such postmodernists as Lyotard, critical systems thinkers are much more circumspect about even using the phrase 'human emancipation'. It has been accepted that Habermas' universalist position, based on the notion of the 'ideal speech situation', has been undermined. Instead, it has become more normal to talk in terms of achieving 'local improvement'. This adjustment, in the face of the postmodernist challenge, does not mean that critical systems thinkers have completely accepted the conclusion that collective emancipation is a dangerous fiction and that self-emancipation is the only proper objective. Universal ethical standards can still be used to evaluate local practices, which may look decidedly dubious in this light. Rather, critical systems thinkers have tempered their argument to reflect the difficulty of generalizing such an idea as emancipation. The current commitment reflects an awareness of the need to be sceptical of any claims to emancipation – either universal or local – but still to strive for something beneficial, call it 'improvement', all the same.

Pluralism in systems thinking is about using different systems theories, methodologies and methods in combination. There have been developments here at all three levels.

The reader will recall that one of the main criticisms of TSI was that it uncritically adhered to Habermas' early theory of human interests. This theory seemed to allow it to operate at a metalevel to the paradigms, allocating appropriate methodologies to different aspects of a problem situation as appropriate. Critical systems thinkers have now largely accepted that it is untenable to believe, in the manner of TSI, that paradigm incommensurability can be resolved by reference to a metatheory. Gregory (1992, 1996), for example, has argued for 'discordant pluralism' against the 'complementarist' version, based in Habermas' work, that she sees as dominating TSI. Discordant pluralism suggests that the differences between paradigms should be emphasized rather than 'rationalized away'. This is a useful clarification and one that points the way forward to the kind of pluralism that can deliver the greatest benefits for systems thinking. In CSP a meta-methodology is required that accepts and protects paradigm diversity and handles the relationships between the divergent paradigms. This meta-methodology must accept that paradigms are based on incompatible philosophical assumptions and that they cannot, therefore, be integrated without something being lost. It needs to manage the paradigms, not by aspiring to metaparadigmatic status and allocating them to their respective tasks, but by using them critically. Paradigms have to confront one another on the basis of 'reflective conversation' (Morgan, 1983). Critique is managed *between* the paradigms and not controlled from above them. No paradigm is allowed to escape unquestioned because it is continually confronted by the alternative rationales offered by other paradigms.

A contribution from Mingers and Brocklesby (1996) helps to explain what developments have occurred at the methodology and methods levels. They provide an overview of the different possibilities that they believe can exist under the label of 'pluralism'. Of these, three are to various degrees compatible with CST: 'methodology selection', 'whole methodology management' and 'multiparadigm multimethodology'.

In 'methodology selection', the systems practitioner regards a variety of different methodologies, based on different paradigms, as useful and chooses a whole methodology (such as system dynamics or SSM) according to the nature of the problem context and what he or she is trying to achieve. That methodology, and its associated methods, tools and techniques, is then employed throughout the intervention to try to resolve the problem situation. The System Of Systems Methodologies (SOSM) (see Chapter 2), before it was incorporated into TSI, can be seen as encouraging this form of pluralism.

The second type, labelled 'whole methodology management', again uses whole methodologies based on different paradigms, but this time is prepared to employ them together in the same intervention. The emphasis shifts to how a variety of very different methodologies, and their associated methods, can be managed during the process of intervention. This, of course, is the primary task that TSI sets for itself.

The third type, preferred by Mingers and Brocklesby, is called 'multi-paradigm multimethodology'. This involves using parts of different methodologies together on the same problem situation. Here the whole methodologies are 'broken up' and the methods, models and techniques usually associated with them brought together in new combinations according to the requirements of the particular intervention.

In support of 'multiparadigm multimethodology' are: operational research and management science practitioners who want the freedom to use whatever methods seem appropriate at the time; postmodernists who are quite at home 'mutilating' methodologies to achieve a judicious 'mix and match' of methods; and, these days, most critical systems thinkers. The great merit of allowing methods, models, tools and techniques to be detached from their usual methodologies, and employed flexibly, is that it allows practitioners the maximum freedom to respond to the needs of the problem situation and to the twists and turns taken by the intervention.

There is one caveat, however, imposed by CST on unrestricted multi-method use. This is that, at all times, there must be an explicit recognition of the paradigm(s) the methods are being used to serve. There must be no relapse from 'genuine' pluralism into unreflective imperialism or pragmatism (see Chapter 14). The way CSP achieves this, while allowing the flexible use of methods, is set out in the next subsection.

15.2.3 Metamethodology

TSI went a long way toward providing a suitable metamethodology for CST. In considering CSP as the revised metamethodology, it is worth noting that the basic philosophy, principles and phases of TSI remain pretty much intact. The philosophy embraced can still be described in terms of commitments, now simplified to the three of 'critical awareness', 'pluralism' and 'improvement'. The principles have stood the test of time (the reader is referred back to Chapter 14). Intervention can still be seen as possessing: a 'creativity' phase, which surfaces ideas about the current problem situation; a 'choice' phase, which considers alternative ways of addressing important issues; and an 'implementation' phase during which change processes are managed. Nevertheless, we saw well enough in the previous subsection that changes need making to reflect the reconceptualizing of the nature of a critical systems metamethodology and to allow for more flexible multimethod use.

As a metamethodology, CSP no longer aspires to metaparadigmatic status. Its job instead is to protect paradigm diversity and encourage critique between the paradigms. This needs to take place during each of the phases of the methodology. In order to appreciate the complexity and heterogeneity of problem situations the systems practitioner must, in pursuing 'creativity', consider them from the perspectives of the four different paradigms, perhaps as reflected through the concerns of various metaphors. Engaging in 'choice', the practitioner will be looking at what he or she hopes to achieve in terms of the strengths and weaknesses of different systems methodologies as seen from the paradigms they represent and alternative paradigms. In order to protect the benefits that each paradigm has to offer, he or she will need to be extremely watchful. Political, cultural and cognitive constraints can delimit the range of methodologies it is possible to use and so reduce the potency of pluralism. Similarly, the way 'implementation' proceeds will be continually critiqued through the lenses offered by alternative paradigms. And the results obtained will be evaluated according to the concerns evinced by the different paradigms. Currently, having incorporated postmodernism, CSP manages relationships between the functionalist, interpretive, emancipatory and postmodern paradigms. It is ready and able to include more if they offer radically new ways of seeing and acting.

In order for CSP to protect paradigm diversity during 'creativity', 'choice' and 'implementation', it requires a clear statement of the methodologies that purport to operationalize the perspectives of the different paradigms. For this purpose TSI used existing systems methodologies and their associated methods, models and techniques. CSP sees advantages in specifying the exact nature of 'generic methodologies', representing the functionalist, interpretive, emancipatory and postmodern paradigms. One advantage is that the theoretical link back to paradigms is made explicit; so allowing us to operationalize better and more obviously the hypotheses of particular paradigms and to test the conclusions of these paradigms in real-world interventions. Another is that it makes it possible for us to keep an open mind on the usefulness of the complete set of available methods, models and techniques and to research what they might be capable of delivering for each methodology and paradigm. We are no longer restricted to using, with each methodology, those methods specifically designed alongside it. This extends multimethod flexibility, while ensuring that we can still evaluate the usefulness of methods in support of the various generic methodologies.

I would claim it as one of the great achievements of CSP (see Jackson, 2000) that it has established generic systems methodologies and so freed itself from the specific methodologies it inherited – many of which were underspecified as to their theoretical assumptions. The generic methodologies have been derived in part from the clear dictates of the paradigms to which they correspond. They also take into account existing systems methodologies, which either implicitly or explicitly follow the orientation provided by the relevant paradigm. For example, the 'generic interpretive systems methodology' draws from the philosophy and theory of the interpretive paradigm as well as from strategic assumption surfacing and testing, interactive planning and SSM. It follows as well that it should be possible to recognize the main tenets of the existing systems methodologies, described in Part II, in the appropriate generic methodology (e.g., system dynamics in the generic functionalist systems methodology). The generic methodologies are set out, following the guidelines for 'constitutive rules' of methodologies offered by Checkland and Scholes (1990) and Checkland (1999), in Tables 15.1–15.4. Just two points remain to be made about CSP as a metamethodology.

First, it has been designed specifically as an 'action research' approach. This means that it seeks to contribute to research as well as to improving real-world problem situations. Any use of the metamethodology is, in principle, capable of yielding research findings about: how to manage the relationship between different paradigms; the philosophy and theory that constitutes the paradigms underpinning any of the generic methodologies used; the generic systems methodologies themselves and how to use them; the methods, models, tools and techniques employed; and about the real-world problem situation investigated. Having worked so hard in producing the 'generic systems methodologies', so that all of this can be achieved, it is worth adding a 'reflection' phase to CSP to ensure that research, and the generation of new learning, receives the attention it deserves.

Second, as with TSI, it is essential to use CSP flexibly and iteratively. It is now capable of being adapted to different situations both in terms of the methodologies it employs and the methods, models and techniques it

Table 15.1 Constitutive rules for a generic functionalist systems methodology.

1. A functionalist systems methodology is a structured way of thinking, with an attachment to the functionalist theoretical rationale, and is focused on improving real-world problem situations.

2. A functionalist systems methodology uses systems ideas as the basis for its intervention strategy and will frequently employ methods, models, tools and techniques that also draw on systems ideas.

3. The claim to have used a systems methodology according to the functionalist rationale must be justified according to the following guidelines:

   a. an assumption is made that the real-world is systemic;
   b. analysis of the problem situation is conducted in systems terms;
   c. models aiming to capture the nature of the situation are constructed, enabling us to gain knowledge of the real world;
   d. models are used to learn how best to improve the real world and for the purposes of design;
   e. quantitative analysis can be useful since systems obey laws;
   f. the process of intervention is systematic and is aimed at improving goal seeking and viability;
   g. intervention is best conducted on the basis of expert knowledge;
   h. solutions are tested primarily in terms of their efficiency and efficacy.

4. Since a functionalist systems methodology can be used in different ways in different situations and interpreted differently by different users, each use should exhibit conscious thought about how to adapt to the particular circumstances.

5. Each use of a functionalist systems methodology should yield research findings as well as changing the real-world problem situation. These research findings may relate: to the theoretical rationale underlying the methodology; to the methodology itself and how to use it; to the methods, models, tools and techniques employed; to the real-world problem situation investigated; or to all of these.

makes use of. Critical systems practitioners should exhibit conscious thought in each intervention, about how their approach needs to be moulded to the particular circumstances. They should also be willing to cycle, as many times as necessary, around the four phases of 'creativity', 'choice', 'implementation' and 'reflection'. CSP can now be summarized as in Table 15.5.

15.2.4 Methods

Our consideration of the methods now associated with CSP will include: those that can be employed to support the generic systems methodologies;

Table 15.2 Constitutive rules for a generic interpretive systems methodology.

1. An interpretive systems methodology is a structured way of thinking, with an attachment to the interpretive theoretical rationale, and is focused on improving real-world problem situations.

2. An interpretive systems methodology uses systems ideas as the basis for its intervention strategy and will frequently employ methods, models, tools and techniques that also draw on systems ideas.

3. The claim to have used a systems methodology according to the interpretive rationale must be justified according to the following guidelines:

   a. there is no assumption that the real world is systemic;

   b. analysis of the problem situation is designed to be creative and may not be conducted in systems terms;

   c. models are constructed that represent possible 'ideal-type' human activity systems;

   d. models are used to structure debate about changes that are feasible and desirable;

   e. quantitative analysis is unlikely to be useful except in a subordinate role;

   f. the process of intervention is systemic and is aimed at exploring purposes, alleviating unease and generating learning;

   g. the intervention is best conducted on the basis of stakeholder participation;

   h. changes are evaluated primarily in terms of their effectiveness and elegance.

4. Since an interpretive systems methodology can be used in different ways in different situations and interpreted differently by different users, each use should exhibit conscious thought about how to adapt to the particular circumstances.

5. Each use of an interpretive systems methodology should yield research findings as well as changing the real-world problem situation. These research findings may relate: to the theoretical rationale underlying the methodology; to the methodology itself and how to use it; to the methods, models, tools and techniques employed; to the real-world problem situation investigated, or to all of these.

those offering guidelines for using the metamethodology itself; and those that can enhance the use of CSP in other ways.

TSI dealt in 'whole' methodologies, like system dynamics, strategic assumption surfacing and testing, soft systems methodology and the methods devised explicitly to support them. It has since been argued that systems practitioners must be allowed much greater freedom to tailor their use of methods, models and techniques to the exigencies of the problem situation they are seeking to intervene in. CSP recognizes that the link between a methodology and the methods traditionally associated with it

Table 15.3 Constitutive rules for a generic emancipatory systems methodology.

1. An emancipatory systems methodology is a structured way of thinking, with an attachment to the emancipatory theoretical rationale, and is focused on improving real-world problem situations.

2. An emancipatory systems methodology uses systems ideas as the basis for its intervention strategy and will frequently employ methods, models, tools and techniques that also draw on systems ideas.

3. The claim to have used a systems methodology according to the emancipatory rationale must be justified according to the following guidelines:

   a. an assumption is made that the real world can be systemic in a manner alienating to individuals and/or oppressive to particular social groups;
   b. analysis of the problem situation must take into account who is disadvantaged by current systemic arrangements;
   c. models are constructed that respond to the sources of alienation and oppression;
   d. models are used that allow everyone to participate properly in addressing the problem situation;
   e. quantitative analysis may be useful especially to capture particular biases in existing systemic arrangements;
   f. the process of intervention is systemic and is aimed at ensuring fairness;
   g. intervention is conducted in such a way that the alienated and/or oppressed begin to take responsibility for their own liberation;
   h. changes designed to improve the position of the alienated and/or oppressed are evaluated primarily in terms of empowerment and emancipation.

4. Since an emancipatory systems methodology can be used in different ways in different situations and interpreted differently by different users, each use should exhibit conscious thought about how to adapt to the particular circumstances.

5. Each use of an emancipatory systems methodology should yield research findings as well as changing the real-world problem situation. These research findings may relate: to the theoretical rationale underlying the methodology; to the methodology itself and how to use it; to the methods, models, tools and techniques employed; to the real-world problem situation investigated; or to all of these.

can be broken. It is, therefore, happy to see existing methodologies 'decomposed', giving the systems practitioner access to the full range of methods, tools and techniques to use in combination as he or she feels appropriate, in support of the generic systems methodologies that are being employed in the intervention. So, for example, the Viable System Model (VSM), originally designed as a functionalist device, is freed up for use to

Table 15.4 Constitutive rules for a generic postmodern systems 'methodology'.

1. Postmodern systems practice is a way of thinking and acting, with an attachment to the postmodern theoretical rationale, and is focused on improving real-world problem situations.

2. Postmodern systems practice uses systemic and antisystemic ideas as the basis for its intervention strategy and will frequently employ methods, models, tools and techniques that also draw on systems ideas.

3. The claim to have used systems thinking and systems ideas according to the postmodern rationale may be sustained locally according to the following guidelines:
   a. an assumption that the real-world is constructed in such a way through discourse that particular groups and/or individuals are marginalized;
   b. intervention in the problem situation is designed to reveal who is marginalized by existing power/knowledge structures;
   c. diverse forms of pluralism are used to surface subjugated discourses and to allow marginalized voices to be heard;
   d. diverse forms of pluralism are used to allow relevant stakeholders to express their diversity and, possibly, grant a 'consent to act';
   e. quantitative analysis is unlikely to be used except as part of the process of deconstruction;
   f. the process of intervention takes the form of local strategizing and subversion in an endeavour to promote diversity;
   g. the intervention is conducted in such a way that conflict is reclaimed, and diversity and creativity are encouraged;
   h. changes are evaluated on the basis of exception and emotion.

4. Since postmodern systems practice can take different forms in different situations and be interpreted differently by different users, each use should exhibit conscious thought and/or an emotional response about how to adapt to the particular circumstances.

5. Each case of postmodern systems practice may yield research findings as well as changing the real-world problem situation. These findings may relate: to the theoretical rationale underlying the practice; to the 'methodology' for applying a postmodern systems approach; to the methods, models, tools and techniques employed; to the real-world problem situation investigated; or to all of these.

help the interpretive, emancipatory or postmodern systems methodologies. Of course, it will have to prove its worth, particularly when it finds itself serving purposes very far from those originally intended. As long as we consciously monitor the performance of methods, models and techniques

Table 15.5   The CSP metamethodology.

Creativity	
Task	To highlight significant concerns, issues and problems
Tools	Creativity-enhancing devices employed to ensure that the perspectives of the four paradigms receive proper attention
Outcome	Dominant and dependent concerns, issues and problems
Choice	
Task	To choose an appropriate generic systems methodology or methodologies and a variety of suitable methods, models and techniques
Tools	Methods for revealing the strengths and weaknesses of methodologies, methods, tools and techniques, including paradigm analysis, previous experience, etc.
Outcome	Dominant and dependent generic systems methodologies and appropriate methods, etc. chosen for use
Implementation	
Task	To arrive at and implement specific positive change proposals
Tools	Generic systems methodologies and appropriate methods, etc. employed according to the logic of CSP
Outcome	Highly relevant and co-ordinated change, which secures significant improvement in the problem situation according to the concerns of the different paradigms
Reflection	
Task	To produce learning about the problem situation, the metamethodology itself, the generic systems methodologies and the methods, etc. used
Tools	Clear understanding of the current state of knowledge about these
Outcome	Research findings that, for example, feed back into improving earlier stages of the metamethodology

against what we expect them to achieve for different methodologies, we will continually learn just how flexible we can be in their use.

In summary, CSP allows practitioners the greatest possible freedom in their choice of models, tools and techniques – as long as it is clear which generic systems methodology they are being employed to help. CSP can draw methods from the full range of existing systems methodologies, and anywhere else, as long as it uses them in an informed way.

It is necessary now to say something about what guidelines can be offered to help operationalize CSP.

I have, elsewhere (Jackson, 2000), compared the critical systems practitioner with a holistic doctor. Confronted by a patient with pains in her stomach, the doctor might initially consider standard explanations, such as overindulgence, period pains or irritable bowel syndrome. If the patient failed to respond to the usual treatment prescribed on the basis of an initial diagnosis you would expect the doctor to entertain the possibility of some more deep-seated and dangerous malady. The patient might be sent for X-ray, body scan or other tests designed to search for such structural problems. If nothing was found, a thoughtful conversation with the patient might suggest that the pains were a symptom of anxiety and depression. Various forms of counselling or psychological support could be offered. Or, perhaps, a knowledge of the patient's domestic circumstances, and bruises elsewhere on the body, might reveal that the patient was suffering at the hands of a violent partner. What should the doctor do in these circumstances? Finally, perhaps the patient just needs another interest – such as painting or golf – to take her mind off worries at work.

We would expect a 'holistic' doctor to be open to all these possibilities and to have appropriate responses and 'treatments' available. To my mind, the critical systems practitioner, probing with his or her functionalist (positivist and structuralist), interpretive, emancipatory and postmodern perspectives, is similarly taking a holistic approach to organizational and societal problems.

We can illuminate the procedure further if we return to the conception of dominant and dependent methodologies that was present in the original TSI. It was argued that the difficulties associated with multiparadigm practice can be managed if an initial choice of dominant methodology is made, to run the intervention, with a dependent methodology (or methodologies), reflecting alternative paradigms, in the background. The relationship between dominant and dependent methodologies can then change as the intervention proceeds in order to maintain flexibility at the methodology level. In our medical analogy, above, the doctor began with the equivalent of a functionalist methodology as dominant, but was willing to shift to interpretive, emancipatory or postmodern methodologies as required.

This remains, for me, an extremely powerful idea because it allows the intervention to proceed in a theoretically informed way (making research possible), and with less confusion to the participants, while as far as feasible protecting paradigm diversity. As long as we are explicit about our initially dominant methodology and are ready to switch paradigm and methodology, then that initial choice does not exclude us from introducing alternative methodologies, based on different paradigms, as required.

There is still the issue of what would make us switch methodology once an intervention has begun. Let us say we begin an intervention with the interpretive approach as dominant. It is possible that an occasion will arise when a model introduced, simply to enhance mutual understanding, will appear to 'capture' so well the logic of the problem situation that a shift to a functionalist position will seem justifiable. The model will then be taken as a representation of reality and a shift made, which establishes the functionalist methodology as dominant. Similarly, there will be occasions when the ethics of the analyst or relevant stakeholders are so offended that the shift to an emancipatory rationale becomes clearly necessary. And, finally, it may sometimes seem appropriate, in the interests of subverting tradition and introducing some fun into an organization, to adopt a postmodern orientation.

For completeness, it should be remarked that there is some theoretical justification for the strategy of alternating dominant and dependent methodologies. The philosopher Althusser (see Jackson, 2000) conceived the social totality as a system that, at various times, is dominated by one of its 'instances': economic, political, theoretical, ideological, etc. In order to act to change the social totality, Althusser argued, you need to understand the relationships between these 'instances', how each is developing and which one is dominant in a particular era of history. We are simply replacing the notion of alternating, dominant 'instances' with the idea of 'improving goal seeking and viability', 'exploring purposes', 'ensuring fairness' and 'promoting diversity', each becoming the dominant concern of an organization for some period of time.

There are two other sets of ideas that can help us further enhance the way we use CSP.

Checkland's distinction between Mode 1 and Mode 2 uses of SSM (see Chapter 10) can, with benefit, be transferred to CSP. An academic, imbued with CSP and in a position to set up a study, is likely to start from the metamethodological level, choose dominant and dependent methodologies and operate with a range of methods and models appropriate to the methodology dominant at a particular time. This allows the academic, according to his or her inclinations, to research the process of critique between paradigms, the theoretical assumptions of the paradigms, the robustness of the methodological rules, and the usefulness of certain tools and techniques for serving a particular purpose. This would be a formal Mode 1 use of CSP, where the metamethodology guides the intervention. A CSP-aware manager or management consultant will, on the other hand, be more likely to use CSP in a Mode 2 manner. The intervention will be dominated by the concerns and pressures of the immediate problem situation. The participants will employ whatever methods, tools and techniques happen to come readily to hand. However, the metamethodology might be used, during the course of the intervention, to help those involved reflect on what was happening and perhaps open up new possibilities. CSP could also be employed, after the event, to analyse what had occurred and draw research lessons from the intervention. In practice, most actual applications are likely to be somewhere between the extremes of Mode 1 and Mode 2.

Second, it is worth reminding the reader of two other forms of 'pluralism' that have not been given much attention hitherto by CSP, but have been brought to the fore by Taket and White (2000) using their postmodern lens. These are (see Chapter 13) pluralism 'in the modes of representation employed' and 'in the facilitation process'. CSP will be enhanced once it embraces these additional aspects of pluralism.

15.2.5 Recent developments

In this chapter I have begun to sketch out a research programme that will lead to new developments in CSP. This includes: testing the various methods, models, tools and techniques available in the service of different rationalities; clarifying the constitutive rules for the different generic methodologies and ensuring they transfer the propositions of the different paradigms into practice; reviewing the philosophy and theory of each paradigm against what happens in practice; and learning better how to facilitate reflective conversation at the metamethodological level.

This research programme is under way and, in the next section, we review one CSP intervention that produced some very interesting results.

15.3 CRITICAL SYSTEMS PRACTICE (CSP) IN ACTION

The intervention took place in Kingston Gas Turbines (KGT) over a three-year period, between 1997 and 2000. KGT has been in the business of manufacturing gas turbines since 1946 and, at the time of the study, employed around 2,000 personnel. KGT's existing structure was of a 'matrix' type, with the primary design, sales, production and production-support departments cross-cut by support functions, such as finance, quality, human resources, information technology, plant maintenance and contracts. In 1997 it embarked on an ambitious 'double the business' strategy. As part of this, all staff were to participate in interdisciplinary teams, which would seek to analyse and solve the company's problems.

The intervention was carried out by Alvaro Carrizosa, first as an MSc student and then as a change agent/researcher, funded by the company and, at the same time, undertaking a PhD. I was his academic supervisor. The intervention has been described before: in detail in Carrizosa (2002) and in outline in Jackson (2000). The aim here is not to replicate these reports, but to use the intervention to illustrate the main elements of CSP as set out earlier in this chapter.

The three-year intervention can be seen as evolving through five 'projects', labelled here Projects 1–5.

Project 1 was undertaken for the Proposals Department, which was responsible for working up formal tenders to submit to customers for jobs. This 'proposals' project was concerned with the consequences of the 'double the business' strategy for the way the department managed its internal and external relations.

Brief flirtations with hard systems thinking and organizational cybernetics as dominant methodologies (the idea of generic systems methodologies had not been fully formulated) ended because of the degree of pluralism in the problem situation. The SOSM pointed to a soft, or interpretive, approach as an appropriate response, and this remained dominant during the rest of Project 1.

The various issues and problems facing the Proposals Department were unearthed through interviews and informal conversations and captured in a rich picture. Discussion of the rich picture yielded various themes that demanded further consideration: communication themes, structure themes, uncertainty themes, efficiency themes and roles themes. Metaphor analysis was used to engender creative thinking about possible futures that would dissolve the problems as they currently existed. Participants were encouraged to develop their own original metaphors, but the TSI 'set' was also employed to ensure that the perspectives of the different paradigms were all taken into account. In general terms, the participants favoured the 'organism' metaphor as a way of viewing what the future should be like. It seemed necessary to become more customer- and market-orientated in order to survive and prosper in what was becoming an extremely turbulent environment. The project, at this point, inevitably started to involve the Sales Department, and five 'relevant' systems were outlined that described structures for sales that would enable it to react more flexibly to the environment. The VSM was used to explore one of these alternatives. The outcome of considering possible 'feasible and desirable' changes was recommendations for changing the structure of the Sales Department to give it more of a project management orientation.

The success of this project led to Alvaro being hired by KGT to help with Project 2, which was about organization structure. This was called the PIT project because it was undertaken by a group of middle managers known as the Process Implementation Team (PIT Group). It arose as a result of dissatisfaction with previous restructurings, which had established the matrix and the various interdisciplinary teams spread across the company. There was a feeling that the technical knowledge, on which the engineers prided themselves, was becoming diluted because they were no longer in such close contact with one another. Moreover, the capacity to transmit information and learning from one part of the organization to another also seemed to be reduced.

Project 2 was governed throughout, we can see now, by functionalism. The main impact of systems thinking was to significantly expand the boundaries of what was being looked at. So, what began as a search for solutions in terms of the layout of offices and departments turned into a review of communication systems generally, then organizational structures, then to the vision and strategy that needed, in the minds of the members of the PIT Group, to inform organizational structure. Receiving little help from top management on vision and strategy, the PIT Group seized the opportunity to focus on five business processes that had a direct link to the market. A new organizational structure was proposed built around these business processes. The new arrangements were presented to top management and, following some minor changes, were approved for immediate implementation without further consultation.

Project 3 – 'the thinking space' – was born of the realization by those middle managers charged with implementation that not all members of the organization understood, let alone agreed with, the changes proposed by the PIT Group and now adopted by senior management. They determined to set up a forum for discussion about how the reorganization should actually be implemented. They hoped this would help ameliorate any negative consequences that might follow from the autocratic way in which plans for the new structure were adopted and imposed. The focus became what characteristics a thinking space should have in order to permit open discussion of how implementation might proceed. It was felt all participants should be able to disseminate their views and reflections on the evolving situation. This sharing of multiple perspectives would help promote and enrich communication, reflection and learning, and eventually encourage co-operation among those involved. Alvaro's role was to constantly bring new perspectives to bear on the issues being discussed.

The dominant generic systems methodologies, during Project 3, were the interpretive and the emancipatory, with the postmodern in a subsidiary role. This can be seen as a reaction to the overwhelming functionalist rationale that dominated Project 2. The aim became to increase the 'collective competence' of those directly contributing to the thinking space and even among those who were not contributing, but nevertheless were interacting with those involved. To assist in achieving this, rich pictures, root definitions, conceptual models, the VSM, system dynamics models and metaphors were all introduced and used. Carrizosa (2000) lists the 'properties and characteristics' of the thinking space as they were eventually codefined by the researcher and the participants:

- an action language, focusing on actors and activities in everyday work;
- structured conversations that helped the actors address the most relevant issues;
- coequal actors engaging in equal participation and able to freely express their viewpoints;
- a systems approach that helps actors define what is important to them;
- an activity, a way of doing and acting, not another company programme;
- the researcher as actor;
- a dynamic process.

The thinking space, enacted on this basis, played an important role in encouraging participation and learning during the various projects undertaken as the new organizational structure was implemented. Its success led to the idea that it should become a permanent part of continuous learning in the company beyond the implementation activity. Projects 4 and 5 stemmed from this ambition.

Project 4 – 'the book' – consisted of writing a book about the experiences of participants in implementing the new organizational structure. The book was produced in an interactive manner with different actors contributing their thoughts on change processes and how they could be brought about effectively. The multiple perspectives available from the participants were further enriched by discussing Senge's ideas on organizational learning (see Chapter 5) and relevant aspects of complexity theory derived from the work of Stacey (see Chapter 7). As well as allowing self-reflection, and exchange and enhancement of viewpoints, the book permitted issues of power relations and constraints on action to be addressed. The book allowed the participants to structure and share their thoughts on Project 3 and so consolidate their learning. The new 'organization theory' that was then held in common, and objectified in the book, could become the basis for new purposeful action.

The book project continued the pursuit of the interpretive and emancipatory rationales established in Project 3 (with the postmodern 'dependent') through the very novel device of cowriting a book. It remained open how the experience of cowriting and the contents of the book would be taken forward in later problem-resolving exercises.

In fact, Project 5, addressing the problem of creating 'an integrated business approach' in KGT, drew upon both the book and the knowledge gained of what was required for a thinking space. Known as 'the walls workshops', Project 5 allowed participants to engage in completely open communication about the complex issues facing KGT and how to tackle them. Everyone was encouraged to contribute and, once discussions on a particular issue had reached a certain level, to represent the results on walls accessible to all actors. The representations were in the form of systems diagrams and various other visual artefacts. They expressed possible options and actions to be taken, new perceptions and interpretations of problems, possible causes and effects, suggestions for local and more global improvements, etc. The representations could be continuously modified and updated. The discussions taking place were therefore available for scrutiny, validation or revision, and feedback. By the end of the project this approach had become readily accepted in KGT and was still being used in 2002.

The walls workshops project clearly had a strong postmodern element to it, as well as continuing the emancipatory and interpretive themes established in Projects 3 and 4.

The intervention in KGT illustrates most aspects of good CSP.

The critical systems commitments of critical awareness, pluralism and improvement were honoured throughout. The change agent/researcher brought with him some critical awareness of the strengths and weaknesses of different systems approaches, and this was revisited by himself and others as experience was gained of their use in the particular circumstances of KGT. Improvement was a constant theme and was judged, in the different projects, according to the concerns of a wide variety of paradigms and methodologies. Pluralism was adhered to in a variety of ways. Most of the projects had clearly defined creativity, choice and implementation phases (though not always in that order!) and pluralism was used in each of these. At the theoretical level, as the intervention progressed, pluralism began to take on the sophisticated form of a pluralism of 'generic systems methodologies'. At the level of methods, the freedom to mix and match was fully exploited. There was an instance (Project 1) of the VSM used in support of a dominant interpretive methodology. In Project 3, system dynamic models and the VSM were employed alongside rich pictures, root definitions, conceptual models, etc.

There were numerous shifts of dominant and dependent methodologies during the intervention. Project 1 started as functionalist, but ended as interpretive. Project 2 was functionalist. Project 3 and 4 were governed by interpretive and emancipatory rationales, with postmodernism in the background. In Project 5 postmodernism came forward to share dominance with the interpretive and emancipatory approaches.

The KGT intervention began as a Mode 1 exercise, but soon became more Mode 2. By the time of Project 3, the situation was very definitely determining what aspects of systems thinking could be usefully brought to the intervention. The change agent/researcher was continually having to learn more systems thinking in order to keep up and reflect on what was happening in the problem situation. At a further step removed from the action, I was trying, in a Mode 2 manner, to make sense of what was going on with reference to critical systems thinking.

The metamethodology of CSP certainly showed itself to be responsive to the changing circumstances in KGT, adapting its dominant methodologies as necessary and using a vast array of methods, models, tools and techniques as they became suitable. Its natural flexibility with respect to clients, methodologies and methods was added to, in postmodern terms, by pluralism in the use of different 'modes of representation' and 'facilitation'. Indeed, it is in these areas that the intervention demonstrated much of its originality.

Finally, CSP proved itself as an approach to action research. As well as bringing about changes in KGT, much was learned about CST and CSP. Carrizosa (2002) details learning in respect of 'pluralism', 'improvement' and the 'role of the agent'. Even more significant, perhaps, are his conjectures about the particular situations in which CSP can be properly operationalized. He calls these circumstances 'platforms' and sets out two elements that must be present for such platforms to come into existence. First, facilitator(s) and participants must be willing to engage in pursuing 'collective competence' – part of which will mean them becoming competent in multi-methodology practice. Second, the involved actors need to see what they are doing as a continuous mutual research endeavour.

The KGT project was an exhilarating experience. The period 1997–2000 was a time of great turbulence in KGT, with new ownership structures, changes in organization design and major initiatives of all kinds. At times it seemed that the only thing that did remain constant was the existence of our critical systems study, exploring purposeful change in KGT. The change agent/researcher and his supervisor emerged even more convinced of the need to employ, in intervention, a pluralism of perspectives and theoretical positions and to use methods and models according to the needs of the particular moment.

15.4 CRITIQUE OF CRITICAL SYSTEMS PRACTICE (CSP)

The purpose of creative holism is to learn about and harness the various systems methodologies, methods, models and techniques so that they can best be used by managers to respond to the complexity, turbulence and heterogeneity of the problem situations they face today. As we saw in Chapter 14, it was a criticism of TSI that, because it was reliant on the methodologies and associated methods that it had inherited, it lacked a degree of responsiveness in addressing complex, dynamic and diverse problem situations. CSP has sought to overcome the problems of TSI in order that the promise of creative holism can be realized.

A key element in this has been the delimitation in CSP of the four generic systems methodologies seen as relevant during each of its phases. In order to be holistic during creativity it is necessary to view the problem situation from the perspectives of the functionalist, interpretive, emancipatory and postmodern paradigms – often mediated through the range of metaphors.

Choice and implementation too benefit from consideration and use of methodologies clearly owing allegiance to different paradigms. It is again the complexity, heterogeneity and turbulence of problem situations that suggest systems practitioners need a pluralism that encourages the use together of different methodologies based on alternative paradigms. We should seek to benefit from what each paradigm has to offer. This is not to dismiss the usefulness of sometimes employing just one methodology, in an 'imperialist' fashion, to guide the use of a variety of methods, tools and techniques. But, it is to insist that such an approach needs to be followed self-consciously and in a way that permits change of paradigmatic orientation. Pluralism can provide its greatest benefits only in the context of paradigm diversity.

Three further strengths of CSP can also be associated with the development of the generic systems methodologies.

First, they offer us very different ways of evaluating the success of an intervention. Functionalism looks for efficiency and efficacy, the interpretive approach for effectiveness and elegance, the emancipatory approach for empowerment and emancipation, while postmodernism values exceptions and engaging the emotions. We will not succeed on all these criteria in any one intervention, but it seems beneficial to pay attention to all of them over some longer period of involvement.

Second, the generic systems methodologies have eased the separation of methods, models and techniques from the host methodologies they were originally developed to serve. They can now be employed freely, as required by the problem situation, as long as this is consciously in the service of one or other of the generic methodologies. TSI dealt in whole methodologies, like organizational cybernetics or Soft Systems Methodology (SSM). It is now possible to break these up and extract relevant methods so that, for example, the VSM can be used alongside root definitions and conceptual models. This gives systems practitioners immense flexibility. They are able to draw on a wide variety of tools, from whatever source, and employ them in combination to respond to the complexities of the problem situation they are intervening in and the dynamics of that situation as it changes. And they can still use them in an 'informed' way.

Finally, it is essential that managers and their advisors are in a position continually to improve the CSP metamethodology, and the methodology and methods it uses. The generic systems methodologies assist by enabling research to take place. They are clear about the theoretical assumptions on which they are built and how they seek to convert these into practice. It is therefore possible to reflect on how valuable the different paradigms are in helping us to understand the social world and to improve the performance of the methodologies designed to apply their insights. By ensuring they are consciously employed in the service of one of the generic methodologies, we can also gauge the usefulness of methods, models and techniques for different tasks and try to improve them.

Of course, critics will point to certain issues that CSP has not yet fully addressed. The critical systems practitioner is required to hop between conflicting paradigms. Often he or she will be operating from within a paradigm to explore a problem situation and intervene in it according to the dictates of that paradigm. He or she then needs to move to other paradigms to critique what he or she has been doing to that point and to see if the problem situation needs reconceptualizing. We have already noted Brocklesby's (1997) concern about the severe 'cognitive difficulties' faced by individuals required to work in different paradigms. In his view it is unlikely, if by no means impossible, for individuals to become multimethodology-literate. But there is an even greater concern stemming from the same source.

CST has abandoned the claim, based on Habermas' work and underpinning TSI, to have metaparadigmatic status. CSP manages relationships between paradigms that it knows are incommensurable. What, therefore, does the systems practitioner do when the paradigms start telling him or her different things and pushing him or her to act in different ways? An easy solution (apparently approved by Midgley, 2000) is always to favour one paradigm over the others. The answer to the questions 'how should we view this problem situation?' and 'what should we do now?' can always then be provided, in the last resort, by the preferred paradigm. But, this is 'theoretical imperialism' and is ruled out for CSP because of its ultimate commitment to pluralism at the theoretical level. The way forward, and it seems a sensible one, is to value the fact that, while CSP can provide the manager or systems practitioner with holistic awareness and guidance, it cannot ultimately take responsibility for choice away from her or him. Managers, informed by creative holism, still have decisions to make that will draw on their own ethical positions, their own conceptions of right and wrong.

Of course, we are then dragged back into discussion with postmodernists about the methodology-user and the particular social context that has formed his or her identity. As Midgley (1997) argues, any approach to pluralism in systems thinking must take into account the dynamic interaction that occurs between the subject who wishes to take action and the power–knowledge formations that form the identity of the subject. This is interesting and important stuff.

15.5 THE VALUE OF CRITICAL SYSTEMS PRACTICE (CSP) TO MANAGERS

The five primary benefits listed for TSI are preserved in CSP. The following five points are, therefore, in addition to those:

- CSP reduces the multitude of different systems methodologies to just four generic types.
- At the same time CSP provides managers with access to all the various methods, models, tools and techniques developed as part of those

methodologies. This is their toolkit from which they can freely (and in an informed manner) choose, as circumstances demand.

- CSP is clear that, although considerable guidance of a holistic nature can be provided to managers, they will still be confronted with ethical choices.
- CSP points to the need to evaluate management action, in the long-term, using measures based on efficiency, efficacy, effectiveness, elegance, empowerment, emancipation, exception, emotion – and ethics.
- CSP eases the task of doing research, as well as taking action, in the managerial domain. Managers should therefore benefit from action researchers continually updating and improving CSP.

15.6 CONCLUSION

CSP provides a basis for action research and must continue to develop by enhancing the theory–practice relationship. An appropriate research programme is in place, and this should ensure the further development of creative holism.

Another vital element is the establishment of more educational and training programmes that embrace the challenges of teaching CST and CSP. In this way the 'cognitive' and 'cultural' constraints preventing the wider adoption of creative holism by managers and systems practitioners can be overcome.

REFERENCES

Brocklesby, J. (1994). Let the jury decide: Assessing the cultural feasibility of Total Systems Intervention. *Systems Practice*, **7**, 75–86.

Brocklesby, J. (1997). Becoming multimethodology literate: An assessment of the cognitive difficulties of working across paradigms. In: J. Mingers and A. Gill (eds), *Multimethodology: The Theory and Practice of Combining Management Science Methodologies* (pp. 189–216). John Wiley & Sons, Chichester, UK.

Carrizosa, A. (2000). Enacting thinking spaces towards purposeful actions: An action research project. Unpublished paper, University of Lincoln, UK.

Carrizosa, A. (2002). Platforms for critical systems practice. PhD thesis, University of Lincoln, UK.

Checkland, P.B. (1999). *Systems Thinking, Systems Practice*. John Wiley & Sons, Chichester, UK (with a 30-year retrospective).

Checkland, P.B. and Scholes, P. (1990). *Soft Systems Methodology in Action*. John Wiley & Sons, Chichester, UK.

Flood, R.L. (1990). *Liberating Systems Theory: On Systems and Inquiry*. Plenum, New York.

Flood, R.L. and Jackson, M.C. (1991). *Creative Problem Solving: Total Systems Intervention*. John Wiley & Sons, Chichester, UK.

Flood, R.L. and Romm, N.R.A. (1996). *Diversity Management: Triple Loop Learning*. John Wiley & Sons, Chichester, UK.

Gregory, W.J. (1992). Critical systems thinking and pluralism: A new constellation. PhD thesis, City University, London.

Gregory, W.J. (1996). Discordant pluralism: A new strategy for critical systems thinking? *Systems Practice*, **9**, 605–625.

Jackson, M.C. (2000). *Systems Approaches to Management*. Kluwer/Plenum, New York.

Midgley, G. (1997). Mixing methods: Developing systemic intervention. In: J. Mingers and A. Gill (eds), *Multimethodology: the Theory and Practice of Combining Management Science Methodologies* (pp. 291–332). John Wiley & Sons, Chichester, UK.

Midgley, G. (2000). *Systemic Intervention: Philosophy, Methodology and Practice*. Kluwer/Plenum, New York.

Mingers, J.C. and Brocklesby, J. (1996). Multimethodology: Towards a framework for mixing methodologies. *Omega*, **25**, 489–509.

Mingers, J.C. and Gill, A. (1997). *Multimethodology – The Theory and Practice of Combining Management Science Methodologies*. John Wiley & Sons, Chichester, UK.

Morgan, G. (ed.) (1983). *Beyond Method: Strategies for Social Research*. Sage Publications, Beverley Hills, CA.

Munro, I. and Mingers, J. (2002). The use of multimethodology in practice: Results of a survey of practitioners. *Journal of the Operational Research Society*, **53**, 369–378.

Pirsig, R.M. (1974). *Zen and the Art of Motorcycle Maintenance*. Bodley Head, London.

Taket, A.R. and White, L.A. (2000). *Partnership and Participation: Decision-making in the Multiagency Setting*. John Wiley & Sons, Chichester, UK.

Conclusion

Creative holism, a new development in systems thinking, wants to provide managers with the joint benefits of holism and creativity so that they can do their jobs better. Holism by itself confers many advantages over traditional, reductionist approaches in dealing with complexity, change and diversity. As systems thinking has developed it has discovered a variety of different ways of being holistic, based on different paradigms and metaphors. We are now able, therefore, to be creative in the way we approach being holistic. Creative holism enables us to use different systems approaches, reflecting alternative holistic perspectives, in combination. Perhaps we cannot use all the various systems approaches at once, but they can be employed creatively, over time, to promote together overall improvement in the problem situations managers face. This is the essence of creative holism.

No doubt creative holism will seem difficult. But then, managerial work is becoming more complex, turbulent and diverse. Most managers are likely to find themselves, on a regular basis, confronted by messes made up of interacting issues, such as the need to increase productivity, become more market-centred, improve communications, adopt fairer recruitment and promotion strategies, and motivate a diverse workforce. They will also find themselves having to prioritize between the demands made on them because of lack of time and resources. They cannot tackle them all at once. This all seems like common sense. Creative holism is in tune with this common sense. It recognizes that excellent organizational performance depends on managers paying attention to improving goal seeking and viability, exploring purposes, ensuring fairness and promoting diversity. And it offers critical systems practice, which provides guidelines on how to tackle in a holistic and balanced way, using various systems approaches, the messes that managers so often confront. Creative holism responds to the everyday problem situations that managers have to deal with.

It is one of the satisfactions of systems thinking that its insights translate between levels. If we move beyond the organizational to the societal and world levels, we find that the same imperatives for improvement, highlighted by creative holism, continue to be crucial. We are unlikely to improve things unless we pay attention to efficiency and effectiveness, mutual understanding, fairness and diversity. And we need to understand the interactions between these and treat them holistically. Few of us will get the opportunity to practise our systems thinking on the world stage. Perhaps, though, if we pay attention to each and all of these things, as managers in organizations, our actions will have a resonance beyond our immediate environments and, in some way, contribute to global improvement. This is a nice thought. Most managers, as well as doing a good job, would like to make things better rather than worse for future generations.

Index